THE
PROFESSIONAL
WRITER
IN
ELIZABETHAN
ENGLAND

THE
PROFESSIONAL
WRITER
IN
ELIZABETHAN
ENGLAND

A Study of Nondramatic Literature

BY

Edwin Haviland Miller

HARVARD UNIVERSITY PRESS
Cambridge, Massachusetts
1959

to the memory of

HYDER EDWARD ROLLINS

PREFACE

Exactly fifty years ago Phoebe Sheavyn published *The Literary Profession in the Elizabethan Age* (1909), the first, and up until the present time the only, work that describes the beginnings of professional authorship in England. Miss Sheavyn concentrated upon the relation of writers to patrons and upon the economics of publication, within the limitations of the material available to her. Her findings were essentially repeated in H. G. Aldis' "The Book Trade, 1557–1625," in *The Cambridge History of English Literature*, and were not fundamentally altered or expanded in *Shakespeare's England*.

In the last half century, however, substantial contributions have been made in the Elizabethan field, many of which have added to our information about the literary profession. Perhaps foremost has been the appearance of *A Short Title Catalogue*, to which every Elizabethan scholar is indebted in more ways than he can ever acknowledge; the revision, now in preparation under the direction of William A. Jackson and Francis Ferguson, with the assistance of other American and English specialists, will make this indispensable compendium more indispensable. In a remarkably short period of time bibliography has changed from a dilettante's plaything to one of the most important, and precise, tools of literary analysis. The labors of R. B. McKerrow, W. W. Greg, and Fredson Bowers in this field have given us insight into the operations of the Elizabethan printing houses, as well as information about the writer's relation to the stationer, the tangled subject of copyright, and the payments authors did or (frequently) did not receive. The last fifty years have also seen an imposing number of monographs of individual authors. We now know a great deal more about Spenser, Gascoigne, Greene, Lodge, Gabriel Harvey, Munday, Chettle, Dekker, Gosson, Whetstone, Rich, Turbervile, and others. In addition, the modern literary critic benefits from new and more accurate editions than were available when Miss Sheavyn wrote. Beginning with McKerrow's exemplary treatment of Nashe, we now have the monumental Spenser Variorum, the Dekker of Bowers, J. B. Leishman's skillful and meticulous *The Three Parnassus Plays*, the poetic miscellanies and collections of broadside ballads to which Hyder E. Rollins devoted his loving attention for over twenty years, the additions to the Dekker canon prepared by F. P. Wilson, and the numerous reprints edited by G. B. Harrison. As my notes readily demonstrate, my debt is particularly great to Louis B. Wright's analysis of popular taste and of Elizabethan bestsellers, *Middle-Class Culture in Elizabethan England*.

Of subjects germane to a discussion of the Elizabethan literary profession, perhaps most attention has been devoted to patronage. Within the past few years interesting treatments of Sir Philip Sidney and the Earl of Leicester as patrons of literature have appeared; the preliminary articles of Professors Virgil Heltzel, Dick Taylor, Jr., and Franklin B. Williams, Jr. have whetted the curiosity of all scholars. Professor Heltzel is completing what will undoubtedly be the most exhaustive discussion of patronage in this period. Professor Taylor is analyzing possibly the greatest Elizabethan and Jacobean patron, the third Earl of Pembroke. Professor Williams' index of dedications and commendatory verses, with all the auxiliary but fascinating sidelights he outlines in a recent article, will become an important tool and a vital source of information.

My obligation to these studies and to many others (omission of mention is not to be construed either as ignorance or as denigration) my extensive notes cannot possibly make clear enough. For scholarship is a cooperative undertaking, and my investigations have correspondingly benefited from those of others in the field.

In this study I have concentrated upon professional writers, those who, for various reasons, did not, or could not, emulate the lofty contempt of amateurs for the printing press, and who therefore became a part of the new commerce of publication. I have dealt mainly with authors and publication in the last half of Elizabeth's reign. For, until roughly 1580 there had been few professionals among English writers: the humanists early in the century had written for idealistic and utilitarian reasons, not for pecuniary gain, and the translators in the first fifteen years after Elizabeth's succession had been supported by statesmen like Burghley and Walsingham and other nobles and noblewomen. But, in the last two decades of the century, young men, fresh from the universities or from the wars, came to London in order to wrest a livelihood from authorship. Since few of them obtained patronage on a continuing basis, they were in effect servants of the stationers. It is these professionals and this new marketplace in St. Paul's Churchyard that I have examined. For the most part I have ignored the dramatists, since they wrote directly for the stage and with but few exceptions evinced little interest in publication. Rewards, as many hacks and many poets with little talent for dramatic composition discovered, were much better in the theaters than in the printing houses.

I have attempted to analyze the Elizabethan writer both

in terms of his society and in terms of the new profession he struggled to create, the literary profession. First, I have examined his middle-class origins and his uneasy, vacillating acceptance of the unformulated assumptions of his culture, which deemed authorship a vain and somewhat suspect activity. Then, though fully aware of the difficulties, I have discussed the audience for books in the sixteenth century and the even more treacherous subject of taste. Next, turning to the more specific relations of authors, I have observed his associations with patrons, with stationers, and with governmental and nongovernmental agencies that suppressed books. Finally, I have recorded the trickeries of literary conycatchers, the hacks who shrewdly exploited the marketplace, and often themselves, and who in their sweat and their poverty founded Grub Street.

I have modernized all titles, with the understandable exception of *The Faerie Queene.* In quoting Elizabethans I have attempted to impose some uniformity upon my sources, which include both original editions and modern reprints, by expanding all contractions except the ampersand, by normalizing *u, v,* and *i,* by omitting redundant italics. The erratic spelling and punctuation of Elizabethan stationers and authors I have retained.

It is with warmest pleasure and a great deal of humility that I make the usual acknowledgment to persons who have been unusually kind to me over a period of years. To Dr. Louis B. Wright and his staff at the Folger Shakespeare Library I am indebted for a most profitable summer as a research fellow at that incomparable institution. The long hours I have spent in the Houghton Library at Harvard have been made pleasant by the kindnesses of Professor William A. Jackson, Dr. W. H. Bond, and the staff in the reading room. I am glad to record my appreciation to the librarians at the Boston Athenaeum, the Boston Public Library, the Library of Congress, and Simmons College. For answers to queries and for photostats I am indebted to the curators of rare books at the Henry E. Huntington Library, the British Museum, and the Bodleian. Like every one else in the field, my work has been made easier by the availability of the University Microfilm series. Professor Herschel Baker, of Harvard University, was kind enough to read my manuscript and to offer constructive comments.

In discussing Elizabethan publishers I have reported the caustic observations of professional writers of that age, and occasionally added a few of my own. For the record, however, I must add that the Harvard University Press bears no resemblance to the sixteenth-century printing establishments described in these pages. I have been impressed with and grateful for the courtesy and intelligent suggestions of those who have guided this book through the press.

Finally, and sadly, I record my debt to Professor Hyder Edward Rollins. Many years ago he suggested that I investigate the history of professionalism in the Elizabethan era. While I was doing research, he was always ready to answer questions and to make helpful suggestions. Though, I realized later, his health was failing, he examined an early draft of this manuscript with such care and thoroughness that I still remain in awe. It was characteristic of the man, however, that, after reading the manuscript, he apologized because he feared that he had not done a satisfactory job. I dedicate this work to the memory of a scholar and a teacher who took more pride in the accomplishments of his students than in his own monumental contributions to scholarship.

PREFACE

Errors in fact and opinion I herewith declare my own. Whatever virtues there may be I willingly attribute to my friends — and to that academic Griselda, my wife.

E. H. M.

Simmons College
September 1958

CONTENTS

If the historian be long, he is accompted a trifler: if he be short, he is taken for a summister: if he commend, he is twighted for a flatterer: if he reproove, he is holden for a carper: if he be pleasant, he is noted for a jester: if he be grave, he is reckoned for a drooper: if he misdate, he is named a falsifier: if he only but trip, he is tearmed a stumbler: so that let him bear himselfe . . . as uprightlie and as conscionablie as he may possible, yet he shall be sure to find them that will be more prest to blab foorth his pelfish faults, than they will be readie to blaze out his good deserts.

— Holinshed, *Chronicles of England, Scotland, and Ireland*

CHAPTER ONE

AUTHORS IN THEIR MILIEU

In the walks near St. Paul's Cathedral, from early morning until dusk, an observer saw a cross section of Tudor society. The modish courtier with his mincing walk and his affected, almost Arcadian, speech, met his friends, male and female, and chattered with the nervous intensity of his kind. The lawyer, his palm about to be greased with the necessary ointment, an angel, soothed his client and promised that the never-ending litigation would end next term-time. The conycatcher, sometimes camouflaged as a courtier, sometimes as a country bumpkin, leaned casually against a wall and inventoried his victim. Women, some honest and some not, waited with excited titters for beaux known and unknown. Youthful apprentices, free of drudgery in the shops of their masters, paraded with their wenches, or ogled the not-so-honest women. Solemn men from the provinces talked with city friends and frequently implored landlords and brokers for leniency. Beggars and broken-down soldiers, indifferently cast adrift in an age which provided few bonuses and gratuities for people maimed in defense of the nation, implored alms in piteous tones and in malodorous rags. There was a hubbub of voices, the fashionable diction of London intermingled with the earthy dialects of the provinces, strenuously gay soprano voices contrasted with desperately anxious bass tones. The drab walls of St. Paul's accentuated the colorful costumes of the strollers. Fops, attired in their international regalia which a moralist like Philip Stubbes never wearied of condemning, resembled lollypops more than men. Women with their ruffs, cuffs, and accouterments rivaled in the flesh the fabricated glitter of the mistresses sonneteers extolled. The homespun of the country cousin or the apprentice, worn because of economic circumstances or because of religious conviction, served to highlight the garish fashionable costumes, just as the sober, well-scrubbed countenances of the religious on their way to the cathedral itself set off the artificial glitter of painted men and women.

Not everyone was engaged in conversation, in striking modish postures, or in importuning passers-by. Many were on their way to shops in the churchyard. Some wandered over to the bookstalls, attracted by the bright signs of the proprietors or lured by the bookseller who had begun his vigil for customers at seven in the morning. Some shops were substantial structures in which printers lived and transacted business; others were simply booths or shelters intended for business. The poles of the booths were decorated with newly printed ballads, title pages which meticulously enumerated the contents in types of various sizes, and eye-alluring (but often ugly) woodcuts. On the shelves were pamphlets of a few signatures, inexpensively printed and stitched, substantial "novels" or collections of tales, handsome (and expensive) tomes for the discriminating and the wealthy, and the better designed imports from foreign printing houses. There were books for every taste. The religious found prayer books and moral treatises. Pretentious ladies could select romances which complemented their poodles. Practical ladies found books on childbirth, recipes, home cures for illnesses. Horsemen could learn in easily digestible form all the diseases horses are heir to. Yeomen (if they were willing to credit theory above their own experiences) were able to choose among many long treatises on cultivation, grafting, the care of bees, the enrichment of the soil. For apprentices, at a halfpenny, there were ballads and descriptions of two-headed monsters, and, for a few pence more, cony-catching exposés. The learned were able to have their erudition in translation or in Latin. Fops, if they read at all, did not have to search long for eroticism, or they could select one of the handsome volumes with ribbons to match the ladies' favors adorning their hats. Merchants discovered factual and fantastic "true" accounts of voyages and foreign lands, or, if they wished to be well informed, there were reports of recent events newly translated by some industrious (and hungry) printer's hack. Those interested in poetry had the choice of songs and sonnets, plays tragical and comical, epitaphs of famous men glorified for eternity before their remains were placed in crypts, narratives patriotic and recreational, translations of Ovid and Ariosto, or *The Faerie Queene*.

While Velvetbreeches, self-consciously puffing on his new pipe, read off titles and flaunted his (limited) knowledge of French, and while Clothbreeches sought out books reflecting his solemn (and sometimes stolid) concern for the moral and social foundations of the nation, authors themselves often hovered nearby. Since, except for the two university presses, all printing was confined to the city, writers of necessity came to London and, more specifically, to St. Paul's Churchyard, where stationers had their shops and their presses. The sight of an author with a recently completed manuscript or of a translator haggling with a stationer over his commission was not unusual. For sixteenth-century London was small and compact, and relations between writers, publishers, and purchasers were intimate and personal. Authors were able to observe courtiers fingering their wares, as we read in Dekker's *The Gull's Hornbook,* and many a writer did not conceal his disgust when a customer spurned his book. Although by 1600 publication had long since become a business venture operated by shrewd merchants, impersonality in the form of modern advertising techniques had not yet overtaken it. And so authors addressed prefaces to their readers, and often to their publishers, hurling indiscriminately encomia rarely equaled in our own day of stupendous claims and invective seldom duplicated (let alone ventured) in later centuries. Or, like Ralph Rabbards, "Gentleman, studious and expert in Alchemical Artes," they frankly discussed typographical errors and recommended, "If in reading hereof thou shalt note any fault in matter or forme, that thou wilt curteously note the same and send it unto me, or the house of Peter Bales in the Olde Bayly, to bee corrected uppon the next generall impression, there being but a small number of these bookes imprinted, remayning at this time in his handes to be privately delivered to the learned & desirous thereof." [1]

In the shadows of a great religious edifice, then, a vigorous, if not always thriving, enterprise was carried on. Here publishers, booksellers, writers, and purchasers mingled, some excited by the fever of sales but others disillusioned by the meager returns from "a thriftlesse, and a thankelesse occupation," some prosperous and others in need. For professional beggars were by no means without companions; professional writers were penniless, exploited offshoots of the business created by the invention of the printing press. Parnassus may have been in fantasy an idyllic haven of artistic delight; in reality it was a business transaction consummated in St. Paul's Churchyard with merchants who little resembled the gods of Olympia. It was personal, intimate, and frequently disenchanting.[2]

Yet the disenchanted never ceased regurgitating tracts. If they were unrewarded or inadequately rewarded, they did not long abandon their quills and their manuscripts. Robert Greene, Richard Robinson, Thomas Churchyard, and Barnaby Rich, to name only four of the most prolific Elizabethans, composed their pamphlets and their poems so rapidly that it seemed as though the wells of inspiration (and duplication) were bottomless. They had the literary fever — a virus which they shared with many of their contemporaries. Gentlemen somehow stole moments from other pressing duties to produce folios. Sir Philip Sidney, so Aubrey informs us, jotted down "notions" for his *Arcadia* while hunting. Archbishop Parker hoped Cecil had leisure to revise one of the epistles for the Bishops' Bible. Students of law in the various Inns of Court neglected jurisprudence for collections of modish trifles like John Grange's *Golden Aphroditis*. Edward Hake, bailiff and subsequently mayor of Windsor, wrote *News out of Paul's Churchyard*. Henry Arthington, "prisoner," completed *The Seduction of Arthington by Hackett* "from my poor chamber in the Counter, this 25. of Februarie. 1592." Even a woman or two ventured into print. In *The First Part of the Mirror of Princely Deeds and Knighthood* Margaret Tyler defends with a proverb her feminine right to appear as a translator and to write of battle: "It is no sin to talke of Robinhood, though you never shot in his bow." Although the products of the untalented are drab and occasionally almost painful, there was a healthy vigor about publication in the age of Elizabeth when almost everyone, at least it sometimes seems so, glanced coyly at the printing establishments and brought to this century-old business some of the recklessness of young love.[3]

To use John Florio's wonderfully English figure, "this our paper-sea" disturbed humanists, moralists, authors of integrity, and perhaps some readers. King James in a proclamation of 1610 took royal cognizance of the "itching in the tongues and pennes of most men, as nothing is un-searched to the bottome . . . from the very highest mys-teries in the Godhead, and the most inscrutable Councels in the Trinitie, to the very lowest pit of Hell." Decades earlier Roger Ascham, humanist and schoolmaster, lamented the use to which the English presses were put: "But now, the ripest of tong, be readiest to write: And many dayly in setting out bookes and balettes make great shew of blossomes and buddes, in whom is neither, roote of learning, nor frute of wisedome at all." Similar fears about the loss of standards were voiced by, among others, Hake, Cross, Joseph Hall, and Samuel Daniel. Thus, hardly a century had elapsed after the introduction of the printing press into England before misgivings about mass production and mass taste were heard.[4]

Just as England's destiny was shaped by middle-class statesmen in the sixteenth century, so middle-class writers and printers dominated the printing trade and, for better or worse, gave to literature a middle-class foundation. Since aristocrats, whether of the well-pedigreed or new variety, affected disdain of vulgar print, and subordinated art to pursuits worthy of courtiers, there could be no other foundation. Philip Sidney, Edward Dyer, Fulke Greville, and Walter Ralegh, for instance, wrote quantities of material which they circulated in manuscript, but they were first servants of the queen, poets only in their idleness. They steadfastly clung to a Renaissance tradition made obsolete by the printing press.

A few authors came from substantial middle-class families. John Donne's father, for instance, was a wealthy citizen, a warden of the Ironmongers' Company. Thomas Lodge's father, a wealthy grocer and a lord mayor of London, was bankrupt before his death, but his son had £1000 to squander after he returned to London from Trinity College, Oxford. Breton was also a member of an affluent family, at least until his mother married George Gascoigne. Neither Lodge nor Breton had Donne's contempt of the printing press; they were but hacks, bringing to their writings not genuine talent but an ambitious enthusiasm. John Lyly, who penned a middle-class *Courtier,* was the son of a yeoman, "whose wealth and degree of cultivation had raised him into the class of the landed gentry." Robert Tofte, a poet of small talent, was the son of a fishmonger, but, after he inherited a considerable estate from his maternal grandfather, he became a "Gent." and proudly disdained professionalism.[5]

The families of most Elizabethan writers were of moderate means. Ben Jonson's father was evidently not an overly successful clergyman, nor was his stepfather prosperous. Spenser, the son of a journeyman in the art of clothmaking, was one of the poor scholars maintained by the Merchant Taylors, and Richard Hooker, the most glorious voice of Anglicanism, came from a poor Exeter family. Michael Drayton's sire was a tanner or a butcher, Christopher Marlowe's a cobbler, Stephen Gosson's a joiner and freeman of Canterbury, Thomas Kyd's a London scrivener, George Peele's a slater, Anthony Munday's a draper, John Webster's a merchant tailor, John Stow's a tallow-chandler, and Henry Chettle's a dyer. It seems appropriate in light of his poetry that Robert Herrick's father was an expert goldsmith. The Goldsmiths' Company, to which his grandfather had belonged, rewarded James Mabbe with twenty-nine nobles when he became master of arts at Cambridge. John Marston lived at Wilton, where his father was chamberlain to the Herberts. Henry Lok (or Lock), the author of *The Return from Parnassus,* was born into the family of a mercer, as was William Browne. Daniel was the son of a music-master. As everyone knows because of Greene and Nashe's cruel taunts, a Saffron Walden ropemaker named Harvey had three sons who attended the university and made reputations in education, medicine, and the ministry. Yet Greene was in all probability the child of a saddler in Norwich, and Nashe came of a family unknown and undistinguished.[6]

Children of tradesmen, then, from London and the provinces, from urban rather than agricultural backgrounds, constituted the majority of Elizabethan professional writers. Their parents were evidently ambitious for their children. For Elizabethan professionals, with such well-known exceptions as Shakespeare, Jonson, and Drayton, were generally graduates of universities. To Cambridge went Spenser, Marlowe, Nashe, Gabriel Harvey, Lok, John Dee, Abraham Fraunce, and Joseph Hall. Oxford claimed, perhaps not always proudly, Lodge, Daniel, Florio, Dyer, William Camden, Sir John Davies, Hooker, Peele, Lyly, Francis Beaumont, Marston, Mabbe, and Thomas Rogers. A few, Greene, Francis Meres, and possibly Donne, were graduates of both universities. The celebrated finishing schools, the Inns of Court, included in the earlier generation of Elizabethans such men as Gascoigne, Turbervile, Grange, Hake, Arthur Golding, and

Sir Thomas North; and, later in the century, Lodge, Donne, Sidney, Francis Bacon, Hooker, Beaumont, Marston, Sir John Davies, and Rogers. Thus, Elizabethan professionals entered in large numbers "the company of educated men." [7]

Education, however, has little to do with artistic genius. Shakespeare's small Latin and less Greek came from his training at Stratford. Drayton also escaped the universities, but he was tutored in classical poetry in the home of Sir Henry Goodere, and studiously absorbed English history, folklore, and traditions before he undertook his survey of England in *Poly-Olbion*. Two of the important antiquarians of the period, John Stow and John Speed, were tailors and devoted historians of London and England. The patriarchs of the Elizabethan Grub Street, Munday, Churchyard, Rich, and Richard Robinson, were unlearned — and proud of it. At least they never tired of immodestly emphasizing their lack of education. But they were undoubtedly graduates of grammar schools. Thomas Deloney, a silk-weaver by vocation and a novelist by avocation, was more talented in his medium than most of the university graduates; certainly he at least equaled famous wits like Greene and Lodge.

These tradesmen and sons of tradesmen, whether trained at the universities or in apprenticeships, faced a difficult problem. Obviously in varying degrees they had literary talent, some for drama and poetry, some for translations, some for journalism. But what were they to do with their talents after they left the universities or completed their apprenticeships? Only the theater was sufficiently well-organized, and at least somewhat considerate of authorship, to furnish a livelihood. Poetry and livelihood have rarely been synonymous. Translators depended upon the largesse of patrons, when they could be found, and upon enlightened publishers. Journalists in the absence of newspapers had at best uncertain employment in printers' establishments.

The plight of the university graduate in many respects was more serious than that of the tradesman-author or the soldier-author. The artisan at least had his trade and sometimes his livery company to shelter him; the soldier could find a war in the sixteenth century (Ireland was there for the English to die in), service in the household of some noble warrior, or, more rarely, a royal pension. But the military did not lure the middle class — then or now. (Burghley, the most indispensable of Elizabeth's bourgeois advisors, has this to say about rearing children: "Neither by my consent, shalt thou train them up to the wars.") They were not interested in gracing arms with learning, like the idealized courtier of Castiglione, nor would they demean themselves in the trades of their fathers. Furthermore, by common agreement university graduates qualified as gentlemen. Yet the label of "gentleman" was virtually meaningless, since it included everything and in effect nothing. Thus, "a Marlowe or a Greene is a young man uprooted." Professor Harbage continues: "He is detached from his class but without the means of becoming fully accredited in any higher class, yet with heightened aspirations; discontent and disillusion stalk him from the moment he steps out into the world." [8]

Despite the uncertainties and risks of authorship, to London came the university wits and the literary-minded artisans. Perhaps they expected to conquer like the Scythian shepherd Tamburlaine. They duplicated only the conqueror's verbalism; his victories they could not achieve. For London was a city of promise and a city of vested mercantile interests. Publication was controlled by the Stationers' Company, which had safeguarded its own interests by laws but which had understandably (and profitably) neglected to provide protection for authors, who soon discovered that the profession provided not even minimal security. Other means of livelihood they had to find. For, as Ingenioso observes in *The Return from Parnassus,* "wit is but a phantasme and Idea, a quareling shadowe, that will seldome dwell in the same roome with a full purse, but commonly is the idle follower of a forlorne creature." [9]

About 1580 Gabriel Harvey wrote to Spenser: "As for my selfe, howsoever I have toyed, and trifled heretofore, I am nowe taught, and I truste I shall shortly learne . . . to employ my travayle and tyme wholly, or chiefely on those studies and practizes that carrie, as they saye, meate in their mouth." In all honesty he cannot encourage Spenser "to goe forward, unlesse ye might make account of some certaine ordinarie wages, at the leastwise have your meate and drinke for your dayes workes." Harvey had a hectic and short-lived career as a don at Cambridge. Spenser passed almost his entire life in governmental service in Ireland. Daniel tutored William Herbert and Anne Clifford, daughter of the Countess of Cumberland, and later became a groom of the privy chamber in Queen Anne's court. Rich, Churchyard, Munday, and Marlowe were professional informers. Gascoigne and Whetstone, as well as Rich and Churchyard, were first soldiers, then writers. Munday, Nashe, and Lyly supplemented their income (and gained favor) by becoming hacks of the episcopacy in the Marprelate controversy. Whether for economic reasons we do not know, Lodge eventually became a physician, and Marston, Hall, Gosson, Meres, and Thomas Bastard, clergymen. Some writers like Harvey and Nashe accepted employment in printers' shops, just as many playwrights became Henslowe's hacks. Lodowick Lloyd, once sergeant-at-arms to Elizabeth and a prolific compiler of curiosa, a kind of earlier and duller Coryat, after James's succession "learned to make glasses and spectacles." [10]

With the notable exceptions of Shakespeare and Spenser, the lives of Elizabethan authors comprise case histories of poverty. Even Jonson, "the wittiest fellow of a Bricklayer in England," who was the recipient of gifts unusual for their size in an era of parsimony among patrons, was, if *An Epistle Mendicant* is to be accepted literally, destitute toward the end of his career. More than twenty years after the poet's death John Lane wrote melodramatically of Spenser,

> When verbale drones of virtuous merit scant
> suffred that gentile poet die of want,

and thereby augmented a legend which it has taken three centuries to disprove. For we now know that two weeks before his death Spenser was paid £8 (to obtain today's equivalent the sum should be multiplied by fifteen or twenty) for bearing letters from Sir Thomas Norrys to Sir Robert Cecil and the privy council. Since governmental officials and patrons recognized Spenser's genius, his lot, economically speaking, was better than that of most of his fellow professionals. He did not of course support himself through his art, as Cuddie and Colin Clout make abundantly clear, but bitterness did not paralyze him.[11]

Drayton was not so fortunate, nor so energetic. He grew up in the household of Sir Henry Goodere. After his master's death Drayton became the charge of Lady Lucy Harington and later of Sir Walter Aston. At the same time, probably in desperation, he turned to the most remunerative form of writing in the Elizabethan age, the drama. But neither playwriting nor poetry provided lasting security: Drayton lacked the dramatic talents of his greater contemporaries, and his poetry failed to produce adequate income either from readers or patrons. In the preface to the second part of *Poly-Olbion* he reveals that he undertook this "Herculean labour" because his friends had persuaded him "that there is scarcely any of the Nobilitie, or Gentry of this land, but that he is some way or other, by his Blood interressed therein." Drayton's friends were probably as romantic as the poet himself, "for instead of that comfort, which my noble friends (from the freedome of their Spirits) proposed as my due, I have met with barbarous Ignorance, and base Detraction." After this failure his bitterness increased, and at his death he was a poor man. "Honest Mr. Michael Drayton," Peacham observes, "had about some five pound lying by him at his death." The inventory of his estate amounted to £24 8s. 2d.[12]

Lodge laments the loss of his inheritance in *An Alarum against Usurers* (1584), one of the familiar prodigal-son tales of the era; and in *Scylla's Metamorphosis* (1589) he bewails his failure to prosper in the literary profession:

> What fruites of former labours doe I finde?
> My studious pen dooth traffique for a scorne:
> My due deserts are but repaid with winde;
> And what I earne, is nought but bitter mourne:
> > In which accompt I reap but this advise,
> > To cease to clime, and live contented wise.

At some time during the 1590's Lodge became a physician and, according to Anthony Wood, "was as much cried up to his last for physick, as he was in his younger days for his poetical fancy." If Lodge's medical practice paid as poorly as his literary works, he was indeed a desperate man. Probably, however, medicine afforded him security since he prepared translations of Josephus (1602) and Seneca (1614), weighty tomes with little sales appeal. "Too long time surfeited upon time-pleasing," Dr. Lodge forsook the trifles of his youth and the uncertain lot of the literary professional.[13]

Nashe was eager to deny Gabriel Harvey's imputation of poverty — "my muse never wept for want of maintenance" — yet six months earlier, in *Pierce Penniless* (1592), he had publicly acknowledged it with extravagant rage:

I sate up late, and rose earely, contended with the colde, and conversed with scarcitie: for all my labours turned to losse, my vulgar Muse was despised & neglected, my paines not regarded, or slightly rewarded, and I my selfe (in prime of my best wit) laid open to povertie. Whereupon (in a malecontent humor) I accused my fortune, raild on my patrones, bit my pen, rent my papers, and ragde in all points like a mad man.

A year later Nashe, who oscillated between Tamburlaine-like assertiveness and self-debasing fawning, hailed Sir Robert Carey as his deliverer: "Through him my tender wainscot Studie doore is delivered from much assault and battrie: through him I looke into, and am lookt on in the world; from whence otherwise I were a wretched banished exile." But he soon lost favor with the Careys, for he was to become "Danter's man." In 1596 he admitted that when "the bottome of my purse is turnd downeward, & my conduit of incke will no longer flowe for want of reparations, . . . I prostitute my pen in hope of gaine; but otherwise there is no newfanglenes in mee but povertie, which alone maketh mee so unconstant to my determined studies." [14]

In the early 1580's these young aspirants to literary fame began to congregate in London, where they nursed their fantasies and reluctantly accepted their poverty. Fervently desirous of acceptance among gentlemen and hostile to vulgar commoners, they often affected the dress and manners of what since has become known as the artist-type or the bohemian. Greene stalked about with the handsome peak which the beardless Nashe admired, but Gabriel Harvey, who "was altogether unacquainted with the man," ridiculed Greene's "fonde disguisinge of a Master of Arte with ruffianly haire, unseemely apparell, and more unseemelye Company." Somehow bohemia, at least in the pictures drawn by writers as well as by philistines, manages a peculiar cross between characteristics of the criminal, or ruffian, and the overgroomed Pateresque esthete. To the practical middle class, authors were eccentrics in strange attire, and to the aristocrats they were pretenders and frequently nuisances. Jonson records a revealing anecdote: "One day being at table with my lady Rutland, her husband comming in, accused her that she keept table to poets." [15]

An anonymous letter-writer to the privy council protested Gascoigne's admission to the position of burgess of parliament:

Item he is a common Rymer and a deviser of slaunderous Pasquelles againste divers personnes of greate callinge

Item he is a notorious Ruffianne and especiallie noted to be bothe a spie; an Atheist and godlesse personne

But the Puritan innately suspicious of art and artists did not have to fabricate stories or to speculate; writers were only too willing to wash their linens in public confessionals. In explaining why "Poems and sonnets of love" are "foolishly odious in this Age," Giles Fletcher, himself the author of the sonnet sequence *Licia* (1593), frankly admits that "many base companions are the greatest Writers." The year before, in his posthumous *Groatsworth of Wit,* Greene had not minced words in unveiling his own indiscretions and those of his former friends. In their acrimonious feud Gabriel Harvey insisted that Nashe's private life belied his protestations of penitence in *Christ's Tears over Jerusalem.* With arrogant self-righteousness Harvey urges his opponent to "reforme his publique, &

redresse his private enormities, & with a sincere vow I sweare him frendship." [16]

Almost from the beginning alcoholism was associated with literary professionals. Nashe, in the preface to *Menaphon,* deplores "their immoderate follie, who affirme that no man can write with conceit, except he takes counsell of the cup." Greene's banquet of Rhenish wine and pickled herring became a classic tale of the short, intoxicated life of a bohemian author. Someone wrote a burlesque elegy on Turbervile's death: "Dinge Donge, cease nowe the bell, he loved a pot of stronge ale well." Drayton, we are told in *The Second Part of the Return from Parnassus,* "wants one true note of a Poet of our times, and that is this, hee cannot swagger it well in a Taverne, nor dominere in a hot-house." The *Parnassus* plays bristle with pointed jests attempting to link the tavern with "Can quaffing hucksters." Webbe observes tartly, "Pottical, poeticall (I should say), heades I would wyshe at their worshipfull comencements might in steede of Lawrell be gorgiously garnished with fayre greene Barley, in token of their good affection to our Englishe Malt." [17]

For hacks and artists alike sought Parnassus in taverns, inspiration in sack, beauty in not-so-divine drunkenness or in unclassical whores. "As Anacreon died by the pot," Meres observes with surprisingly little pretense of morality for one later to become a clergyman, "so George Peele by the pox." Of these pleasure-bent, diseased, hungry writers we can probably accept, but without his vindictive glee, what Harvey reports of Greene: "They that have seene much more, then I have heard; (for so I am credibly informed) can relate straunge, & almost incredible Comedies of his monstrous disposition." For we are dealing not with saints but with men susceptible to fleshly attractions, among whom, according to Meres, Drayton, almost alone, "is helde for a man of vertuous disposition, honest conversation, and wel governed cariage, which is almost miraculous among good wits in these declining and corrupt times." [18]

Because authors were filled with guilt when they turned their backs upon their parents for the shoddy retreats of Shoreditch, they viewed themselves as prodigal sons. Lyly in *Euphues* made the prodigal son into a fashionable formula for tales, and Whetstone, Lodge, Greene, and others imitated him. But this was more than a fashion: the prodigal-son story was a thinly disguised means of relating their own experiences. Although only Greene dropped the pretense of fiction in his *Groatsworth of Wit,* desire for pleasure and escape from middle-class restraints, uneasiness in the midst of desired pleasure, eventual revulsion, and the meek return to their bourgeois parents — all had counterparts in their own experiences. Munday, the cloth-worker-author, like many other young Elizabethans who ignored the admonitions of grave Ascham to shun travel, journeyed to France and Italy: "My wilde oates required to be furrowed in a forreyne ground." There in ways unspecified he betrayed his parents. When he returned to England, fleeing the lures of Italianate vice, he felt compelled to confess his waywardness publicly in *The Mirror of Mutability* (1579). Though penitence literature was not without sales appeal (it has what journalists call "human interest"), the contrition of a Munday was more than a vendible utterance: it was the sincere statement of a man unable to shrug off the moral training of his youth.

The most celebrated prodigal in this era of prodigals was the most popular pamphleteer of the sixteenth century, Greene. The personal charm and amiability of Shoreditch's most colorful citizen concealed a stricken conscience. Greene turned his back on his Norwich family after he left the universities in order to write volumes for the stationers of St. Paul's Churchyard. For a time he made money, especially when he wrote for the stage, but he squandered it quickly on prostitutes and other vain pleasures. About 1588 he returned to Norwich, where a preacher so frightened him with the prospects of eternal conflagration that for a short time he reformed his life — and produced a few repentance tales to salve his conscience and replenish his purse. Within a few months, back in his London haunts, he once more swaggered as Robin Greene, and in "unseemely Company" blasphemed with Marlowe, caroused with Nashe, and sapped his strength, physical and moral, with whores and cozeners. Harvey's catalog of Greene's vices is accurate except perhaps in minor details. In *Groatsworth of Wit,* written in the last month of his short life, in August 1592, Greene essentially corroborates Harvey. So intent was he to make himself into an example for wayward English youth that with inverted pride he termed himself the worst of sinners, and he summoned to penitence, in the tones of a Robert Parsons, his "quodam acquaintance," Marlowe, Nashe, and Peele. Although he had burned the candle at both ends, Greene had never extinguished the morality of Norwich in his amoral bohemia. In his squalid room with his squalid mistress he died a true son of the bourgeoisie.[19]

The rebellion of these prodigal sons, like Greene's, did not extend much beyond a self-conscious and superficial flouting of society's customs. Fundamentally, Elizabethan writers accepted the premises as well as the fears and the aspirations of Tudor culture.

"Profite," or utility, was an obsession with English humanists, a yardstick which precluded theory and abstract speculation and minimized aesthetic experience. In his typically humanistic treatise, *The Governor,* Elyot in effect describes the Cromwells, Starkeys, and Cecils — Tudor middle-class governors. Future governors are to read utilitarian and moral treatises. When they read poetry they are to search out what is useful to their careers. Homer they may read, for from him "as from a fountaine proceded all eloquence and lernyng. For in his bokes be contained, and most perfectly expressed, not only the documentes marciall and discipline of armes, but also incomparable wisdomes, and instructions for politike governaunce of people." Elyot concludes, "I only desire that they have, in every of the saide bokes, so moche instruction that they may take therby some profite.[20]

Elyot's utilitarian and ethical approach to literature also anticipates that of critics and authors at the end of the century. In the *Aeneid* Elyot finds that hunting, wrestling, running, "or other lyke exercise" will profit the governor. Lodge singles out "the practice of a dilligent captaine"; Webbe points to "the valoure of a worthy Captaine and valiaunt Governour, together with the perrilous adventures of warre, and polliticke devises at all assayes"; and Sidney asks, " Who readeth Aeneas carrying olde Anchises on his back, that wisheth not it were his fortune to perfourme so excellent an acte?" Webbe feels compelled to rationalize his pleasure in Spenser's *Shepherd's Calendar* by dwelling upon its useful morality: "The occasion of his worke is a warning to other young men, who, being intangled in love and youthful vanities, may learne to looke to themselves in time, and to avoyde inconveniences which may breede if they be not in time prevented." As zealously as a Puritan, Webbe employs two favorite sixteenth-century words, "profit" and "commodity." [21]

Gabriel Harvey's notation in his marginalia epitomizes much of the spirit of the age: "Ite, et praedicate (non sedete, et scribite)." In colloquial diction: be up and doing, don't sit around scribbling foolish fancies. Thus "the new learning," to which C. S. Lewis somewhat harshly joins "and the new ignorance," formulated, or perhaps only verbalized, the cultural pattern of sixteenth-century England.[22]

At the same time the age had a strongly moralistic frame of mind. Personal pleasure was suspect — and not only among Puritans. Although Puritans like Gosson and Stubbes became notorious for their indiscriminate (and excessively vigorous) attacks upon stage plays, bawdy tales, and romances, Ascham, a humanist, was no less hostile, though his language was slightly more temperate. In his reply to Gosson, Lodge is no less stringent than his Puritan adversary:

I abhorre those poets that savor of ribaldry: I will with the zealous admit the expullcion of such enormities: poetry is dispraised not for the folly that is in it, but for the abuse whiche manye ill Wryters couller by it. Beleeve me the magestrats may take advise (as I knowe wisely can) to roote out those odde rymes which runnes in every rascales mouth, savoring of rybaldry. Those foolishe ballets that are admitted make poets good and godly practises to be refused.

Nashe alleges that "tender youth ought to bee restrained for a time from the reading of such ribauldrie, least, chewing over wantonlie the eares of this Summer Corne, they be choaked with the haune before they can come at the kernell." [23]

Sidney, Harington, and others argued idealistically the noble mission of poetry in order to refute Agrippa's denunciation,

. . . an Arte, that was devised to no other ende, but to please the eares of foolishe men, with wanton Rithmes, with measures, and weightinesse of sillables, and with a vaine jarringe of wordes, and to deceive mens mindes with the delectation of fables, and with fardels of lies. Wherefore, shee dothe deserve to be called the principall Authoure of lies, and the maintainer of perverse opinions.

But most Elizabethans were troubled: If poetry can encourage man to noble behavior, then it can seduce him to evil. Nashe cautions "that we dwell not so long in Poetry that wee become Pagans." Harvey urges Spenser, after he peruses the enclosed "Verses and Rymes," "to abandon all other fooleries, and honour Vertue, the onely immortall and surviving Accident amongst so manye mortall and ever-perishing Substaunces." [24]

Authors, then, not only engaged in an activity of questionable usefulness to society, but also, if they chose not to produce didactic treatises, threatened the moral order. Finally, there was the question of propriety: in maturity one put away childish things. In *The Art of English Poetry*, Richard Puttenham minimized his work as "but the studie of my yonger yeares, in which vanitie raigned." His was a widespread notion. Lodge in his maturity translated moral treatises, and Greene vowed to deny his own nature and to ape Gower rather than Chaucer. "Jack Donne" the Dean wished to forget. John Chamberlain, although an Elizabethan man-about-town, reacted like a solid citizen after reading "certain verses of our Dean of Paules [Donne] upon the death of the Marquis Hamilton, . . . though they be reasonable wittie and well don yet I could wish a man of his yeares and place to geve over versifieng." For, in the sixteenth and early seventeenth centuries, as Harvey observes, "lyttle or no writing will now serve. . . . All writing layd abedd as taedious, & needles. All is now, in bowld Courtly speaking, and bowld Industrious dooing. Activity, praesent bowld Activity." And, to prove Harvey's point, there is Greville's report of an interview with Sir Robert Cecil in which the courtier had expressed his intention of writing a life of Elizabeth: Cecil "descending to question me, why I would dreame out my time in writing a story, being as like to rise in this time as any man he knew." [25]

As if Tudor society had not created difficulties for authors, aristocratic amateurs who could not resist the temptation to trifle in poetry and occasionally in prose scorned, or pretended to scorn, the printing press and the readers who purchased books in St. Paul's Churchyard. Indeed, by the end of the century anyone who wished to demonstrate his gentlemanliness confined his scribblings to manuscripts or, if his work somehow chanced to fall into a stationer's hands, protested — in print — his innocence.

Just as Elyot's *Governor* became a manual for bourgeois magistrates and politicians, so Castiglione's *Courtier* expressed the ideals of amateurism. Although Castiglione's comments are in actuality ambiguous and subject to almost any construction a courtier chose to place upon them, Elizabethans generally construed them to mean: that writing was a permissible diversion to be indulged in only when there were no urgent matters of state; that poems and other amateur effusions were to be kept private and circulated in manuscripts among friends; and that under no circumstances were amateurs to accept compensation for their trifles.[26]

Authors of humble origins were placed in an untenable position: to attain gentlemanly status they had to avoid manual labor, yet if they chose authorship as a profession, they lost caste in the eyes of gentlemen. Spenser, for example, anxious to retain the favor of the Earl of Leicester and other aristocrats, published *The Shepherd's Calendar* anonymously, but he had "doubts" about printing other manuscripts. He confessed to Gabriel Harvey: "I was minded for a while to have intermitted the uttering [publication] of my writings, leaste, by overmuch cloying their noble eares, I should gather a contempt of my self, or else seeme rather for gaine and commoditie to doe it, for some sweetnesse that I have already tasted." In other words, he feared loss of status and the scornful attribution of desire for "gaine and commoditie." [27]

These writers could not afford the luxury of amateurism; they had neither inheritances nor estates, and they had few prospects of obtaining substantial positions at court. Amateurs, on the other hand, were usually either of noble birth or of the landed gentry. Donne and Tofte, sons of wealthy burghers, were exceptions. Edward de Vere, seventeenth Earl of Oxford, was the most aristocratic of amateurs. Sidney belonged to the new nobility of the sixteenth century. Ralegh, Greville, Dyer, Richard Carew, Arthur Golding, and Turbervile stemmed from the gentry. Richard Barnfield, according to Wood, was born "of genteel parents in the county of Stafford." With few exceptions, then, amateurs came from families of means and social position and from rural England rather than from urban centers. They were, in short, of conservative stock. Perhaps it is also of some significance that, with the exception of Sidney and Carew, these amateurs matriculated at Cambridge and later became members of the various Inns of Court.[28]

Unlike professionals, amateurs channeled most of their energies and talents into nonliterary pursuits. The activities and careers of the Earl of Oxford, Ralegh, and Sidney are too well-known to be recapitulated. Turbervile wrote no books after 1575, when he was about thirty-one, and was able to "imbrace a wife, with wealth and coyne enough." Greville was a scholarly courtier and, paradoxically, a somewhat crabbed Calvinist. Carew dabbled in literature only in times of respite from his duties as a country squire. After a literary career of approximately ten years Barnfield retired to manage his estates in Staffordshire, and

Golding, probably a professional for many years, left London about 1580 and returned to Exeter to take charge of his estate and to spend more of his time in litigation than in composition.[29]

Amateurs and their imitators invoked much too facilely the God-Mammon dichotomy, which is still fashionable in certain artistic circles. The pure artist loathes money; mountebanks worship lucre and prostitute their talents. This is the cry of writers attempting to rationalize their failures. Spenser, Shakespeare, and Jonson united business acumen and artistic genius. Donne wrote some of his greatest poetry — the *Anniversary* poems, for example — for splendid fees, and Spenser undoubtedly for a substantial reward composed one of the loveliest poems in the language, *The Prothalamion*. Daniel's talent was not spoiled by the sinecures bestowed upon him by the Countess of Pembroke. Art cannot be explained in terms of payments. Geniuses and quacks have written for money. In fact, as Dr. Johnson observed, no one but a blockhead writes except for money.

More serious than the refusal of the amateurs to accept money for their creative works (many of them, incidentally, pursued Elizabeth's purse strings with unseemly zeal) was their reduction of literature to a pastime. For, by their insistence that art was of secondary importance and that they trifled in poetry only in their leisure, they not only minimized the aesthetic experience in order to glorify an essentially amorphous principle of social obligation (their version of Tudor "utility"), but also reduced the status of the serious literary craftsman to that of a toiler of a lower social order. Justifiably, George Pettie protested, "Those which myslike that a Gentleman should publish the fruites of his learning, are some curious Gentlemen, who thynke it most commendable in a Gentleman, to cloake his arte and skill in every thyng, and to seeme to doo all thynges of his owne mother witte as it were." Puttenham was even more forthright than Pettie in his strictures against the subterfuges of amateurs. "I know very many notable Gentlemen in the Court that have written commendably, and suppressed it agayne, or els suffred it to be publisht without their owne names to it; as if it were a discredit for a Gentleman to seeme learned, and to shew him selfe amorous of any good Art." In fact, though he probably was not aware of the implications, his conclusion reads like a refutation of Castiglione's *Courtier*:

Since therefore so many noble Emperours, Kings, and Princes have bene studious of Poesie and other civill arts, and not ashamed to bewray their skils in the same, let none other meaner person despise learning, nor (whether it be in prose or in Poesie, if they them selves be able to write, or have written any thing well or of rare invention) by any whit squeimish to let it be publisht under their names, for reason serves it, and modestie doth not repugne.

For he rightly singled out the weaknesses in Castiglione's portrait and in literary amateurism: learning is as important as arms to the nation, and art is more than a graceful accomplishment to entertain women.[30]

In final analysis, however, more important that the frequently discussed, and overemphasized, aristocratic contempt of print is the cultural attitude toward art and the artist. "Use" was the byword of humanist, Puritan, critic, and courtier. Literature was scrutinized in terms of ethical presuppositions. Not one voice was raised in England during the century to defend art on aesthetic grounds; the only difference between the artist and nonartist was the former's vague defense of literary standards. No one of importance dared to defend recreation and simple pleasure. It seemed that everyone distrusted art: the humanist because of his concern for the social welfare, the Puritan because of his mania for God's work, the nobleman because of his devotion to the abstract ideal of the well-rounded courtier, the bourgeois because of his indifference to a useless, unprofitable activity. The public chorus, then, appeared to be unanimous. Fortunately for Elizabethan authors and readers, the situation was not so desperate as it appeared. Solemn pontification of moralistic truisms was a public duty; the practice was not as consistent as the monotonous pronouncements.

But, while England established herself as mistress of the seas, while commerce was expanding with remote countries and intrepid adventurers (and exploiters) were opening up new lands to merchants in search of new frontiers, while Elizabeth with her political genius brought peace and solidarity to a nation that had been rent asunder through internal rivalries, while the Elizabethan and Jacobean stage became a national institution and English music achieved international fame — many artists and creators felt themselves consigned to the periphery of their society. They looked in vain to find their niche in a materialistic world. The audience for their books, so they declaimed with typical Elizabethan positiveness, consisted of clowns and louts without taste. Maecenases were rare; Maecenasses, to borrow Nashe's pun, were willing to pay hacks to immortalize their vulgarity. Meanwhile Spenser's Cuddie went in rags, unesteemed and unregarded.

CHAPTER TWO

THE AUDIENCE

OFTEN the Elizabethan professional stood in St. Paul's Churchyard, not far from the bookstalls, watching fops, merchants, ladies, and apprentices who glanced with calculating eyes at the tracts, perhaps even at his own latest "trifle," each buyer wanting his money's worth according to his own taste.

Some readers lookes,   for newes from forrayne lands,
A custome old,   that no new world can leave,
Some buyes new bookes,   that coms from writers hands,
To see what works,   the laboring wit can weave.
Some steps in hast,   and leanes on Stationers stall,
To aske what stuffe,   hath passed Printers Presse,
Some reades awhile,   but nothing buyes at all,
For in two lines,   they give a pretty gesse:
What doth the booke,   contayne such schollers thinke,
To spend no pence,   for paper, pen, and inke.

Superciliously these readers, or would-be readers, picked up, thumbed noisily, and cast aside books as though they were bolts of material rather than products of the imagination. "A farme for those," Churchyard concludes, "is better than a book," since "farmes profit brings." [1]

Invariably purchasers asked, "What's new?" A book several months old was like last season's costume, something to bestow upon the poor. "I have noted," Webster writes, "most of the people that come to that Playhouse, resemble those ignorant asses (who visiting Stationers shoppes their use is not to inquire for good books, but new bookes)." Before begrudgingly parting with their pence (let alone their shillings), customers had to be reassured by the bookseller that what they were purchasing was the latest thing. In haggling they could demonstrate to themselves and fellow shoppers, as well as to the bookseller, that they knew a thing or two about the merchandise of printers' row — like the gentleman described by Rowlands, who, despite his "knowledge," finally parted with his sixpence.

GENTLEMAN. But were's the new Booke thou tel'st me off, which is it?

PRENTICE. Marry, looke you sir, this is a prettie odde conceit, Of a Merrie meeting heere in London, betweene a Wife, a Widdow, and a Mayde.

GENTLEMAN. Merrie meeting, why, that Title is stale: Ther's a Booke cal'd, *T'is merry when knaves meete.* And ther's a Ballad, *T'is merry when Malt-men meete:* and besides, there's an olde Proverbe, *The more the merrier:* And therefore I thinke sure I have seene it.

PRENTICE. You are deceived, sir, Ile assure you, for I will bee disposed upon all the Bookes in my Shoppe that you have not seene it; t'is another manner of thing then you take it to bee, sir: For I am sure you are in Love, or at least will bee, with one of these three: or say you deale but with two, The Widow and the Mayde; because the Wife is another mans commoditie: is it not a prettie thing to carry Wife, Madye, and Widdow in your pocket, when you may as it were conferre and heare them talke togither when you will? . . .

GENTLEMAN. Nay, if your Booke be of such excellent quallitie and rare operation, wee must needes have some Traffique together. Heere take your money, i'st six-pence?
PRENTICE. I certaine tis no lesse, sir. I thanke yee sir.[2]

Like all relations in the small Elizabethan society, those between authors and buyers were intimate. Custom had decreed (and sales no doubt demanded) that writers cajole "gentle readers" in prefaces designed to flatter and to advertise the contents of a book. But by 1600 many customs had been discarded — for several reasons: authors were flooding bookstalls and were outstripping the demand of the book-buying public; and writers, more self-assertive than in earlier days, refused to bottle up their wrath and prostrate themselves before readers. In addition, it had become fashionable to flay the audience and to strike a verbal pose of independence. Hence, Dekker spoke out fiercely:

Yet to mainteine the scurvy fashion, and to keepe Custome in reparations, he must be honyed, and come-over with *Gentle Reader, Courteous Reader,* and *Learned Reader,* though he have no more Gentilitie in him than Adam had (that was but a gardner) no more Civility than a Tartar, and no more Learning than the most errand Stinkard, that (except his owne name) could never finde any thing in the Horne-booke.

By so doing he probably achieved a type of catharsis not possible in the more impersonal relation between author and reader in later centuries.[3]

Since Elizabethans were seldom content to express hatred in abstract terms, they created a repulsive stereotype of their audience. What they disliked apparently had to be translated into graphic pictures; such had been the influence of allegory upon the intellectual and emotional responses. Thus authors inveighed against the literary equivalent of allegorical evil with the choleric intensity with

which moralists attacked sin. "You (that are Readers),"
Dekker proclaims, "are the most desperate and fowlest
players in the world." "Readers in these times," Florio
avers, are "most part sicke of the sullens, and peevish in
their sicknes, and conceited in their peevishnes." Shall I
write, cries Marston,

> To please each hound? each dungie Scavenger,
> To fit some Oyster-wenches yawning jawes?

Marston cannot tolerate a situation in which "each dung-
hill pesant" has "free perusall" of his "well labor'd lines"
and some "perfum'd Castilio . . . blast with stinking
breath, [his] budding Muse." [4]

As one would expect, authors pictured readers as stupid
louts proud of their stupidity. Drayton almost despaired
of coming into print again after the reception of *Piers
Gaveston*: "The fonde censures of the sottish and absurd
ignorant had altogether discouraged me . . . theyr dull
eyes, so over-clowded with mistie ignorance, as never able
to looke into celestiall secrets of divine Poesie, thereby to
discerne the right and true method of a perfect and exquisite Poeme." Maliciously, Middleton writes,

> I fat with joy to see how the poor swains
> Do box their country thighs, carrying their packets
> Of writings, yet can neither read nor write:
> They're like to candles, if they had no light;
> For they are dark within in sense and judgment
> As is the Hole at Newgate.

And Marston, still dissecting readers, queries,

> Shall each odde puisne of the Lawyers Inne,
> Each barmy-froth, that last day did beginne
> To reade his little, or his *nere a whit*,
> Or shall some greater auntient, of lesse wit,
> (That never turn'd but browne Tobacco leaves
> Whose sences some damn'd Occupant bereaves)

Lye gnawing on thy vacant times expence?
Tearing thy rimes, quire altering the sence? [5]

With obvious delight Gascoigne illustrates the critical ineptness of readers. In the 1560's Churchyard and Camell had engaged in a dull fliting, the allegations of one producing a short pamphlet by the other, sometimes in torturous prose and occasionally in something remotely resembling poetry — all in all, a controversy that must have aroused only the interest of the participants. "The contentions," Gascoigne charges, "betwene maister Churchyard and Camell, were (by a blockheaded reader) construed to be indeed a quarell betwene two neighbors. Of whom that one having a Camell in keping, and that other having charge of the Churchyard, it was supposed they had grown to debate, bicause the Camell came into the Churchyarde." Other readers confused "jeast" and "sad earnest," Gascoigne continues. "Laugh not at this (lustie yonkers) since the pleasant dittie of the noble Erle of Surrey (beginning thus: *In winters just returne*) was also construed to be made indeed by a Shepeherd. What shoulde I stande much in rehersall how the L. Vaux his dittie (beginning thus: *I loth that I did love*) was thought by some to be made upon his death bed?" In other words, "they take Chalke for Cheese." [6]

What actually rankled with the author was not so much the misconstruction of his phrases as the necessity of exposing his wares on the bookstalls of St. Paul's Churchyard. In spite of his education and his desire for gentlemanly status, circumstances compelled him, like his bourgeois father, to "swink and swat" for a livelihood and to resort to a marketplace where his books were subject to the caprices of illiterate purchasers. Though he protested, like Marston, making his "soule a merchandize, Seeking conceits to sute these Artless times," he recognized the absence of alternatives. The professional, generally speaking, was too much a part of the restless, compulsive age, and too imbued with the bourgeois dream of success, to retreat to the sidelines with Daniel. If people refused to read his books, they were not to be cajoled in the mellow, resigned tones of *Musophilus*; they were to be cudgeled with Nashean invective.[7]

This picture of an audience slobbering in its stupidity, however, was a fantasy of writers. Literacy produced the printing press, and literate readers purchased its products. Literacy enabled the Stationers' Company to increase from one printer to such numbers that the government had to impose restrictions. Such a trade could not flourish in an illiterate nation: apprentices, printers, and booksellers had to be able to read. Literate parents, desirous that their children get on in the world, sent them to grammar schools and then to the universities, where they became "wits" and frequently made snide remarks about ignorant readers. "You know well," the father in one of Hollyband's dialogs observes, "it were better to be unborne than untaught." Such had been the attitude of generations of Englishmen and their rulers. A statute of 1406 decreed "that every man or woman, of what estate or condition that he be, shall be free to set their son or daughter to take learning at any manner of school that pleaseth them within the Realm." [8]

Before the Englishman sought God and the arts, he sought a livelihood; hence capitalism was the most important factor in eradicating ignorance. Trade required bookkeeping and accounts; merchants, in order to best competition, both native and foreign, had to communicate with business prospects, and many merchants understood and wrote Latin, the language of trade as well as of law and diplomacy. Apprentices to these merchants were valuable according to their mastery of the rudiments of learning, and craftsmen had to keep records for their guilds. (As early as 1478 the goldsmiths would not accept an apprentice "without he canne writte and Rede.") Many shopkeepers kept accounts in Latin; the record-book (1520) of John Dorne, a bookseller in Oxford, is mostly in Latin. According to Professor Campbell's analysis of the signatures of approximately three thousand yeomen to wills, bonds, and other legal documents, "between 60 per cent and 70 per cent of those involved could write their own names." Although it cannot be assumed that these yeomen were therefore capable of reading and writing, Miss Campbell comes to the conclusion that "it was no extraordinary thing for yeomen to possess some books and to be able to read them." [9]

Equally persuasive as statistics produced by modern research is the testimony of the Elizabethan leatherseller-translator, Richard Robinson:

Those letters, therefore doe I deeme not onely to bee throughly learned: but also scarcely can I thinke any man in a free citty can or may deserve the name of a witty Citizen withoute the knowledge of learninge: for how without learning can we attaine not only unto the high knowledge of liberall sciences, but also thereby learne manye small artes or faculties: neither can merchandize it selfe or husbandry, be in sufficient savety without them: for these do keepe the memory of things past, they instruct posterytye: they annexe and compare thinges done and past, unto thinges yet to come, and do keepe a perpetuall reckoninge of all our whole lyfe.

For, beneath the idealistic (and conventional) flimflam of his last sentence is the realistic awareness that only the literate succeed. Even though he was later to be disillusioned with the literary profession, his grammar-school education at Newark had prepared him to become a competent translator and for a while to receive favors from important men of the realm. He had got on as his illiterate forebears never had.[10]

So mercantilism had imprinted on English minds the pragmatic necessity of education in an economic system based upon complex financial arrangements and trade agreements. The middle class early perceived the need of academic training for success in a nonfeudal society, just as courtiers recognized the practical nature of Castiglione's precepts for preferment in the new monarchies that depended more upon intelligence than upon military prowess. Neither commerce nor government in the sixteenth century could flourish without the support of educated men and women. Writers, however, were incapable of objectivity: they singled out the *nouveaux riches* for censure but ignored the large numbers of literate people produced by an economic system which they tended to scorn because it scorned them.

Catholicism supported education in ways that Puritans failed to appreciate. For centuries nunneries had provided elementary education to women; priests in villages had served as teachers of children (not all priests were baptized in ignorance, as sixteenth-century Protestants intimated); grammar schools had been established near churches in all parts of England. Catholicism reflected, if it did not always direct, the national interest in education. Puritanism, on the other hand, with its lower-class appeal and with its evangelistic insistence that every one should read and interpret the scriptures for himself, made education almost synonymous with godliness. But it is erroneous to attribute solely to Puritanism the demand for biblical translations or to credit this new movement with the edict of Henry VIII in 1543 expressly forbidding the reading of English Bibles by artificers, apprentices, and journeymen. Long before the appearance of the nonconformists, merchants, Catholics, and Anglicans had encouraged people to read. However, while Catholics and then Anglicans were preoccupied with their vain efforts to suppress heretical writings, and while Henry VIII's government was often more interested in confiscating church property than in preserving long-established schools and free education, Puritans remonstrated. Lever, for example, implored the King not to permit covetous men to usurp and sell charitable schools "to the utter disconforte of the poore, to the grevous offence of the people, to the most miserable drounynge of youthe in ignoraunce, and sore decaye of the Universities." [11]

Earlier in the century humanists had determined to reform the educational system, to broaden the curriculums, and to revitalize humane values placed in jeopardy by materialism and by the conspicuous waste of many nobles. Realistically they interested themselves in pedagogical procedures, trained teachers, and composed textbooks. According to Bennett, 40 per cent of the seven hundred books printed by de Worde early in the century were educational treatises. Cheke, Lily, Ascham, and Mulcaster have become famous names in English education. More important perhaps than their practical reforms were the living examples of humane culture these humanists set to the nation and the eloquence with which they voiced their faith in education. In *Utopia*, More envisaged a land in which, in Caspari's words, "the whole people should be raised to a high intellectual and moral level by general education." More's idealism was transmitted to the greatest of Tudor humanist-educators, Sidney and Spenser.[12]

Although too pragmatic to dream of an utopian society, Henry VIII and Elizabeth were monarchs of the new style, well-schooled for their political roles in an increasingly complex world order and astute in surrounding themselves with intelligent aides. These shrewd rulers indulged themselves in delights which sometimes remind us of sophomoric excesses, but their fopperies and the antics of courtier-clowns could not hide the intellectual climate in the English court. Nor did hermaphroditic hangers-on obscure the fact that power rested with the educated. All foreign observers, hostile though they were at first, cannily appraised the intelligence of the Tudors and their courts.

Together, then, merchants, Christians, humanists, and Tudor rulers, although they frequently clashed over other matters, and although their motivations were markedly different, recognized the utility of education; and all contributed to England's transformation from an insular power into an empire, an empire that could come into existence only with a well-trained, literate people.

For centuries Englishmen had been attending schools. Many did not go beyond the petty schools, where they learned to read and write English, but increasing numbers went on to the grammar schools, where they were exposed (not without pain) to the traditional Latin curriculum. In 1400 there were approximately four hundred grammar schools in England for a population of slightly over two million. In the sixteenth century Marjorie Plant finds that the country was better provided with grammer schools than in modern times. The government inquiry into chantries and the continuance of schools (1546) brought to light the fact that there was approximately one school for every 8300 people. In 1865 the report of the Schools Inquiry Commission showed that population had outstripped the rate of increase in schools, so that there was only one school for every 23,000 people. In 1546, Miss Plant adds, there were four schools for London's 44,000 inhabitants; and in 1600, the climactic year in this study, according to Brown, there were 361 grammar schools in England, fewer than in the fourteenth century but more than in the middle years of the century. Brown has estimated that "some twelve thousand boys were being educated in the grammar schools at this period [1600], which is one in 375 of the population, as compared with one in 180 to-day [1931]." [13]

"There are great number of Grammer schooles through out the realme," Harrison writes in 1577, "and those verie liberallie indued, for the better reliefe of poore scholers, so that there are not manie corporat townes now under the queenes dominion, than hain not one Gramar schoole at the least, with a sufficient living for a maister and usher appointed to the same." It was the destruction of these schools — in Lever's words, "founded of a godly intent to brynge up poore mennes sonnes in learnynge and vertue" — that had aroused the religious and moral wrath of Puritans against sixteenth-century robber barons. Fortunately, opposed to the despoilers were public-spirited men intent upon preserving educational facilities. Thomas Magnus, in 1532, refounded the Newark grammar and singing school; his indenture prescribed that "two priests should freely teach and instruct all persons and children that at Newark aforesaid come to school with them and be disposed to learn." The anonymous author of *The English Courtier and the Country Gentleman* also testifies to the opportunities of the poore: "These common Schooles (whereof in England are many) . . . receave all sortes of children to bee taught, bee their parents never so pore, and the Boyes never so unapt." According to Tawney, the register at Repton reveals that among the first twenty-two names were five gentlemen, four husbandmen, nine yeomen, two websters or weavers, one carpenter, and one tanner.[14]

Nor was the education of Elizabethan women so neglected as some contemporary males wished, or as some modern scholars by omission have suggested. Education of women has almost as long a history as that of their alleged superiors, a fact obscured by their exclusion from the universities and from most grammar schools until the seventeenth century. Noblewomen as early as Anglo-Saxon times had received rudimentary training in nunneries, and, later, daughters of wealthy burghers had been educated by nuns or tutors. Humanists early in the sixteenth century boasted to foreign scholars of the accomplishments of English women. Margaret More, Neale informs us, had "perfect mastery of Greek and Latin, some knowledge of philosophy, astronomy, physic, arithmetic, logic, rhetoric, and music." The erudition of Queen Elizabeth, trained by a later humanist, Roger Ascham, was celebrated at home and abroad. On one occasion a naive foreign diplomat decided that he could safely vent his wrath at the queen's perennial procrastination by lecturing her and the court in Latin. Elizabeth reportedly answered him in a dazzling (and devastating) extemporaneous Latin oration.[15]

Female education was not confined to the upper classes. The edict of 1406 provided for education of both sexes. On the basis of her study of bequests in the fifteenth century, Miss Thrupp observes that "this evidence is not enough to show whether education was actually as general among the women as it was among the men of the merchant class, but one may infer that it was quite commonly within their reach." Her conclusion is strengthened by the discovery that women in this century held many important business positions and had the same needs for literacy as their merchant fathers and husbands. (In this connection it is significant that widows of stationers frequently assumed management of their husbands' businesses.) Evidently, however, feminine education had not become a fixed national policy by 1550, when Thomas Becon railed against the neglect of women and recommended: "That by public authority schools for women-children be erected and set up in every Christian comonweal, and honest, sage, wise, discreet, so-ber, grave, and learned matrons made rulers and mistres-ses of the same, and that honest and liberal stipends be ap-pointed to the said school-mistresses." By 1581 the situation had apparently improved, for Mulcaster, who was an ex-pounder of custom rather than an innovator, devotes a chapter of his *Positions* to feminine education: "Our coun-trey doth allow it, our duetie doth enforce it, their aptnesse calls for it, their excellencie commandes it." From which we can probably conclude, as Adamson and Rowse do, that girls were now often admitted to grammar schools. Perhaps by this time more Englishmen were ready to agree with Richard Hyrde: "He that had leaver have his wife a fool than a wise woman, I hold him worse than twice frantic." [16]

In 1533 Thomas More had conjectured that 40 per cent of the English people were able to read. If the population at that time was four or five millions, as Adamson suggests, almost two million people were able to read. By the end of the century it seems logical to suppose that the number of illiterates had been sharply reduced, and that literacy had kept ahead of population growth. Fifty per cent in 1600 appears conservative, especially when one recalls that after the middle of the century livery companies as well as nobles and merchants had founded, or refounded, gram-mar schools, and that by the end of the century books were produced in greater numbers than ever before.[17]

That education at the end of the sixteenth century in-cluded all classes and probably both sexes can be inferred from the ominous warnings of gloomy prophets. Writing in 1592, Giles Fletcher reports that in the eyes of the fash-ionable education had lost prestige: "Now it is grown to this pass, that Learning is lightly respected; upon a persuasion that it is to be found everywhere: a thing untrue and unpossible." Early in the next century Bacon maintained that "there being more scholars bred than the State can prefer and employ, . . . it must need fall out that many persons will be bred unfit for other vocations, and unprofitable for that in which they were bred up, which fill the realm full of indigent, idle and wanton people." [18]

Impressive as statistics pertaining to schools and literacy may be, they are in final analysis inconclusive, unfortunately, since there is no way of knowing what and how frequently these literate men and women read. Fifteenth-century merchants, Miss Thrupp is forced to conclude, displayed little "intellectual curiosity." Probably they approved the logic of Breton's Countryman:

Now for learning, what your neede is thereof I know not, but with us, this is all we goe to schoole for: to read common Prayers at Church, and set downe common prises at Markets; write a Letter, and make a Bond; set downe the day of our Births, our Marriage day, and make our Wills when we are sicke, for the disposing of our goods when we are dead: these are the chiefe matters that we meddle with, and we find enough to trouble our heads withall. . . . What more learning have we need of, but that experience will teach us without booke? We can learne to plough and harrow, sow and reape, plant and prune, thrash and fanne, winnow and grinde, brue and bake, and all without booke.[19]

Many members of the nobility and the gentry agreed with the opinion of the gentleman described by Richard Pace, who shouted with fury that "gentlemen's sons ought to be able to blow their horn skilfully, to hunt well, and to carry and train a hawk elegantly; but the study of letters is to be left to the sons of peasants." Other parents who in the abstract revered education exercised, to quote Geoffrey Fenton, "mor care to entertaine horsriders and falkners for the delight of their trifling fancy, then to provide good and lerned scholemasters to breath knowledg and manors into their precious children." Nor is this statement any more surprising than the Countryman's logic. Education has always been a good thing, but personal pleasures are even better.[20]

Since there is no exact correlation between literacy and reading in the sixteenth or in any other century, there is no reason to suppose that large numbers of Elizabethans rushed to bookstalls and bought books as rapidly as stationers printed them. Many (perhaps most) people had learned to read for utilitarian reasons, and their interest in reading was limited by what they construed, either narrowly or broadly, as beneficial to their success. Reading was no more popular or fashionable in Elizabethan times than in our own. Indeed Copland's complaints to an author in 1518 require little alteration to be made applicable to modern readers.

> At your instaunce I shall it gladly impresse,
> But the utterance, I thynke will be but small.
> Bokes be not set by: there tymes is past, I gesse;
> The dyse and cardes, in drynkynge wyne and ale,
> Tables, cayles, and balles, they be now sette a sale.
> Men lete theyr chyldren use all such harlotry,
> That byenge of bokes they utterly deny.[21]

Hence there was some truth in the embittered indictments of readers by authors, particularly by those who refused to compile manuals for economic or religious improvement, to popularize through sensationalism, or to jingle with Tusser and other rimesters who prettified the commonplace. On the other hand there were mitigating factors. Though many books (usually ephemera) sold for a few pence, the important ones of the century sold for shillings, and people earning £10 annually could not afford such prices. Thus, there was an economic factor that barred most Elizabethans from the "treasures" of authors. Second, books were easy to come by only in London, Oxford, and Cambridge, where stationers were permitted to print and sell. People in the provinces could buy books at fairs or from an occasional hawker who roamed through smaller towns, or of course they could come to London. Religious books they could obtain more easily because nonconformists carried on a vigorous traffic in heretical works, especially near the ports, and because conforming clergymen were anxious to counteract religious propaganda. Third, most people were so busy "swinking and swatting" for a livelihood, in trade or in agriculture, that they had neither time nor energy for reading.

"We in England divide our people commonlie into foure sorts," Harrison writes, "as gentlemen, citizens or burgesses, yeomen, and artificers, or laborers." Unquestionably the largest reading audience came from the first group, which Harrison further describes:

Of gentlemen the first and cheefe (next the king) be the prince, dukes, marquesses, earls, viscounts, and barons: and these are called gentlemen of the greater sort, or (as our common usage of speech is) lords and noblemen: and next unto them be knights, esquiers, and last of all they that are simplie called gentlemen; so that in effect our gentlemen are divided into their conditions.

Those "simplie called gentlemen" included graduates of the universities, military captains, and those able to "live without manuall labour." Writing in 1601, Thomas Wilson estimated that there were approximately five hundred knights and sixteen thousand country gentlemen. Unfortunately he did not speculate as to the number of nonlanded gentlemen who had achieved their status through educational and professional attainments. Tawney has advanced the not unreasonable estimate that this class comprised slightly over 6 per cent of the entire population.[22]

Harrison's "citizens or burgesses" included what we would now elusively describe as the middle class. Harrison's category, however, is equally elusive. For this group consisted of wealthy merchants engaged in foreign and domestic trade, manufacturers, small merchants or shopkeepers, retailers, and skilled craftsmen who had completed apprenticeships in livery companies. Because extremes in wealth and intellectual interests were great, "citizens" advanced in large numbers to the class above. Thomas Smith's career was a typical Elizabethan (or Deloney) success-story, the rise of a merchant to affluence and to powerful position in court circles. Thomas Bodley, in Manningham's words, "was at first but the sonne of a merchant, untill he gave some intelligence of moment to the counsell, whereupon he was thought worthie employment, whereby he rose." He became the enterprising founder of one of the world's great libraries, "perpetuall preservation, support & maintenance" of which, he writes, "dothe greatly surpasse all my other worldly cares." At the other extreme were the more typical bourgeois whose tastes and outlook Louis B. Wright has ably described in *Middle-Class Culture in Elizabethan England*.[23]

The yeomen were the rural middle class, below the gentry but above husbandmen and peasants. They were, Harrison comments, "free men borne English, and may dispend of their owne free land in yearlie revenue, to the summe of fortie shillings sterling." Yeomen like their urban counterparts were ambitious and often improved their status in society: many became landed gentlemen; others, however, migrated from the provinces to the cities to seek their fortunes. These yeomen were industrious and God-fearing, and literate too, but it is not known whether they read more than the Bible and practical guides to success. One thing is certain: few had sufficient means to purchase books in quantities. In spite of incomplete information their story has been admirably told in Mildred Campbell's *The English Yeomen*.[24]

About Harrison's last group we know even less. The lower urban and rural orders — unskilled laborers, semi-literate farm workers, and artisans of little learning — were born in poverty, grew up to toil, married to have a partner to share their toil, bred more toilers, and died in poverty. Some, of course, rose to the middle class, but most remained where they were conceived.

The reading habits and tastes of these groups present formidable difficulties. Evidence in any genuine sense is fragmentary, and what little there is must be cautiously evaluated. Lyrical praise in dedications, for example, cannot be accepted at face value. If it could be, then virtually every nobleman and lady in England, as well as the wealthy burgher and the successful public official, was godlike in erudition and lived in a library perusing old and new masterpieces. University wits and poseurs frequently paraded learning gleaned from commonplace books and easily accessible compendiums of Renaissance knowledge. Many an Elizabethan professed a learning he had not. Nor are writers and custodians of class entitled to uncritical acceptance. The slanted attacks of the former upon readers were rarely answered (perhaps not even read), because the public cared little what indigent authors had to say. Arbiters of class were also filled with prejudice and sometimes with arrogance, and their comments contained but partial truths. Elizabethans were masters of propaganda — religious, political, and social; and like all propagandists they sorted their "evidence" to conform to pre-established conclusions. Finally, because class lines were fluid, it is not always easy to classify. Is Bodley, for instance, to be con-

sidered a merchant or a gentleman? In view of these difficulties, the slenderness of the evidence and the biases of
commentators, conclusions can only be inferential.

Gentlemen, in Harrison's inclusive definition, though
smaller numerically than any of the other groups, unquestionably constituted the most important Elizabethan reading audience, at least of the works posterity has deemed
significant. But this class was by no means homogeneous
either in taste or in temperament. It contained many erudite men as well as dilettantes with no taste or literary dis-
cernment, courtier-statesmen like Sidney as well as fops like
the Earl of Southampton, discriminating members of the
gentry like Richard Carew as well as the Elizabethan
counterpart of Squire Western.

Literature was actively encouraged by a small group of
the nobility, the Sidneys, the Herberts, the Countess of
Cumberland and her daughter Anne Clifford, and the Russells. Beginning with the Countess of Pembroke, both major and minor poets were "mothered" by noblewomen.
Only Spenser among the great poets, probably because he
was prospering in Ireland, escaped direct feminine influence, and even he dedicated many of his poems to patronesses. Nashe, who had groveled before Sidney's sister a
few years earlier, complained, "I hate these female braggarts that contend to have all the Muses beg at their doors."
Despite Nashe's bitter sally, born no doubt of his rejection
by "female braggarts," these were intelligent women, perhaps occasionally precious, but at the same time not without sensitivity and acumen. Lucy Harington, later Countess of Bedford, encouraged and, more important, supported Drayton, Donne, Jonson, and others; she could
hardly have chosen more wisely. Many of these women
were also amateur writers. Meres calls the Countess of Pembroke, perhaps a little too extravagantly, "a most delicate

Poet." The title page of *The Countess of Montgomery's Urania* (1621) reads: "Written by the right honorable the Lady MARY WROATH, Daughter to the right Noble Robert Earle of Leicester, And Neece to the ever famous, and renowned Sr Phillips Sidney knight, And to the most excelent Lady Mary Countesse of Pembroke late deceased." Although none of these ladies contributed anything of consequence to the history of English literature, their enthusiasm for belles-lettres and their amateur effusions are not to be dismissed lightly.[25]

Only the Sidneys and the Herberts (note the link through Mary Sidney's marriage to Henry Herbert) equaled the ladies in encouraging nondramatic poets. Again these men were amateurs themselves, of genius in the case of Philip Sidney. Wilton, which was "like a College," according to Aubrey, in Mary's time, was in William Herbert's "an Academie, as well as Palace, and was (as it were) the Apiarie, to which Men, that were excellent in Armes, and Arts, did resort, and were carress't; and many of them received honorable Pensions." There for almost a half-century the Sidneys and Herberts sheltered poets and like their Renaissance forebears in Italy actively encouraged the arts.[26]

Aubrey's description of the library at Wilton reveals the literary interests of the Sidneys and Herberts:

Here was a noble librarie of bookes choicely collected in the time of Mary, Countesse of Pembroke. I remember there were a great many Italian bookes; all their poets; and bookes of politie and historie. Here was Dame Julian Barnes of Hunting, Hawking, and Heraldry, in English verses, printed temp. Edward the Fourth. . . . A translation of the whole book of Psalmes, in English verse by Sir Philip Sydney, writt curiously, and bound in crimson velvet and gilt; it is now lost. Here was a Latin poëme, a manuscript, writt in Julius Caesar's time. Henry Earle of Pembroke was a great lover of heraldrie, and collected curious manuscripts of it, that I have seen and perused; e.g., the coates of armes and short histories of the English nobility, and bookes of genealogies; all well painted and writt.

Among the 221 books contained in the library of the Earl of Bedford, on the other hand, 161 were religious treatises and only 11 titles were "of a literary character." Perhaps like Rutland, Bedford did not share his wife's fondness for poets and literature.[27]

Libraries of other noblemen also emphasize Bedford's indifference to literature. John Dudley, Earl of Warwick, had in his collection between 1545–1550 one romance (*Sidrach and King Bochas*) and four plays (three by John Heywood, one anonymous); the rest were religious tomes, classics (sometimes in the original, sometimes in translation), and utilitarian treatises. The recusant William Lord Howard was evidently interested in saintliness and practical affairs, for his library consisted primarily of Catholic works in Latin and histories, almanacs, and legal treatises. Chief Justice Edward Coke, through his marriage to the widow of Sir William Hatton, nephew and heir of Sir Christopher Hatton, received the latter's diversified library, which consisted of " 'Lawes of England; Civill Lawe; Approved Histories; Philosophy, Rethoricke, Grammar, Lodgicke and Schoolebookes; Phisicke and Naturall Philosophie; Poetrie; Dictionaries; Severall Sciences' (including a generall section subtitled 'Tracts and Discourses', and another 'Antiquities and Rarities')." The records of book purchases by Henry Percy, ninth Earl of Northumberland, also reveal a catholic selection of Elizabethan books. Percy bought *The Mirror for Magistrates* (1587 edition), *The Shepherd's Calendar, The Life and Death of Sir Philip Sidney,* Daniel's *History of England,* Chapman's *Iliad,* Florio's *Second Fruits,* as well as Holinshed, Bullinger, Machiavelli in French, and Speed's

Chronicles. It is disappointing that Percy for the most part cited only sums of money paid to stationers and booksellers, since he was said to have averaged £200 annually for books while he was in prison.[28]

Because of their governmental responsibilities and because of the sixteenth-century utilitarian orientation, Elizabeth's advisors, although not unlearned, were neither zealous patrons of artists nor avid readers of the great literature being published in the time. That Burghley, according to Peacham, "to his dying day would always carry Tully's *Offices* about him either in his bosom or his pocket" is significant: a practical and astute politician, he valued manuals of conduct because they directly related to his duties as an official. It is hardly surprising that, according to his most recent biographer, Burghley ignored the arts for the art of government. During the early years of the queen's reign, Walsingham and Burghley, it is true, had encouraged translations by members of the Inns, but these translations had a useful purpose, to train and develop an informed citizenry. Walsingham was also interested in the voyages compiled by Hakluyt, as most practical men were enamored of the new horizons of commerce and power.[29]

While the famous amateurs of the age were conversant with native and foreign books and more than parrots of university education and fashionable chatter, other members of the nobility and the imitation courtiers, the fops who affected anything so long as it promised preferment, made a mockery of Castiglione's manual with their dilettantism, their posturing, and their ludicrous affectations. "Mark you Amoretto, Sir Radericks sonne," we read in *The Second Part of the Return from Parnassus:*

He is one that wil draw out his pocket glasse thrise in a walke; one that dreames in the night of nothing but muske and civet, and talkes of nothing all day long but his hauke, his hound, and his mistres; one that more admires the good wrinckle of a botte, or the curious crinkling of a silke stocking, then all the witt in the world; one that loves no scholler but him whose tyred eares can endure halfe a day togither his fliblowne sonnettes of his mistres, and her loving pretty creatures, her munckey and her puppet.

There is no evidence that the Earl of Southampton was anything more than, in Hotson's words, a "vain, fantastical, amorous, and hare-brained young sprout of the New Nobility," who admired the decadent eroticism of *Venus and Adonis* and *Lucrece*. Like the character in the *Parnassus* play many a dandy exclaimed: "Let this duncified worlde esteeme of Spencer and Chaucer, Ile worshipp sweet Mr Shakspeare, and to honoure him wil lay his *Venus and Adonis* under my pillowe." Moffett informs readers that Sidney had

kept far aloof from those noblemen (if such as they are noble) who, averse to the Muses and in some degree robbed of their minds (as if husks of men rather than men), despise literature; who without sensibility, without the smack of any learning, gulp down sensual pleasure with greedy mouths, who actually feel disgust at knowledge (the ambrosia, the nectar, the garden, the ocean main, the clothing, of the mind!) and toss it aside.[30]

This group was, then a fickle audience of fashionable apes who lauded the new until something newer came along. Their guides were novelty and exclusiveness. Of them Niccols writes: "Many idle humorists whose singularity allowes nothing good, that is common, in this frantik age, esteeme of verses upon which the vulgar in a Stationers Shop, hath once breathed as of a peece of infection, in whose fine fingers no papers are holesome, but such, as passe by private manuscription." Common print was not to soil their beautifully gloved hands, nor were ideas to sully their minds.[31]

Although fops must be recreated from literary burlesques, there is no such difficulty with that man-about-town and Elizabethan Pepys, John Chamberlain, whose gossipy letters to his friend Dudley Carleton are still extant. This son of a wealthy ironmonger matriculated at Trinity College, Cambridge, in 1570, but did not take a degree. Without occupation or profession he spent most of his life in London, avidly gathering tidbits of all kinds from his prominent friends and scanning the bookstalls for the newest books. As soon as it appeared in London, Chamberlain sent his friend a copy of James's *Basilicon Doran.* "I come even now from reading," he writes to Carleton on December 16, 1608, "a short discourse of Quene Elizabeths life written in Latin by Sir Franc: Bacon. Yf you have not seen nor heard of yt, yt is worth your inquirie." In Donne's *Devotions upon Emergent Occasions* he found "many curious and daintie conceits, not for common capacities, but surely full of pietie and true feeling." Usually Chamberlain and his correspondent evinced more interest in the latest trifles than in books of substance. Carleton in France and Chamberlain in London frequently exchanged fashionable trivia. In September 1598, Chamberlain noted that he had received "ballads, bookes and babies" and "Aldegondes tedious discourse." In December of the same year he sent Carleton "such pedlarie pamflets and threehalfpeny ware as we are served with; make the best use you can of them, and use your owne censure, but yf I be not deceved some of the satires are passable." He writes again in January 1599: "I send you here certain odde epitaphes and epigrammes that go under the name of pasquills." In March he transmitted to Carleton "three or fowre toyes to passe away the time";

these toys included two newsletters, Thomas Moffett's *The Silkworms and Their Flies,* and, interestingly, a mutilated copy of Hayward's *Henry IV,* with a "transcript" of the Latin dedication to the Earl of Essex which had aroused the wrath of the government. (Chamberlain found "no such buggeswords" in the dedication.) With *Basilicon Doran* he sent along an unnamed work which "will serve when you have leysure to laugh, for both in the matter, and manner of setting yt downe you shall finde pretty knavery." [32]

Except for Greene's portrait of Clothbreeches, writers were as severe in their castigations of the gentry as of the fops. Rich assails "malapert clownes,"

. . . that have no vertue of the minde to crake of, but of their oxen, of their sheepe, and how many hogges they have in their backeside, that are so choaked up with the carkes and cares of the worlde, that they can not rellish those things that savour of wit, to whose cares the lowing of a kow is better pleasing, than a Lecture of Logicke.

In *Every Man in His Humor* Jonson has Master Stephen ask his uncle for a book of hawking and hunting because "the hawking, and hunting-languages now a dayes . . . are more studied then the Greeke, or the Latine." One husband Dorothy Osborne will not have: "He must not be so much a country gentleman as to understand nothing but hawks and dogs, and be fonder of either than of his wife." The gentry will have nothing to do, the author of *The English Courtier and the Country Gentleman* caustically observes, with "mad headed knaves, that bee properly learned." They will read only "diverse pleasant bookes," such as *Sir Guy of Warwick, The Ship of Fools,* or *A Hundred Merry Tales,* since "these pretty and pithy matters, do some times recreate our mindes, cheefely after longe sittinge, and losse of money." [33]

This of course is biased criticism. In fiction and in reality Squire Western had his opposite. The opposite of this literary stereotype was the humanely learned Richard Carew, who was both translator and author. According to a manuscript written by his son,

. . . my father (from my childhood) took all the care he could to have me bred up in learning, well knowing the value thereof by the sweet fruits he still gathered of his own, which he always increased by his (almost incredible) continual labour; for without a teacher he learned the Greek, Dutch, French, Spanish and Italian tongues . . . He ever delighted so much in reading . . . for if he had none other hindrance, going or riding he would ever have a book and be reading.

In Carew's library were the works of Virgil, Homer, Ariosto, Leo Africanus, Pliny, Roger of Havedon, Polidore Vergil, Holinshed, Chaucer, Surrey, Spenser, Marlowe, Shakespeare, Daniel, and Sidney. Although as criticism this passage in *The Excellency of the English Tongue* is scarcely remarkable, it reveals the range of Carew's reading:

Will you have Plato's vein? read Sir Thomas Smith. The Ionic? Sir Thomas More. Cicero's? Ascham. Varro? Chaucer. Demosthenes? Sir John Cheke, who in his treatise to the rebels hath comprised all the figures of rhetoric. Will you read Virgil? take the Earl of Surrey. Catullus? Shakespeare, and Marlowe's fragment. Ovid? Daniel. Lucan? Spenser. Martial? Sir John Davies, and others. Will you have all in all for prose and verse? take the miracle of our age, Sir Philip Sidney.[34]

In recording "the true patterne for a Gentleman to imitate," Whetstone outlines "the chiefest course of his studie": theology, health or physic, civil laws and the statutes, "Militarie Knowledge," "Government, and Civill behaviours," cosmography, history, and heraldry. In the years 1576 and 1577, William Carneshaw, one of the gentry lovingly described in Rowse's *Tudor Cornwall — Portrait of a Society,* almost fulfilled Whetstone's regimen. He read Cartwright, Latimer, Fox, Bullinger (probably in Golding's translation), *The Bishop of Winchester's Sermon before Edward VI,* and Calvin's *Epistles.* In addition to this rich diet in theology he perused a new history of the Turks, Vegetius (the military historian), Sir Humphrey Gilbert's account of his explorations, Ficino's books on astrology, and a pamphlet depicting the Spanish destruction of Antwerp. Nor does this account, according to Rowse, "exhaust the tale of his reading." Another country gentleman, John Ramsey, had in his library the works of William Perkins, Du Bartas, Ariosto, Spenser's *Faerie Queene,* Sidney's *Arcadia,* and Daniel's poems and histories. Here then are three excellent illustrations of learned members of the English gentry.[35]

Merchants were caricatured as moneybags, ignorant boors, and immoral Machiavellians, yet this class was less homogeneous than Harrison's gentlemen. Bodley was the first of the great middle-class bibliophiles who have created notable book collections and have interested themselves in the nation's cultural heritage with an energy and zeal not shared by many members of the upper classes. Nicholas Yonge, a London merchant, was an enthusiastic admirer of music. Daily to his home came, in his own words, "Gentlemen and Merchants of good accompt (as well of this realme as of forreine nations)" to practise Italian madrigals in books he had imported from Italy and other countries. Yonge himself wrote a preface for (and probably subsidized) *Musica Transalpina* (1588), and he and his friends unquestionably provided an audience as well as economic support for the native madrigalists who were about to compose some of England's greatest music. It is logical to assume, since words and music in Elizabethan songs are inseparable, that these musical amateurs were appreciative of the new poetry, not contemptuous as contemporary satirists would have us believe. The Whiteways, successful merchants of Dorchester, had in the early seventeenth century a library of over one hundred books, "on law, philosophy, religion, history, medicine, military strategy, language, heraldry, drama, astronomy, poetry, and manners" — a collection not unlike that of noblemen and gentry. Among the authors were Aristotle, Galen, Justinian, Castiglione, Rabelais, Tasso, Boccaccio, William Lambarde, and Puritan divines like Richard Greenham and John Brinsley. Notably absent, because the Whiteways were Puritans, were English poets and dramatists; in fact, except for Rabelais, Tasso, and Boccaccio, entertainment was eschewed for informational and religious treatises.[36]

The tastes of these men had nothing in common with the interests of the great masses in the middle class who, in the words of S. I. (or S. J.), had "many hinderances, Want of bookes, want of sufficient maintenance, want of time, and many other lets." Many of these people craved entertainment, education in capsule form, and sensationalism. For them there was Richard Halseton's *Strange and Wonderful Things* (1595), "penned," the title page states, "as he delivered it from his own mouthe." For an audience eager for sensations Greene wrote his cony-catching revelations:

A Notable Discovery of Coosnage. Now daily practised by sundry lewd persons, called Connie-catchers, and Crosse-biters. Plainely laying open those pernitious sleights that hath brought many ignorant men to confusion. Written for the general benefit of all Gentlemen, Citizens, Aprentices, Countrey Farmers and yeomen, that may hap to fall into the company of such coosening companions.

Although his work was dedicated to the same cross section

of the population, it was patently intended for the unso-
phisticated reader who was fascinated by the machinations
of "lewd persons," who naively thought he could avoid
the confusion of the ignorant by learning to outwit
sharpsters, and who could be duped into believing that
he was reading a tract approved by gentlemen. For good
measure the title page promises diverting education ("With
a delightful discourse of the coosnage of Colliers"), flatters
the intelligence of the readers ("Nascimur pro patria"),
and vouches for the authoritativeness of the exposés ("By
R. Greene, Maister of Arts"). The crude woodcut shows a
human-like rabbit holding playing cards in either hand,
surrounded by a pair of dice, a cup, and a tankard. Greene
and printer John Wolfe had omitted nothing.[37]

The kind of fare these readers sought is "that which
most my soule excruciates," according to Sir John Davies,

> And if a Brick-bat from a Chimney falls
> When puffing Boreas nere so little bralls:
> Or else a Knave be hangd by justice doome
> For cutting of a Purse in selfe-same roome:
> Or wanton Rig, or letcher dissolute
> Doe stand at Pauls-Crosse in a Sheeten Sute:
> All these, and thousand such like toyes as these
> They clap in Chronicles like Butterflees,
> Of which there is no use.

The "Chroniclers" were the balladmongers and the authors of one-signature tracts on earthquakes, macabre
events, or some new freak with two heads recently born in
a remote shire of England. For almost four centuries they
have been the recipients of brickbats from Davies and his
kind.[38]

Critics like Davies ignore the interest the middle class
had in religious books, manuals for self-improvement, and
utilitarian treatises. The title page of Thomas Hilles's *Art*

of Vulgar Arithmetic (1600) promises "knowledge pleasant for Gentlemen, commendable for Capteines and Soldiers, profitable for Merchants, and generally necessarie for all estates and degrees." Hilles's treatise is by no means a debased popularization of mathematics; it undoubtedly served a useful purpose for those interested in teaching themselves. Edward (or Edmund) Coote's *English Schoolmaster,* designed as a guide to teach the ignorant and foreigners how to read and write, had over forty editions between 1596 and 1684. For his purposes Coote adopts "that plaine rudenesse, which may fit the capacity of . . . such men and women of trade, as Taylors, Weavers, Shopkeepers, Seamsters, and such other, as have undertaken the charge of teaching others." The popularity of Coote's manual testifies to the success of his instruction and to the widespread desire to help oneself.[39]

Deloney wrote expressly for craftsmen and laborers, whose tastes were little different from (and certainly no worse than) those of many people in the classes above. This son of a silkweaver ("the Balleting Silke-weaver") composed many broadside ballads; so popular were his verses ("triviall trinkets and threedbare trash," according to Nashe) that they circulated until the eighteenth century. Equally successful were his novels, *Jack of Newbury,* dedicated to clothworkers, *The Gentle Craft,* dedicated to shoemakers, and *Thomas of Reading,* a collection of tales about weavers. Deloney's tracts had a threefold appeal: he related bawdy anecdotes similar to, and sometimes borrowed from, the popular jest-books of the period; he modernized medieval romances by having craftsmen play central roles in implausible plots; and, finally, his success stories reflected the aspirations of his readers. Ribald entertainment, "escape" literature, and bourgeois wish-fulfillment. The jest-book material Deloney related in pithy, alehouse dialogue.

A typical story, in *Jack of Newbury,* concerns a knight who, after seducing a maid, is tricked into marrying her when, unknown to him, she disguises herself as a wealthy widow; thus the maid becomes an honest woman and the knight a wealthy man — and their sins have been rewarded. In Deloney's bourgeois variations upon old romances, Sir Hugh (*The Gentle Craft*) becomes a shoemaker after Winifred spurns his love, and the princes Crispine and Crispianus become apprentice shoemakers. The romance of Duke Richard and Margaret serves as a framework for brief tales concerning Thomas of Reading, who personifies *noblesse oblige* among clothworkers.[40]

Deloney's greatest appeal, however, stemmed from his success tales. Unlike Nashe, who stigmatized the Harveys with their ropemaker origin, or Greene, whose hero, Clothbreeches, belonged to the gentry, Deloney delighted in the achievements of craftsmen. In *Jack of Newbury* appear many accounts of clothiers who gain the favor of the king, and who, unlike sycophantic courtiers, with manly bluntness present their grievances to him. In Jack's home — a good bourgeois establishment with the proper accouterments of success — are portraits of fifteen men of low descent who have achieved eminence. Shoemaker Simon Eyre becomes lord mayor of London and wealthy; and Lusty Peachey, another affluent shoemaker with a retinue of expensively clad workmen, but not unmanned by his wealth, puts two upstart sea captains in their places. These stories reflect the goals of the middle-class aspirant: regardless of origin each man has the opportunity to rise to high station; if he is industrious he will some day be wealthy and virile, like Thomas of Reading and Peachey, and surround himself with symbols of success (portraits, expensive furnishings, fine clothing, and servants); and his patriotism and loyalty to the throne will reap rewards.

In other words, everything has a price, and morality is conveniently subordinated to success, as in Simon Eyre's shrewd deception of a Greek merchant and his apprentices. Deloney, anticipating Alger's pluck-and-luck formula and the bourgeois work-and-pray ritual, portrayed in his fiction the dreams of his class.

"But aware, keep bak, make room noow, heer they cum! And fyrst, captin Cox, an od man I promiz yoo: by profession a Mason, and that right skilfull, very cunning in sens, and hardy az Gawin; for hiz tonsword hangs at his tablz eend." Thus, Robert Laneham, a London merchant, whose robust, breathless style tingles with comic overexuberance, introduces Captain Cox, a mason of Coventry who obviously had succeeded in this world. "Great oversight hath he in matters of storie," Laneham informs us, and catalogs the romances in Cox's library, a collection rivaling Don Quixote's in quantity. In addition, "in Philosophy, both morall & naturall, I think he be az naturally overseen," Laneham avers, and promptly lists the most bizarre assembly of philosophical books ever gathered together: *The Ship of Fools, The Highway to the Spital House, A Hundred Merry Tales, The Book of Riddles,* Cox's "Philosophy" had unmistakable affinities with the hundred or more naughty ballads and songs "fair wrapt up in Parchment and bound with a whipcord" and with his "Allmanaks of antiquitee." "To stay ye no longer heerin," Laneham concludes, "I dare say hee hath az fair a library for theez sciencez, & az many goodly monuments both in proze & poetry & at afternoonz can talk az much without book, az ony Inholder betwixt Brainford and Bagshot, what degree soever he be." If Cox shared Laneham's lusty indifference to taste and intellectual distinctions, as the titles in his amazing library suggest, he must indeed have been a wonderful companion in alehouse literary discussions.[41]

It is not unlikely that the most eager readers were found among women. For centuries noblewomen had constituted an important market for books, a fact recognized by Castiglione, who urged his courtier to acquaint himself with literature because "he shall by this meanes never want pleasant intertainments with women which ordinarily love such matters." Lady Anne Clifford was said to have read Montaigne, Sidney, Cervantes, Spenser, Daniel, and many other writers. Donne observed that "she knew how to discourse of all things, from predestination down to slea-silk." Jonson's Lady Wouldbe studied physics, music, philosophy, and poets.

> I would have
> A lady, indeed, t'have all, letters and arts,
> Be able to discourse, to write, to paint.

Despite Volpone's groans, Lady Wouldbe flaunts her knowledge of poets — Dante, Petrarch, Ariosto, Tasso, and Aretine — and delivers her critical pronouncements with fashionable (and seductive) eloquence.

> I'le discourse
> (And't be but only, sir, to bring you a-sleepe)
> How we did spend our time, and loves, together,
> For some sixe yeeres.

Volpone gasps for "some power, some fate, some fortune" to rescue him from this "well-read" woman intent upon seduction by literary allusion.[42]

Wives of merchants and shopkeepers read books of all kinds, probably more commonly than their husbands. The wealth of their spouses afforded them leisure, and since they were as ambitious as their husbands to rise socially — materialistic aspirations are often fused with cultural aspirations — they aped noblewomen. *Euphues,* for example, was popular in court circles and soon became modish in the middle class. Dekker speaks of "euphuized" women, and Nashe describes "Mistres Minx, a Marchants wife, . . . finical in her speach, as though she spake nothing but what shee had first sewd over before in her Samplers." So numerous were female readers that men, their conservatism and security in jeopardy, shared Volpone's groans. The Earl of Northampton advised his son not to educate his daughters — "the wiser the waywarder." King James, when introduced to a maid able to speak and write Latin, Greek, and Hebrew, asked with laconic masculine practicality, "But can she spin?" It is probably of middle-class women that puritanical Thomas Powell writes in *Tom of All Trades:* "Let them learne plaine workes of all kind, so they take heed of too open seaming. In stead of song and Musicke, let them learne cookery and Laundrie. And in stead of reading Sir Philip Sidney's *Arcadia,* let them read the grounds of good huswifery. I like not the female poetresse at any hand." [43]

Yet early in the sixteenth century male writers had begun to manufacture guidebooks for women. Vives' *Instruction of a Christian Woman,* translated by Richard Hyrde about 1540, purports to diagram a woman's life from birth to death: "Therefore in the first book, I will begin at the beginning of woman's life, and lead her forth unto the time of marriage. In the second from marriage unto widowhood, how she ought to pass the time of her life well and virtuously with her husband. In the last book, I inform and teach widowhood." Ladies were told how to bear and rear children, how to cook and tend a garden, how to make marriage a success (recognize male superiority!) — in short, how to spend their time from morning to night. Markham's *English Housewife,* according to the title page, discusses "her skill in Physicke, Surgery, Cookery, Extraction of Oyles, Banqueting stuffe, . . . Distillations, Perfumes, ordering of Wooll, Hempe . . . , and all other things belonging to an Houshold." Hugh Platt, who collected *Delights for Ladies, to Adorn their Persons, Tables, Closets, and Distillations,* seductively entreated his readers to

> . . . let my wearied Muse
> Repose her selfe in Ladies lap awhile,
> So, when she wakes, she haply may record
> Her sweetest dreames in some more pleasing stile.

The ladies also had souls, and T. B. (presumably Thomas Bentley) was ready to provide a guide for feminine salvation:

The Fift Lampe of Virginitie: Conteining sundrie forms of christian praiers and meditations, to bee used onlie of and for all sorts and degrees of women, in their severall ages and callings; as namelie, of Virgins, Wives, Women with child, Midwives, Mothers, Daughters, Mistresses, Maids, Widowes, and old women. A Treatise verie needful for this time, and profitable to the Church. . . . 1582.[44]

No more than men did Elizabethan women restrict themselves to books intended to improve their earthly and spiritual life. They read poetry, romances like *Amadis of Gaul* and Sidney's *Arcadia,* Greene's tales, and ephemera of all sorts. Vives warned husbands to keep from their wives poetry and other "trifling books" — "for nature is enough incited to naughtiness, although we put not fire to tow." Lyly, in *Euphues and His England,* made love "to the Ladies and Gentlewoemen of England."

It resteth Ladies, that you take the paines to read it, but at such times, as you spend in playing with your little Dogges, and yet will I not pinch you of that pastime, for I am content that your Dogges lye in your laps, so *Euphues* may be in your hands, that when you shall be wearie in reading of the one, you may be ready to sport with the other: or handle him as you doe your Junckets, that when you can eate no more, you tye some in your napkin for children, for if you be filled with the first part, put the second in your pocket for your wayting Maydes: *Euphues* had rather lye shut in a Ladyes casket, then open in a Schollers studie.

Euphues is stylistically embellished like women's clothes: tropes and rhetorical figures, clusters of proverbs and unnatural natural history allusions, word-plays and alliterations are decorative rather than intrinsic. The consciously contrived aural effects of euphuism, the lengthy mannered letters exchanged by the lovers, the charming poems, and the idyllic pastoral interludes must have been especially pleasing to women who read aloud in small groups. Furthermore, euphuism gave them a distinctive (and easily acquired) speech pattern that flattered and at the same time satisfied their social desires, and the romances permitted escape into an unreal lover's land where Romeo wooed and won Juliet (contrary to the arranged marriages of the era) and amorousness never was stained with sex.[45]

The Elizabethan audience was, then, a heterogeneous group, only a relatively small part of which read books. It had boors, its "illiterate literates," and its intellectuals. As an audience it was neither brilliant nor barbarous. It resembled closely the audiences of succeeding centuries. Tabloids, comic books, lewd stories, factitious success dreams, "inside" revelations of the seamy and sordid differ only in degree, certainly not in kind, from what Elizabethan authors, moralists, and intellectuals deplored in their attacks upon "lowbrows," who, one must never forget, not only appreciated Deloney but also constituted a large section of Shakespeare's audience at the Globe.

CHAPTER THREE

THE TASTE OF THE AUDIENCE

THE taste of any audience is difficult to describe. Critics in every age indict and rage against "bad taste"; their fury is usually premised on arbitrary assumptions that they know what "good taste" is, and that they unerringly know what clowns and louts read and enjoy. Writers themselves are not diffident in condemning the taste of readers, or of those who refuse to purchase their books. Moralists (the religious custodians of taste) assail with intemperate and intolerant zeal those who prefer to enjoy themselves in their three score years and ten rather than to anguish over their immortal souls. Without much articulateness the masses simply know what they like. But in this verbal maze of indictment and clever (but misleading) dualisms — highbrows and lowbrows, aristocrats and philistines, supermen and the herd — the pyrotechnics are more scintillating than informative, the generalizations more glib than reliable, the tendency to expound more common than the desire to discover.

[63]

Even after the historian of taste sifts the dogmatic utterances of articulate contemporaries in order to get at what he believes to be the real situation, he is still confronted with almost insoluble problems. Libraries do not necessarily demonstrate that owners read the books on their shelves. Book collectors are especially prone to follow current fashion and to own what they know they should own. Similarly, though many commentators think otherwise, the presence of a religious book in an Elizabethan household does not conclusively demonstrate that it was carefully perused day after day, and that sixteenth-century Englishmen never ceased worrying about salvation. The secularism of the age — its preoccuption with commerce and business, its desire to get on in the world's terms (like Philocosmus), and the achievements of an essentially non-religious queen — belies the portrait of a bible-reading people. Even the number of editions of a work cannot always be accepted without reservations as indicative of the number of readers. The Bible, for example, has sold in extraordinary quantities for centuries, yet it has been termed, not without justification, "the book that nobody knows." People simply do not preserve ephemeral fare, whether Tudor jest-books and romances or twentieth-century detective books and love stories. Yet presidents, executives, professors, and the white-collar class literally devour detective stories.

And so, without dogmatism and with skepticism (perhaps an euphemism for my own bias), I shall examine the tastes of Elizabethan readers as objectively as I can on the basis of evidence which is often too incomplete to warrant sweeping conclusions.

Because the Tudor age accepted certain shibboleths and reiterated them unendingly (Elizabethans knew only too well what they were supposed to seek in literature), it made little difference who was indicting the taste of readers, whether Puritan, humanist, author, or critic. Literature was to inculcate moral attitudes, to be useful socially and religiously, and to keep people from idleness. It was to please and instruct, but pleasure, as Puttenham acknowledges, was the least of its gratifications.

Puritans did not confine themselves to polemics against stage plays; all literature was their province. Translations of classics and romances were said to enfeeble the reason, introduce pernicious pagan morals, and perpetuate monasticism. In *The Theater of God's Judgment,* Thomas Beard, bachelor of divinity and Cromwell's schoolmaster, alleges that in classical times "prophane writers" related stories, "therein to take pleasure and passe away time, without respecting anie further matter: Notwithstanding the true and principall use of their writings ought to be, diligently to marke the effects of Gods providence and of his justice, thereby to learne to contain our selves within the bounds of modestie and the feare of God." Edward Dering deplores "these dayes in which there is so great licentiousness of printing bookes," and exclaims sanctimoniously: "What multitude of Bookes full of all sinne and abominations have now filled the world! Nothing so childish, nothing so vaine, nothing so wanton, nothing so idle, which is not both bouldly printed and plausibly taken, so that herein we have fulfilled the wickednesse of our forefathers, and overtaken them in their sinnes." Soiled by their own preoccupation with sin, these zealots, almost inhumanly sincere, burned to keep man from pleasure and sensuality.[1]

Equally vehement but somewhat less intolerant were humanistic commentators concerned for the welfare of the nation. Nicholas Udall, for example, lauds the benefits to the "common weale" of translations of the Bible and biblical paraphrases. "For as for newe bookes of trifle-ing vanities and profane argumentes we nede none, there are daily so many writen: but to have such weorkes made common to the publique use of the unlearned multitude, as are the principal best, & have ben written by noble Clerkes of undoubted learning, knowlege, and godlines, therin consisteth such a publique benefite, as . . . is in mine estimacion, worthy publique thankes and regarde." Toward the end of the century Richard Robinson writes like one of the early Tudor humanists:

> By studious practitioners of our age, the workes of sundry auncient authors have made the most fertile increase of fallowed grounds by the sweat of others, which their remisnesse and imperfection had left as wast ground beefore, whereby their fame is more amplified then decreased, vertue more advaunced then abandoned, and the age present & henceforth more edified, then defrauded of so noble benifits of knowledge, and perfection of lyfe.

These critics, in brief, had no patience with literary trivia or books without explicit moral purpose, but they had an utilitarian faith in the pedagogical effects of translations.[2]

While religionists focused their thoughts on immortality, and writers like Udall and Robinson dreamed of the city of God on earth, maintainers of artistic standards conjured up visions of an Elizabethan Parnassus. "I will persecute," Nashe sputters, "those idiots and their heires unto the third generation, that have made Art bankerout of her ornaments, and sent Poetry a begging up and downe the Countrey." Daniel asks,

> Do you not see these Pamphlets, Libels, Rymes,
> These strange confused tumults of the minde,
> Are growne to be the sicknes of these times,
> The great disease inflicted on mankind?

Drayton, in the disillusioned twilight of his career, cursed the "sonnes of Beliall" and "th'hideous braying of each barbarous Asse," the poetic mountebank whose "Accents so untuneable and vile" make foreigners "thinke our braines were meerely mud." Writers have betrayed not only themselves and their art but also their readers.

> These blinded Fooles, on their base Carion feeding,
> Which are (in truth) made ignorant by reading,
> In little time would growe to be asham'd,
> And blush to heare those lowzie Pamphlets nam'd,
> Which now they studie, naught but folly learning,
> Which is the cause that they have no discerning,
> The good from bad.

Sir John Davies, not content with generalizations, cites specific works which have debased literature and corrupted its audience: Churchyard's *Chips* ("Offals of wit"), Harington's *Ajax Metamorphosed* ("His wit . . . defiled mee his maide"), Shakespeare's *Venus and Adonis* ("Lines so drawe [maids] on, To the venerian speculation"), the Harvey-Nashe quarrel, Greene's underworld tracts, the humors of Jonson, the chronicles of trivialities and sensational tidbits, and folios on the brewing of beer.[3]

Thus the increasing body of critical writings toward the end of the sixteenth century underscored the indictments of moralists and humanists. This is understandable, since English critics were children of an age given to moralistic evaluation and for the most part were unoriginal expounders of secondhand platitudes and generalities borrowed from foreign and classical writers. Literature they appraised in the light of what it was supposed to be — and to do — according to the sterile precedents they quoted at length. Hence they lost the particularized aesthetic response in a cloud of lofty generalizations more impressive for sound than for content. In short, English criticism consisted of intellectualizations, or moralizations, unrelated to the emotional and aesthetic qualities of literature. Even the noble Sidney bandied about tired truisms except in the aside in which he comments on "Chevy Chase." Nor were other critics, Jonson excepted, to revitalize an oppressive tradition and to articulate meaningful standards: Puttenham was occasionally acute, but he submerged himself in technical details; Webbe was well-intentioned but, like Meres, devoid of aesthetic sensibility; Nashe possessed more fury than acumen, and Harvey was utilitarian and blusteringly unsympathetic to the aesthetic experience; Greville worshiped a Calvinistic Jehovah and utility; Chapman was a greater poet and dramatist than critic; Daniel, like Sidney, had too much nobility of sentiment and too much respect for precedent, except in his defense of rime. Fortunately, in practice the great Elizabethan writers were as little slaves to classical precedents as the auditors of a Shakespearean play or the readers of *The Faerie Queene.*

And so these tirades of moralists, social critics, and custodians of taste, couched in blunt Elizabethan language, were ineffectual. The audience knew what it liked. And it did not like its soul subjected to merciless analyses, its social responsibility insisted upon in terms of an abstruse cosmic order, or its taste molded to the standards of self-appointed experts. In books many readers sought entertainment more avidly than they craved edification, perhaps because they were unable to differentiate between literature and what Colet termed "blotterature" but, more probably, because they preferred to be humans rather than moral robots.

Harington, whose notorious treatise on privies receives Davies' censure, voices in one of his epigrams the "correct" attitude of intellectual, artist, and moralist:

> All sorts read bookes, but why? will you discerne?
> The foole to laugh, the wiser sort to learne.

[68]

But this is a blatant quarter-truth. Englishmen were not so solemn and pleasure-hating as their public statements (and snobbery) make them appear. The Puritan was not always the glum-faced spokesman of a glum salvation; a humanist like Udall was not so humorless, or sadistic, as to be content to beat knowledge into his students; and just as amateurs composed to entertain their select audience, so professionals wrote for pleasure and to give pleasure to the general public. Yet in public most Elizabethans donned the mask of sobriety and regurgitated a platitude.[4]

When Caxton set up his printing press in England, he established a business which was intended to produce a profit, only incidentally to maintain or foster artistic ideals. Since he was dependent upon the patronage of aristocrats and wealthy burghers, the tastes of that audience determined his selection of books. According to Lathrop, of the seventy-seven books printed by Caxton, thirty-five (45 per cent) can be labeled religious, twenty-two (29 per cent) literary, eleven (14 per cent) informational, and nine (12 per cent) official (statutes.). This list appears to be, within the limitations of a small output, a fairly accurate indication of aristocratic and upper middle-class preference until 1491, the date of Caxton's death. However, as Duff wisely observes, "it cannot be supposed for a moment that at this time and to a considerably later date the products of the printing press in England represented in any way the literary wants of the people."[5]

Wynkyn de Worde catered to a much larger public than his predecessor. In 1500, with a shrewd eye for business, he moved his printing establishment from Westminster to St. Paul's Churchyard, and he decorated his books with what he supposed were attractive, eye-catching woodcuts. He cared little whether these crude blocks were appropriate to the text; his concern was the customer. In his shop the reader found not only religious, literary, informational, and official works, but also jest-books, ballads, romances, and chapbooks. De Worde, then, provided the diversity of printed matter necessary to capture the largest possible audience. In Plomer's words, "he had no high ideals, and his printing was solely a commercial undertaking for profit." [6]

Not many years were to pass before that talented versifier-printer Robert Copland lamented the decline of taste. While books of virtue lie unsold on the shelves, he maintains, readers clamor for "tryfles" and "wanton toyes." For the old they have no use; they seek for "thynges a-new." Then when they tire of novelties they ask for "conceytes . . . of laughyng."

> Have ye the ballad called *maugh murre,*
> Or *bony wenche,* or els, *go from my durre,*
> *Col to me,* or *hey down derry derry,*
> Or *a my hert,* or *I pray you be merry?*

Copland, disgusted with this "baggage, nought worthe in substance," and annoyed that "bokes of virtue have none utteraunce," dramatizes his revulsion in an imaginary dialog with a customer.

> Syr, I have a very proper boke
> Of morall wisedome, please ye their on to loke,
> Or els a boke of comen consolation. . . .
> Tushe a straw man, what should I do therewith?
> Hast thou a boke of the wydowe Edyth,
> That hath begyled so many with her wordes,
> Or els such a geest that is ful of bourdes.
> Let me se, I wyll yet waste a peny
> Upon such thinges, and if thou have any. . . .
> A peny I trow is ynough on bokes.
> It is not so soon goten, as this world lokes.

For his hard-gotten penny the customer seeks amusement, not salvation.[7]

Yet the customer's contempt of "a very proper boke Of morall wisedome" and "a boke of comen consolation" is not substantiated by most modern commentators on Elizabethan taste, who repeatedly single out the popularity of sermons and moral philosophy as illustrative of the religious interests of sixteenth-century Englishmen. Nor is the customer sustained by Edith L. Klotz's analysis of printed books between 1480 and 1640. Miss Klotz tabulates and classifies the products of the presses as recorded at ten-year intervals in the Stationers' Register and in *A Short-Title Catalogue*. (To what extent unregistered and lost books would have altered her computations is, of course, problematical.) Her selective sampling indicates that, except on one occasion (1520), from 33 to 63 per cent of all books published were religious, and the average for the entire period was 44 per cent. It is also significant that literature on only two occasions (1500 and 1600) constituted 30 per cent of the annual output of books, the average for 160 years being but 22 per cent. On the other hand, perhaps we should be surprised that such a large number of literary works was published in an era in which "utility" was the password in most circles, in which religious groups wielded political as well as ecclesiastical power, and in which, for at least a century in the period covered by the analysis, the national climate (both political and economic) was only spasmodically favorable to artistic expression.[8]

But Copland's customer, who stubbornly liked what he liked despite gentle and violent injunctions to study "profitable" books, was not an imaginary creation, for many writers testify to his existence. At the end of the century, Ingenioso, in *The Second Part of the Return from Parnassus*, informs the printer, "I tell thee this libel of Cambridge has much salt and pepper in the nose: it will sell sheerely underhand, whenas these bookes of exhortations and Catechismes lie moulding on thy shopboard." And in *Virtue's Commonwealth* (1603) Cross deplores the lack of interest in moral tracts: "Men are not only otherwise imployed, but also greatly discouraged, for if they set forth any notable booke of divinitie, humanitie, or such like, they are in no request, but to stop musterd-pots." In his preface to *Of the Imitation of Christ* (1580) Thomas Rogers charges that "the sale of good workes be mard manie-times for lack of wel handling" by printers, who also "abuse" the trade by publishing "vaine and vile bookes to the dishonor of God, the infamie of this land, to the confirming of the wicked in naughtines, and alienating of the wel disposed from virtue, I saie, to the discredite of the Gospel." Philip Stubbes, the earnest Puritan who wrote with the raciness of a Nashe and incurred the enmity of Nashe and others, bewails "the corruption of our time, for (alas) now-a-days it is grown to be a hard matter to get a good book licensed without staying, peradventure, a quarter of a year for it; yea, sometimes two or three years before he can have it allowed, and in the end happly rejected too." Yet, "other bookes, full of all filthines, scurrility, baudry, dissolutenes, cosenage, conycatching and the like . . are either quickly licensed, or at least easily tolerate." [9]

Early in Elizabeth's reign, Nicholas Robinson, a minister, made a significant point: "For fashion's sake merchantmen have Bibles, which they never peruse; for fashion's sake some women buy Scripture books, that they may be thought to be well disposed." Toward the end of the century an anonymous writer exclaims, "Woe is me, the playhouses are pestered when the churches are naked. At the one it is not possible to get a place, at the other void seats are plenty." Now moralists are often untrustworthy commentators, tending to see hell's fires in any puff of smoke and to magnify sin until it is unrecognizable even in the eyes of the sinner, but when to their testimony is added that of printers and other less extreme observers, it is time to reconsider. According to Sisson's admirable examination of the printing history of Hooker's *Of Ecclesiastical Polity*, in an age which modern commentators term "religious," printers were not interested in this great monument of Anglicanism "because bookes of that Argument and on that parte were not saleable." Or, in another contemporary comment: "The Printers at that time were fearfull to adventure uppon printing bookes in that kynde for that the bookes of a reverent man being then newly printed were badly soulde." And it took thirteen years to dispose of the first edition of Hooker's masterpiece, consisting of approximately one thousand copies! Vulgar guides to godliness and dull biblical paraphrases, so monotonous as to lead the reader to sin rather than to salvation, evidently sold better, while religious books of profundity had to be subsidized. Such an age is more accurately termed moralistic than religious.[10]

Against this evidence must be placed Stephens' description of "a booksellers shoppe on Bartholomew day at London: the stalls of which are so adornd with bibles and prayer-bookes, that almost nothing is left within, but heathen knowledge," and the imposing number of editions of treatises by Parsons and Perkins, to cite only two popular religious writers of the age. Stephens' assertion is not nearly so impressive as it appears when one remembers that on a saint's day it was good business to display religious books, and when one recalls the testimony of Copland and others as to the indifference with which many, if not most, purchasers viewed moral treatises. Two years before Stephens wrote, Rich asserts, "Those lines that are now put in print if they conteine any matter of pietie, or that are any whit at all entending to honesty, they doe but pester a Stationers stall, and there are very few or none that will bestow one peny of them." He adds that one year after Stephens took pride in what he saw on the book-stalls: "Idle toyes tending to sensualitie, or other like lycencious follie, are set foorth upon their Stalles, in bright and glistering covers, when those Bookes that are eyther drawing to vertue or godlinesse, are throwne into dustie corners." Parsons' *Resolution* was one of the most popular books of the age, issued both in Catholic and Protestant versions, but the graphic depiction of brimstone and the gleeful detailing of the punishments awaiting sinners constitute a salvation horror piece. The book filled Greene and Harington with terror and is still eminently readable, if not precisely terrifying. The writings of Perkins and other puritanical ministers found a ready audience among readers of their persuasion, who probably had neither time nor taste for nonreligious writings. Yet one should not forget Nicholas Robinson's remarks about the fashionable-ness of owning such works, nor should one ignore the fact that in a compact, conforming society like the Elizabethan the person who dared to express his indifference to guides to godliness was ridiculed and inevitably accused of athe-ism.[11]

Finally, at least three other factors tend to make religious treatises appear more popular than they in fact were. Many sixteenth-century poetical satires, romances, and topical pamphlets are known to us only from fragments and from contemporary allusions; how many of these works have been lost we can only conjecture. In other words, unlike devotional works, many popular books were literally read to pieces. The first four editions of Richard Robinson's *Record of Ancient Histories*, one of the most popular books of the seventeenth century, are lost, and there is only one copy extant of each of the printings between 1595 and 1610. Similar gaps appear in the sequence of editions of Deloney's novels. How frequently the "boke of the wydowe Edyth," which Copland's customer wanted and which received an honored place in Cox's library, was reprinted, no one will ever know. Second, the fact that much popular literature was penny literature, cheaply printed and stitched and then devoured by eager readers, contributed to the mortality of these books. Third, while ballads, books of bawdry, romances, and news sheets only appeared sporadically in the registers of the Stationers' Company, religious works (unless heretical) were almost always entered.

In view of contemporary fulminations against non-religious trifles and the statements of printers as to the saleability of "morall bokes," it is not an unrealistic conclusion that, while religious tomes gathered dust on Tudor tables, Elizabethans, long faces in abeyance, sought in books fun and escape from a bleak (socially and religiously) environment. Far too much significance can be attributed to the number of religious books printed in the sixteenth century, and too close a correlation can be assumed between the number of volumes printed and the actual reading of them.

Ballads were the common man's delight — and sometimes, but of course surreptitiously, the nobleman's too. At least Sidney candidly acknowledged his fondness for "Chevy Chase." The reasons for their popularity were obvious enough. Ballads were brief, farcically humorous, or sentimentally tragic, frequently bawdy, almost always topical and "new," poetic in the mechanical singsong fashion that the uncultivated admire, and generally set to a popular tune. In addition, they were inexpensive — one for a halfpence, two for a pence. Thus they elicited an uncomplicated and commonplace emotional response with their irresistible rhythm and infectious music, at a price well within the financial means of most people.

Ballads were much too popular with the masses to be socially or intellectually acceptable, and, in truth, so crude and so blatantly commercial were many of them that only the uncritical and insensitive could tolerate them. Among writers, except for producers like Munday, Churchyard, and Deloney, there was only wholesale condemnation. Nashe laments that "the cockscombs of our daies, like Esops Cock, had rather have a Barly kernell wrapt up in a Ballet then they wil dig for the welth of wit in any ground that they know not." A character in one of the *Parnassus* plays exclaims ironically, "I am in some choller with this assheaded age, where the honorable trade of ballet makinge is of such base reckoninge." Although he deplores the vulgar taste of "the multitude," Spenser is more perturbed by the banalities of the ballad mongers who sell out art and,

> . . . to the vulgar sort now pipe and sing,
> And make them merrie with their fooleries,
> They cherelie chaunt and rymes at random fling,
> The fruitfull spawne of their ranke fantasies:
> They feede the eares of fooles with flattery,
> And good men blame, and losels magnify:
> All places they doo with their toyes possesse,
> And raigne in liking of the multitude.

More specifically, but probably less fairly, Stanyhurst charges that these "wooden rythmours" had never attended grammar schools and hence had not "the paringes of thee Latin or Greeke tongue." Chettle brands "that idel up-

start generation of ballad-singers," and Marston trans-
forms them into alcoholics:

> When every ballad-monger boldly writes,
> And windy froth of bottle-ale doth fill
> Their purest organ of invention.[12]

There was no surcease to these denunciations, nor was
Autolycus without successors. For ballads retained their
popularity well into the eighteenth century, when, according to Thomas Holcroft, they were pasted on walls of cot-
tages and alehouses to "the delight of the vulgar." In fact,
at the safe distance of several centuries these ballads were
to achieve respectability and handsome editions when literary historians turned to the vulgar delights of the vulgar
and enshrined them in scholarly tomes. Such are the vicis-
situdes of taste and of time. With the flux of taste and the
curiosity of posterity authors of artistic integrity are rightly
little concerned; they have always been, however, irked
by the success of popular literature and the economic returns of its producers. Breton, for example, wrote sadly
and somewhat enviously these lines:

> Goe tell the Poets that their pidling rimes
> Begin apace to grow out of request:
> While wanton humors in their idle times,
> Can make of Love but as a laughing jest:
> And tell poore Writers, stories are so stale,
> That penny ballads make a better sale.

Indeed Elizabethan professionals were more envious of the
balladmongers than they cared to admit.[13]

Almost as popular as ballads, and certainly as vehemently
abused, were the medieval romances which sprang up
simultaneously in many European countries, and which
enjoyed an enormous international vogue for many centuries, until the development of the eighteenth-century

novel introduced a popular literary substitute. But it is a mistake to assume that only the ignorant read these romances, as some modern scholars have done, or that within a half century after their appearance in England only the vulgar perused them. They maintained their fascination for upper-class readers into the first quarter of the seventeenth century, after which time they gradually became the literary fare only of the lower classes and eventually tales for children. During the period we are surveying romances had not gone over to the lowbrows, and upper-class readers, sometimes with the mixed emotions of Cervantes' Curate, took pleasure in the exploits of Amadis of Gaul, Bevis of Southampton, and other chivalric heroes.[14]

With artfully chosen words and full realization of the English interest in obtaining useful lessons from literature, Caxton introduces his translation of *Morte Darthur*:

> Noble men may see and lerne the noble actes of chyvalrye, the jentyl and vertuous dedes that somme knyghtes used in tho dayes, by whyche they came to honour, and how they that were vycious were punysshed and ofte put to shame and rebuke; humbly bysechyng al noble lordes and ladyes wyth al other estates, of what estate or degree they been of, that shal see and rede in this sayd book and werke, that they take the good and honest actes in their remembraunce, and to folowe the same. . . . For herein may be seen noble chyvalrye, curtosye, humanyte, frendlynesse, hardynesse, love, frendshyp, cowardyse, murdre, hate, vertue, and synne. Doo after the good and leve the evyl, and it shal brynge you to good fame and renommee.

Yet, despite the acceptable morality and the utility of the work as a model of deportment in Caxton's eyes, sixteenth-century critics of the genre denied the assets cited by the English printer.[15]

A moralist like Vives claims that "these works do hurt both man and woman, for they make them wily and crafty, they kindle and stir up covetousness, inflame anger and all beastly and filthy desire." To Tyndale such books "corrupte the myndes of youth with all clene contrary to the doctrine of christ & of his apostles," and Perkins attempts in *The Foundation of Christian Religion* to dispel the fallacy "that merrie ballads and bookes, as *Scoggin, Bevis of Southampton, &c.* are good to drive away time, and to remove hart quames." Edward Fenton abominates the lies in the stories of knights and the absence of "either grave precept or good example." Ascham argues that romances "were made the moste parte in Abbayes, and Monasteries, a very lickely and fit fruite of suche an ydle and blynde kinde of lyvynge," in order to glorify "manslaughter and baudrye" — a palpably false accusation later repeated by Dering, Nashe, and Rich. With charming naiveté, in 1539, the *Summary Declaration of Faith, Uses and Observances in England* alleges that "Englishmen have now in hand in every Church and place, almost every man, the Holy Bible and New Testament in their mother tongue, instead of the old fabulous and fantastical books of the 'Table Round,' 'Launcelot du Lac,' 'Huon de Bourdeaux,' 'Bevy of Hampton,' 'Guy of Warwick,' &c., and such other, whose impure filth and vain fabulosity the light of God has abolished utterly." [16]

Romances are not only iniquitous but also useless. In the eyes of John Harvey, Gabriel's brother, they are intended "to busie the minds of the vulgar sort, or to set their heads aworke withal, and to avert their conceits from the consideration of serious, and graver matters, by feeding their humors, and delighting their fansies with such fabulous and ludicrous toyes." Fenton witnesses contemptuously "with howe great earnestnesse and delight the unlearned sorte runne over the fruitlesse Historie of king Arthur and his round table Knights, and what pleasure they take in the trifeling tales of Gawin and Gargantua." If one heeds this endless torrent of abuse, the "vulgar sort" were corrupting their morals and undermining the foundations of the nation.[17]

Actually the "vulgar" and "unlearned" were in good company. Unlike Fenton, Thomas Wilson, author of *The Art of Rhetoric* and later Elizabeth's secretary of state, found Arthur and his knights "good sport," and Burghley, who preferred moral treatises to belles-lettres, purchased in his youth the French edition of *Amadis of Gaul*. Although Drayton writes bitterly of "that trash of *Amadis de Gaule*," and Tofte terms it "bitter in Sense, but no thing Sweete att all," Sidney deems it a morally edifying work: "Truely, I have knowen men, that even with reading *Amadis de Gaule* (which God knoweth wanteth much of a perfect Poesie) have found their harts mooved to the exercise of courtesie, liberalitie, and especially courage." Sidney's son Sir Robert, at the time English governor in the Low Countries, asked to borrow the Earl of Pembroke's copy of *Amadis*. The romance, then, was scorned neither by the most famous patrons of literature in the period nor by some of Elizabeth's most esteemed advisors.[18]

In a court in which a skillfully amorous queen demanded and received tokens of passion from noble swains — with as much involvement on her part as the aloof sirens of romances and sonnets — and in a setting in which remnants of medieval pageantry revived in the Iron Age the past glory of chivalry, romances were not without honor. It was only natural that Spenser should transform Elizabeth into the most glorious model of chivalry. It was no less surprising that her court in its expensive festivities reenacted the jousts of romances. On February 26, 1588, Cumberland and Essex made challenge that "they will runne all comers to maintain that the Queen is most worthiest and most fairest Amadis de Gaule." At another royal celebration the Earl of Southampton jousted, according to Peele, as "Bevis of South-Hampton." In the reign of her successor, in 1606, Chamberlain describes "a cartell" in which four knights descended from "Donzell del Phebo, Amadis de Gaule, Palmerin d'Oliva, and Ascapart, wherin besides other ridiculous stuffe, they aunswer their fowre positions in goode earnest." Though the tourneys were "ridiculous" to the sophisticated Chamberlain, whose taste for mock-jousts had probably been jaded by their frequency, Edward de Vere was reported to be so fond of romances that he quixotically thought himself "descended of the doughty Knight of the Swan!" [19]

Aubrey informs us that Thomas Hobbes "spent too yeares in reading romances and plays, which he haz often repented." The serious and sometimes pontifical William Segar is, like Sidney, sympathetically disposed toward romances, because "some egregious acts atchieved and written in the bookes of *Amadis de Gaule, Ariosto, Tasso, King Arthur* of England, and such others doe containe many things, which deserve not to be discredited"; and Sir Thomas Cockaine, in his *Short Treatise of Hunting*, extols Tristram as "the first writer of the exact knowledge of hunting." Robert Ashley, a graduate of Oxford and a lawyer, snatched time during his busiest years to read of the exploits of chivalric heroes. Puttenham confesses to composing "for pleasure a little brief Romance or historical ditty in the English tong" for those "desirous to heare of old adventures & valiaunces of noble knights in times past." Cox, the Coventry mason, was enamored of these tales, and a "Countrey-farmer" spurned Henry Parrot's book of epigrams —

> It may be good (saith he) for those can use it.
> Shewe mee King *Arthur*, *Bevis*, or Syr *Guye*,
> Those are the Bookes he onely loves to buye.

Indeed, it would appear that most people shared the far-mer's joy in books of chivalry, if not the fantasies of de Vere and the woman described by Overbury, who "is so carried away with the *Mirror of Knighthood*, she is many times resolv'd to runne out of her selfe, and become a lady errant." [20]

There appears to be something of Quixote in most peo-ple in their tendency to embellish certain eras — the Na-poleonic in France, the Civil War in America, the Eliza-bethan to later Englishmen — with a romance and a splendor never to be encountered in the city of man. Chivalric tales had such an appeal for several centuries, and their pageantry became more dazzling in contrast with the drabness of daily living, the account books of merchants, and the unheroic business morality of emergent capitalism. In addition, there were the excitement of swift plots and the continuous movement of uncomplicated heroes rescu-ing uncomplicated damsels and living happily forever after in uncomplicated matrimonial (and material) bliss. Final-ly, in the illusionary world of romance good and evil re-ceived their deserts with mathematical exactitude. To "the Chronicle of wasted time" Shakespeare pays tribute in Sonnet 106 — as do St. Ignatius, St. Teresa, Sidney, one-third of whose *Arcadia*, it has been estimated, is traceable to *Amadis of Gaul*, Spenser, whose great poem could not have been written if romances had not preceded it, Jon-son in *The Masque of Oberon*, and, finally, Cervantes. No greater tribute could be paid to a popular literary form.[21]

Amorous stories, jest-books, and erotic poetry were un-der an incessant barrage of hostile criticism from essen-tially the same people who lambasted ballads and romances. Ascham, whose anti-Italian bias had an unhumanistic fierceness, maintains that "mo[re] Papistes be made, by your mery bookes of Italie, than by your earnest bookes of

Lovain." After attributing romances to popish superstition, Dering turns upon native books and charges that,

> . . . wee have multiplied for our selves so many newe delights, that wee might justifie the idolatrous supersticion of the elder worlde: To this purpose we have printed us many baudie Songes. . . . To this purpose we have gotten our Songes & Sonets, our Pallaces of Pleasure, our unchast Fables, & Tragedies, and such like sorceries, moe than any man may recken. Yea, some have bine so impudent, as new borne Moabites, which walow in their own vomit, & have not bin ashamed to intitle their books the Court of Venus, the Castle of Love, & many such other as shameles as these.

The poet Richard Robinson fears that his readers will not "credite" his poetic dreams because they scarcely believe in Jesus and "clappe their handes for Joye" only when Cupid appears; and Bastard claims (not quite accurately) that his epigrams are unread because he does not write "of lewde loves and wantonnesse." On the bookstalls in St. Paul's Churchyard, Rich finds only "Idle toyes tending to sensualitie, or other like lycencious follie." And critics droned on in the fallacious belief that books have the power to corrupt, and that, if these "Bookes of so great vanitie" were burned, as Dering proposes, man could be saved from the immortal but immoral Adam inherent in the species.[22]

When we look beyond the moralistic pronouncements, we discover that the reading of jest-books and bawdy tales was not confined to the semiliterate. In 1578 Spenser presented Gabriel Harvey with *Howleglass, Merry Tales by Master Skelton, Scoggin's Jests,* and *Lazarillo.* (In his *Marginalia* Harvey calls them "foolish books.") After exhausting romances, Ashley informs us, he read Boccaccio and Margaret of Navarre, only to find them more dissolute than the former. Cox, who had enormous gusto for diversion, includes under "Philosophy, both morall & naturall" such works as *The Highway to the Spital House, The Castle of Love, The Hundred Merry Tales,* and some of Skelton's racier poems. Some of the greatest writers of the period, including Marlowe and Shakespeare, did not hesitate to plunder books of "sensualitie," and that self-appointed guardian of public taste, Nashe, circulated in manuscript his realistic description of a visit to a bawdy house, *The Choice of Valentines,* which is no less vulgar than the jest-books of the period and a great deal cruder than the anecdotes that Deloney inserted in his novels. As the fop in *The Return from Parnassus* prefers *Venus and Adonis* to *The Faerie Queene,* so readers and writers in their own ways refused to deny the universal libido, even though like Gascoigne's printer they frequently took refuge in the Horatian rationalization of the spider and the bee:

As the venemous spider will sucke poison out of the most holesome herbe, and the industrious Bee can gather hony out of the most stinking weede, even so the discrete reader may take a happie example by the most lascivious histories, although the captious and harebraind heads can neither be encoraged by the good, nor forewarned by the bad.[23]

Except among Puritans who professed to have their thoughts glued on the endless spaces of eternity and among those who read only for information and clues to success, the reading audience sought pleasure and diversion in books, and many writers, especially popularizers, endeavored to entertain them. After all, the endlessly repeated classical dictum — to please and to instruct — was as familiar to grammar-school graduates as to readers of Sidney's *Defense of Poetry,* and, though it was more ambiguous than its exponents imagined, it did not eliminate entertainment and sanction only solemn moral disquisitions. In truth its ambiguity permitted as many constructions as there were writers and readers.

To Churchyard, a soldier trained in the battlefields rather than in the universities, it meant primarily diversion and laughter — and perhaps a reward from the dedicatee, the Earl of Surrey.

He that sturreth up the heavie myndes to lightsome consaites, is more welcome in every place, then he that overthrowes the weake senses of common people, with curious imaginations, and burthens bothe bodie and mynde, with wordes of greater weight, then common judgement can conceive, and be able to beare. A tale or a toye mirrely delivered, pleaseth moste mennes eares: and an earneste sadde arugment, either rockes a man a slepe, or maketh the hearers awearie.

As an entertainer, Churchyard's intention was better than his achievement: his writings rarely went into a second printing, and his poulter's measure, like "an earnest sadde argument," made his readers "awearie." To a serious artist like Spenser, on the other hand, the dictum meant a fusion of pleasure and moral earnestness. *The Faerie Queene* has all the ingredients of popular entertainment: chivalric heroes and romantic heroines, villains in pursuit of good women's virtue, duels and encounters with strange monsters (sometimes human and sometimes animal), excitement and suspense, and a plot overabundantly filled with complications and fantastic incidents. But this mixture of chivalry, allegory, and contemporary satire is never without the firm control of Spenser's moral vision. No wonder his great poem appealed to practical printers, hacks like Meres, squires like Richard Carew, and intellectuals and artists. In Saunders' words, "Spenser's ability to win and hold a simultaneous popularity with several different audiences is by far the outstanding mark of his career." [24]

Writers more analytical and self-critical than honest Churchyard were aware that entertainment without serious moral purpose won readers among the masses but cost prestige among artists. Thomas Cutwode was reconciled to the situation. After praising Sidney, Daniel, and Spenser, who "are admired & deified almost by the wisest, the lernedst, & the deepest sighted," he declares himself content to be one of those who "are held among the inferior spirits, and are the litle Penates, to countrey, homely and lowe reaching wits, admired by such, and religiously read, though never taken into others hands." But Greene, the most successful writer in the era, was not reconciled to his popularity among "inferior spirits." In the *Vision*, allegedly "written at the instant of his death" (it was probably composed earlier), Greene apologizes to his readers: "I crave pardon of you all, if I have offended any of you with lascivious Pamphleting. Many things I have wrote to get money, which I could otherwise wish to be supprest: Povertie is the father of innumerable infirmities: in seeking to salve private wantes, I have made my selfe a publique laughing stock." The book itself is a debate between Chaucer and Gower as to the merits of Greene's publications. Merry Chaucer approves because "Poets wits are free, and their words ought to be without checke," for "our English Gentlemen are of the mind of the Athenians, that will sooner bee perswaded by a fable, than an Oration: and induced with a merrie tale, when they will not be brought to any compasse with serious circumstances." Moral Gower disapproves:

> Poets quils,
> Ought not for to teach men ils.
> For learning is a thing of prise,
> To shew precepts to make men wise.

In one of his penitent moods at the moment of composition, Greene permits the moralist to triumph and promises to follow Gower's example: "My pamphlets have passed the presse, and some have given them praise, but the gravest sort, whose mouthes are the trumpets of true report, have spoken hardlie of my labours." Fortunately for himself as well as for his readers Greene's decisions were made for revision.[25]

This desire for the approbation of "the gravest sort" led some hacks to place the blame for their huckstering upon pleasure-mad readers in this "humorous" age, just as amateurs permitted printers to bear the onus of the publication they secretly coveted. Dekker, a talented hack writer though he poured forth verbalisms to deny his professionalism, was especially artful in concealing his need for shillings by his elaborate rationalizations of his huckstering. "If I put into your hands a homely piece of Worke," he writes, "I must entreat you to blame the vanitie of our times, which are so phantasticall, that they covet Stuffes, rather slight, to feede the eye with shew, then Substantiall for enduring . . . . I have therefore not . . . swomme against the streame; But followed the Humorous Tides of this Age." Rich was another hack particularly susceptible to delusions about his ability. "To make my selfe sociable with the multitude," he exculpates himself, "I have mingled matters of importance, with matters of small regarde: I know this is the humorous age, and although to reade over fewe things advisedly, profiteth, yet to runne through many things (though slightly) delighteth, and a man that can but tattle this and that (though to little purpose) shall have audience." But Rich had little to offer readers except truisms. Indeed, contemporary indifference to his concoctions has been vindicated by posterity. Even more ingenious than Dekker and Rich is Bastard, who transfers responsibility for his trifles to an avaricious printer eager to pander to popular taste.

> Some will perhaps condemne my foolish veyne,
> For that of Dogs, Lyons, and Apes I speake.
> But if they knewe the cause they would refrayne.
> I doe it onely for the Printers sake.
> The simple must have something for their humour,
> And having somthing they my booke will buy.
> Then gayneth he by whome I am no looser.
> So is he satisfide, and they and I.
> > Some will give sixe pence for a witty touch,
> > And some to see an Ape will give as much.

With such rationalizations are the sidewalks of Grub Street paved.[26]

At least other popularizers attempted to legitimatize entertainment by invoking precedents on the not unshrewd principle that, if the ancients approved, Englishmen had better get in step with tradition. The unknown author of *The Life of Long Meg of Westminster*, a work that went through countless editions in the sixteenth and seventeenth centuries, so justifies his jest-book tales: "Gentlemen, Augustus would reade over Riddles, when he had tossed over Virgils Heroicks, and Cicero would oft Delirat after his weighty affaires; so I hope you will use Long Meg as a whetstone to mirth after your serious businesse: and if shee have any grosse faults, beare with them the more patiently for that she was a woman." But few dared to emulate this writer's example, probably out of self-consciousness and fear that levity degraded.[27]

Breton is a case in point. Actually he had a genuine talent for light entertainment, an accomplishment by no means common in the Elizabethan or any other era. He was neither subtle nor profound, as is transparent in his collections of moralistic aphorisms, and he is sentimental and occasionally cute, as in his model letters and his descriptions of the months and the seasons. For the most part, however, his platitudes are charmingly phrased and his sentimentality disarming. Yet, despite forty years devoted to writing trivia "to passe Idle Time withall," Breton never quite accepted the role of entertainer. In 1597, for example, he seeks a cultivated audience: "I would be glad to please the best spirits; for other, I wish them more perfection of understanding then lavishnesse of speech, and my selfe but the happines to bee out of the censure of the unwise." But four years earlier, in *No Whipping Nor Tripping*, like a popular writer he minimizes his education in order to establish camaraderie with his readers:

> But, pardon me, if that I speake false Latine
> For lacke of learning: I no scholar am:
> My masters gowne deserves no face of Satine:
> I never to degree of Master came.

The Pilgrimage of Paradise (1592), on the other hand, is intended for "the correction of the learned" at Oxford and the Inns of Court. And frequently Breton utilizes prefaces, as modern publishers employ dust jackets, to coax a few pence from the customer. In *The Strange Fortunes of Two Excellent Princes* (1600) he writes, "Let me tell you, that if you will kindlie reade, that is friendlie offred you, and part with a little mony, for a matter of more worth; it maie be you shall have more contentment, then you looke for." In order to sell *The Miseries of Mavillia* (1599) he cajoles his readers: "Me thinks I heare a number say, What meanes this fellowe to fill our eares with miseries? Why? our eyes are full ynough alreadie: tell us some merry tale, if thou wilt have any money of us. Such I answere, A Christmasse song is worth a cup of ale: I am no hyreling for halfe-pence. And this I will tell you, it will

do you no harme, but keep you from worse exercises."
Here he speaks as a professional anxious to sell his books
and anxious to please his audience, despite his self-righteous observation that he is "no hyreling for halfe-pence." [28]

Like Breton, Greene was never quite reconciled to his
success. Popular he was, as the unsympathetic testimony
of Gabriel Harvey demonstrates: "The Countesse of Pem-
brookes Arcadia is not greene inough for queasie stomackes,
but they must have Greenes Arcadia: and I beleeve most
eagerlie longed for Greenes Faerie Queene"; and his popularity continued into the seventeenth century, *Pandosto*
becoming one of the bestsellers of the century. Despite
later qualms, Greene began his career as an entertainer,
possibly of the fashionable, who at the time reveled in the
affected style of *Euphues* and in interminable discussions
of love and deportment. Greene hopes, in *Mamillia*, that
"Gentlemen will take my booke as a toy to passe away the
time, and weigh more of my meaning then of the matter,
and more of my wil, than eyther of my wit, or the worke."
In his foreword to *The Mirror of Modesty* he excuses "such
trash" because a lady "perswaded me that to trouble your
patience was but a small cracke, but to deny a Gentlewom-
an and my freend so reasonable a request a great discredite." "Whatsoever I have done or written," he avows in
Penelope's Web, "I onely desire for my paynes your favorable acceptance, and so wish to you, as to my selfe, to
live fortunate, and dye happy." Like Churchyard, he is
determined not to be "tedious to young mindes" or "with
solemne shewes to foster melancholie." So, in *Planetomachia*, "I have interlaced my Astronomicall discourse with
pleasaunt Tragedies, that your profitable Harvest may be
gleaned together with delightfull paines," for "the minde
wearied with weightie affaires, seeketh assoone to be recreated with some pithie conceipts, as with any deepe con-

templations." In *Menaphon,* "there be as well humors to
delight, as discourses to advise." With justification he
writes in *Pandosto*: "So Gentlemen, if any condemne my
rashnesse for troubling your eares with so many unlearned
Pamphlets: I will straight . . . lay the blame on you
aswell for frendly reading them, as on my selfe for fondly
penning them." [29]

By 1589 he had become, in his own words, "a second
Ovid," a narrator of amorous tales in modified euphuistic
prose. His characters had endlessly debated the profundi-
ties of love and passion with a suitably puritanical lack of
concern for the physical aspects of the subject. But the
events of 1588 had altered the climate. "Hetherto Gentlemen," Greene observes in *The Spanish Masquerado,* "I
have writte of loves, . . . now least I might be thought to
tie my selfe wholly to amorous conceites, I have adventured
to discover my conscience in Religion." In *The Royal Exchange* (1590) he collects "strange definitions, devisions,
and distinctions of vertue and vice," which, he characteristically adds, "may please the gravest Cittizens, or young-
est Courtiers." Then Greene forsakes laughter-loving Chaucer for the didactic Gower, and at the conclusion of his
Vision he promises "to seeke after wisdome so highly commended by Salomon." Repetitiously he apologizes for
"lascivious Pamphleting" (*Vision*), for "frivolous toyes"
(*Never Too Late*), for "wanton Pamphlets" (*Greene's
Mourning Garment*). Now it is "*Farewell to Follie,* and
then adieu to all amorous Pamphlets." Like those of many
actors Greene's farewells went on and on. As late at 1592
he issued another collection of stories, *Philomela,* but only
he assures us, at the printer's "earnest intreatie." [30]

In his cony-catching pamphlets of 1591 he changes like
Diogenes "from a counterfait Coiner of money" to "a cur-
rant corrector of manners," and "I crie out with Salomon,

Omnia sub sole vanitas." But Greene was neither Diogenes nor Ecclesiastes: he still entertained his readers with "pleasant tales" of rogues and racketeers, although he convinced himself that his cony-catching exposés performed a major patriotic service. "I thanke God," he writes in the *Repentance of Robert Greene,* "that hee put it in my head, to lay open the most horrible coosenages of the common Conny-catchers, Cooseners, and Crossebiters. . . . And my trust is, that those discourses will doe great good, and bee very beneficiall to the Commonwealth of England." Only in *Groatsworth of Wit,* when he finally admitted that the life of Roberto was the story of his own life, was he able to drop the mask of the entertainer briefly and to describe his own tormented existence. Yet the imminence of death did not effect a drastic alteration, for in this tract he promises his readers that "if I recover, you shall all see, more fresh sprigs, then ever sprang from me, directing you how to live, yet not diswading ye from love." [31]

The popularity of his works indicates that Greene supplied the Elizabethan audience with the literature it wanted. Always he kept paramount the desire of his readers to be entertained: his characters were the simple heroes and ladies of romances, his prose was clear and idiomatic, and his exposition was straightforward. Although in his remorse he labeled his tracts lascivious, it is difficult to see whom he could have offended. Evil was always punished and virtue rewarded, and everyone must certainly have been content. Finally, he never troubled readers with experimentation, for like all popular writers he was not an innovator: he converted such medieval genres as the dream, the debate, the prodigal-son story, the attack upon social evils into successful Elizabethan entertainment.

As one would expect, the morality of popular literature, despite the Bunyan-like natures of writers like Greene, was innocuous. Not for these authors and their public was Wildean amorality. Evil was evil and good was good, and the denouements of tales made the fact clear that God rewarded and chastised accordingly — the industrious, virtuous man achieving success as concretely evidenced in wealth or in a good marriage, and the indolent, evil man losing both status and his sordid lucre because he had offended God and society. Such was the formula Elizabethan popularizers instinctively evolved to please their public, and the formula remains essentially unchanged centuries later.[32]

The public in its certainty that it knows what it likes and in its insatiable desire for entertainment of the most elementary kind is infuriating both to artists and to critics; yet the fact remains that rarely are writers who were scorned by their contemporaries admired by posterity. (Frequently, however, later critics in effect confirm popular taste by intellectualizing what contemporary readers instinctively appreciated; in other words, with the passage of time lowbrow taste frequently becomes highbrow taste.) Compromisers with the heterogeneous tastes of readers may be geniuses like Shakespeare and Spenser or men of talent like Greene and Deloney or third-rate hacks like Churchyard and Rich. Yet the dynamic tension of reconciling what seems to the aesthete unreconcilable — artistry and popularity, or, in Renaissance terminology, pleasure and instruction — would appear to be at least partly responsible for contemporaneous and timeless success.

CHAPTER FOUR

PATRONAGE: "MECOENAS IS YCLAD IN CLAYE"

By 1600 patronage like many other medieval institutions was obsolescent, but this fact was not to be widely recognized for almost another century and a half, when writers like Pope and Johnson successfully attacked the system, and when conditions in the book trade were so altered that literature provided a livelihood in itself. However, by the end of the sixteenth century hack writers who were not beneficiaries of sustained patronage began to voice their misgivings as to the adequacy of the system and to protest their enforced dependency upon the generosity of the nobles and the wealthy.

Like the concept of order and the moralistic hostility toward usury, patronage was in conflict with a world moving from an agricultural economy and closed society to a capitalistic system and an open society. This benevolent paternalism was suited to a society in which reading was confined to aristocratic circles and in which writers, like scops of earlier centuries, were respected members of noble households. Unlike his successors, the medieval poet was closely identified with his society: he belonged. He not only knew his patrons intimately and, like painters and sculptors, frequently composed by commission, but also he accepted the underlying assumptions of his world. He did not question the subordination of writing to other political and religious interests. To bear arms for the sovereign was more honorable than to wield the pen in the name of the muses. In other words, before one was a writer, one was a member of an integrated society. A Dante placed high value upon his political duties; only in exile did he have time for his masterpiece. A Chaucer was first a servant of the king, then a poet; the former was his vocation, the latter his avocation. Writing in medieval times had its function and its place: it was primarily a courtly exercise for aristocratic diversion. The medieval author did not feel himself degraded or demeaned by his role. In truth, he had a form of psychological security rarely granted to authors in the future.[1]

Unlike medieval poets, university wits, ex-soldiers, apothecaries, religious polemicists, ballad writers, and would-be poets rushed into print and frankly catered to the tastes of a heterogeneous audience, which more often than not they affected to despise. Patrons were sought, even exploited. The medieval lord had never found on his threshold an unknown man with a recently printed book replete with effusive dedications — and a hand outstretched. Intimacy between patron and author was becoming a faded dream of a bygone age. Writers sought patrons as merchants sought new accounts. Since authors had to sell themselves, they strained their verbalistic powers for unhackneyed variations upon the glories of the Maecenases of the age. Because swarms of authors sought patronage (the increase in their number not being equaled by the number of people willing to subsidize art), the tones of these verbal symphonies became more saccharine and cloying. To see (and hear) the difference we have but to place side by side dedications by an amateur and a professional. Sir Thomas Cockaine, who wrote about his avocation in *A Short Treatise of Hunting,* dedicated his work to an old family friend, the Earl of Shrewesbury:

Aswell in respect I had the originall of my said experience under your most noble Grandfather (whose servant I was in my yonger yeares, and brought up in his house) as also in regard that I have receaved many extraordinary favours, both from your said most noble Grandfather, from my honourable good Lord your father, and lastly and most especially from your selfe (my good Lord); who knowing me a professed Hunter, and not a scholler, I make no doubt but your Lordshippe wil affoord my plainnes herein your favourable liking.

Where Cockaine's language is simple and dignified, Richard Robinson's is pompous and affected as he courts the favor of Ambrose Dudley, Earl of Warwick:

I have withall humble and duetiful regard adressed this my poore travell unto your Honors moste noble patronage, as one whose Heroicall vertues in patrociny counterpoysable to the Princely protection of the first noble patrone that Honourable *Augustus* High Marshal of the most sacred Empire that now is. Your Honor assuredly shall by Gods grace, of your godly zeale adorne both patrones & expositors godly purposes, advaunce the honor of God, your Prince, and country: not a little adumbrating by your accustomed clemency the true and unfayned goodwill of me the Translator.

Robinson obviously strains syntax and diction, let alone sense, in order to assuage his need. Perhaps his torturous prose repelled the earl, for Robinson went unrewarded.[2]

Just as the sonneteer elevated his beloved, real or imaginary, into an Elizabethan Beatrice, and the nobleman courted his goddess-queen, so some writers composed almost amorous paeans to patrons, male and female. Barnaby Barnes, for instance, assumes the role of an unworthy suitor to the Earl of Southampton:

> Receave (sweet Lord) with thy thrice sacred hande
> Which sacred muses make their instrument
> These worthles leaves, which I to thee present,
> Sprong from a rude and unmanured lande.

Perhaps this foppish lord demanded such coyness, but humility carried to these extremes demeans art as well as the artist.[3]

Dedications toward the end of the sixteenth century were "manufactured" with the monotonous, repetitious precision of the epistles addressed by the woe-begotten euphuistic lover to his aloof lady. Just as euphuistic letters were mechanically balanced, so dedications lauded the virtues of the Maecenas, compared him to classical patrons, implored protection against carpers (the classical Zoili and Momi), and asked forgiveness for the presentation of trifles. Language was inflated and diction sometimes grotesque, as the writer plodded through the stereotyped litany of Grub Street.

But Shakespeare rebelled in Sonnet 130 against the platitudes of fellow sonneteers and anchored his dark lady on earth, and Rowlands decided to frame "a new found fashion" and to emancipate his "freeborne Muse" from servile dedications.

> *I will not fawne with* Matchles, valorous,
> Rarely renown'd, divine Ingenious;
> Admired wonder, map of clemency,
> Applauded, lauded magnanimity,
> The Mercury of perfect eloquence
> True sphaere of bounty and Magnificence:

> The feirce and crewell warre God at the sharpe:
> Apollo's better on the Lute and Harpe.
> Old Hector's over-match at pike and launce,
> Disgrace to Juno for a stately daunce,
> The very Nonesuch of true courtesie,
> And Treasurer to liberallity.

Not for Rowlands the hyperbole that increased markedly as the gulf between patrons and authors widened.[4]

Like Velvetbreeches and other aspirants, writers sought out Maecenases; they could not wait in their garrets (and starve) until an apathetic society sought them out. On a notable occasion, November 1, 1595, Richard Robinson intrepidly approached Elizabeth as she was going to her chapel at Richmond and gave her *A Third Proceeding in the Harmony of King David's Harp*, his most recent translation of Victorin Strigel: "I making my humble suite unto youre moste gracyus Highnes for some releef in money." For his rashness he received, from Dr. Julius Caesar, Elizabeth's "commendacions," and, more ominously, he was reminded that her "Highnes sett me not on worck, and therefore yow were not to pay me any wages." Even more humiliating was the rebuff of Sir Thomas Egerton, lord keeper of the great seal. When the author presented to him *A Fourth Proceeding in the Harmony of King David's Harp* (1596), Egerton in the presence of six clerks asked, "What have we here? Literae petaces?" and informed the translator that he should have been made privy to the dedication. Humiliated and embittered, Robinson writes in his *Eupolemia*: "Not helping mee pore man for the Commaundements sake, He turned mee away bycause of my poverty." Although he probably misconstrued Egerton's rebuke (Robinson could hardly be expected to comprehend a nobleman's reaction to his opportunism), the translator's experience was doubtless not unusual. Since, as Thomas

Evans observes, "in the multitude of Writers our age hath begotten a scarcitie of Patrons," authors frequently received the beggar's fee — a door shut in their faces. For, as Donne writes,

> . . . they who write to Lords, rewards to get,
> Are they not like singers at doores for meat? [5]

So effusive and so commonplace were the "songs" of men claiming to be authors that an Egerton, inured to the melodies, quickly perceived the materialistic motivation of a Robinson, who, rather than a stipend, wanted employment as a clerk. Patrons scrutinized the cloying language of a dedication for what it did not state, just as the cold eyes of Elizabeth read between the lines of the love letters of her courtiers and suitors. Yet many writers deluded themselves that somehow their verbalistic brilliance concealed their intentions. Although Ulpian Fulwell is satirizing flatterers in the following passage, there can be little doubt that the ruse described and the naiveté of the petitioner typify the conduct of many Elizabethan writers:

I compiled a pleasant Pamphlet, and dedicated the same unto him, in the preface wherof I fed his vayne glorious humor with magnificent Tytles and termes. . . . I waited opportunity to deliver my sayd Pamphlet unto the Patron when I found him in a mery moode (which is a thing specially to bee regarded of all suters) it pleased him so wel to reade his owne commendacions, that hee vouchsaved to peruse the rest, and gave mee his rewarde and good countenance which was the thinge for the which I fished.

Such was the economic insecurity of writers that their only recourse was to indulge in literary diplomacy. If the cat caught the mouse, as Egerton caught Robinson, there was always another prospective patron — as well as another prospective "Literae petaces." [6]

" 'Tis the iron age," Robert Anton laments in the Jacobean era, "and vertue must have Estredge [Ostrich] like concoction, or else die in an Hospital for want of a Patron." Meres writes, "For lacke of Patrones (o ingratefull and damned age) our Poets are soly or chiefly maintained, countenanced, and patronized." Barnfield declares that he cannot exist on the rewards he now receives — the "commendacions" of his dedicatee.

I never then, did write one verse in vaine;
Nor ever went my Poems unregarded:
Then did each Noble breast, me intertaine,
And for my Labours I was well rewarded:
    But now *Good wordes,* are stept in *Bounties* place;
    Thinking thereby, her glorie to disgrace.

But who can live with words, in these hard tymes?
(Although they came from Jupiter himselfe?)
Or who can take such Paiment, for his Rymes?
(When nothing now, is so esteem'd as Pelfe?)
    Tis not *Good wordes,* that can a man maintaine;
    Wordes are but winde; and winde is all but vaine.

After Robinson received only words from Elizabeth, he concluded in his frank autobiographical pages that he came "as a pore man before" and departed "now (by this meanes) become a Poorer." Such was the hapless lot of this "poore humble Orator" and his kind.[7]

Peacham, in *Minerva Britannia* (1612), recalls nostalgically another era in which the wealthy fostered the arts.

The Laurel joyned to the fruitefull vine,
In frendly league perpetually doe growe,
The Laurell dedicate to wits divine,
The fruite of Bacchus that in clusters growe,
    Are such as doe enjoy the world at will,
    And swimme in wealth, yet want the muses skill.

PATRONAGE

This frendship should inviolate remaine,
The rich with Bountie should rewarde the Artes,
The living muse should gratefully againe,
Adorne Moecenas with her learned partes:
    And when his branch is drie, and withered seene,
    By her support, preserve him alway greene.

But this is quixotism, unhistorical and starry-eyed.[8]

The history of English patronage does not demonstrate a firmly established tradition of rewards to poets and creative artists. This is hardly surprising in view of the emphasis upon utility and the attitude toward literature. Second, because of the rise and fall of English nobility in the fourteenth and fifteenth centuries, there was little continuity in aristocratic circles. Most sixteenth-century nobles, including the Tudors themselves, had risen from the gentry and were therefore new aristocracy. The Earl of Leicester's grandfather, for instance, was a taxcollector in the reign of Henry VIII. Third, throughout the sixteenth century, almost to the closing years of Elizabeth's reign, consolidation and peace were the cornerstones of national policy. Hence, translators of utilitarian treatises and propagandists of the government's political and religious policies were more generously rewarded than poets. Finally, the new aristocracy, despite the booty from the confiscation of church properties, was unable to entrench itself economically like the nobility of earlier centuries in the face of the rapid shift of wealth to the merchant class in a capitalistic society. To read the biographies of Sidney, Dyer, Golding, the Earl of Essex, and Walsingham, is to undertake a study of bankruptcy and tangled economic affairs, including elaborate appeals to the queen or Burghley and whining statements of poverty not unlike those of writers; and at death there were encumbered properties and impoverished widows. In light of these facts patronage in England was foredoomed to be erratic.

Writers like Peacham looked back longingly at the early sixteenth century, when humanists, nobles, and prelates welcomed Erasmus to England and apparently showered him with honor and, more importantly, favors. Yet Erasmus' report, in 1514, of his receipts from English benefactors was unsympathetic and at places bitter. From William Warham, Archbishop of Canterbury, he received a living valued at 100 nobles (a noble was the equivalent of 6*s.* 8*d.* silver) as well as gifts totaling 400 nobles during a period of approximately five years. Mountjoy granted him a pension of 100 crowns (500*s.*), and unnamed bishops bestowed gifts of more than 100 nobles. Henry VIII awarded Erasmus 60 nobles for his translation of Plutarch. Not everyone, however, was so generous to the scholar as these patrons. Of Cardinal Wolsey, Erasmus writes: "I am much indebted to him for his singular favour, still following me from of old. But up to date his generosity has not made me the richer by a halfpenny." The niggardliness of John Yonge, Dean of York, so infuriated Erasmus that he substituted a new dedication. Though to an objective observer it may appear that Erasmus was handsomely rewarded (the total of these gifts, without taking into account the possibility of annual pensions, was £245), he was not satisfied. This points up several difficulties in any discussion of patronage: what constitutes adequate compensation is necessarily a matter of opinion about which giver and receiver may be in sharp disagreement, and the value of stipends can only be vaguely judged in terms of such unknowns as the standard of living and the purchasing power of money. Whether or not Erasmus was properly compensated must not entice us into an analysis of economics and personal factors. Two significant points, nevertheless, stand out: the Dutchman received gifts greater than those accorded to most Elizabethan professionals, and as a translator and biblical scholar he was in a much better position to attract the secular and religious hierarchy than a creative writer.[9]

So too in the early years of Elizabeth's reign a group of translators, including Golding, Googe, Hoby, Hall, Turbervile, and Phaer, apparently enjoyed the sustained patronage of members of the privy council. Writers and patrons had a number of things in common: they were university graduates and members of the Inns of Court and for the most part came from the gentry, and some were bound by family ties (Googe was a kinsman and Hoby the brother-in-law of Cecil). This, then, was a closed circle in which relations were personal, and in which all shared similar patriotic and philosophic beliefs. As perpetuators of humanism these men made available in the vernacular the wisdom of the ages, and as practical governors determined to reestablish sound civil policy after the Marian turbulence, they prepared mirrors for magistrates and guidebooks instilling obedience and respect for law and authority. They were, in short, propagandists interested in their own and the nation's welfare.[10]

Since no such ties existed between most professional writers and patrons toward the end of the century, they foundered and termed the Elizabethan the Iron Age. However, they painted the picture blacker than the facts justified; patronage, though not on a scale necessary to sustain the hordes of writers, was not nonexistent. The parsimonious queen did not emulate Italian nobles in largesse to artists. Hence, there is some justification for the conclusion of a recent critic, B. B. Gamzue, "that the reputation of Elizabeth as a patron of letters and learning, has been derived not from her deeds, but largely from legends based upon the many adulatory dedications to her. No such reputation probably was ever more cheaply bought." This harsh judgment, though never articulated with Gamzue's bluntness, was shared by at least some Elizabethan writers and critics. Spenser significantly in *The Shepherd's Calendar* did not qualify his assertion that "Mecoenas is yclad in claye." In his survey of English patronage Puttenham, in 1589, stops with the reign of Mary and cautiously mentions a few pages later "the scorne and ordinarie disgrace offered unto Poets in these dayes . . . for that liberalitie is come to fayle in Princes" — an ambiguous criticism probably directed at Elizabeth. A few years later somewhat melodramatically Peele says that all poets may as well be dead,

> Unless in hope Augusta will restore,
> The wrongs that learning bears of covetousness,
> And court's disdain, the enemy to art.

In the following year, 1594, Sir Hugh Platt charges that if Elizabeth were to raise her "most princelie and prosperous hand," which "hath hitherto borne up her sword and scepter in despight of all her forren and domestical foes to propound some liberall stipende for all such of her ingenious Subjects as should bring forth any profitable or rare particular, for the general good of his prince and Country," people would witness "a new revolution of the first golden age." Until such time "there remaine a secret number of choice wits, who being full fraught of more necessarie, yea more invaluable commodities, then either the East or west Indies are able to affoord, are nevertheless forced to consume their daies in melancholie, & (almost to the hazard of their soules) to burie their talents in the bottomles pit of oblivion." Meanwhile a revealing little verse circulated in the court.

PATRONAGE

Madam,
You bid your treasurer, on a time,
To give me reason for my rhime:
But since that time and that season,
He gave me neither rhime nor reason.

Some attributed the lines to Churchyard, who for years had been begging for a pension. Others assigned the ditty to Spenser, a less likely candidate, since in 1591 he had received an annual pension of £50 from the queen, but, on the other hand, as is well known, Spenser was no friend of Burghley. The authorship, however, is of less importance than the implication that Elizabeth temporized with rimers.[11]

No doubt she did, since she dallied and withheld favors from almost everyone. It is probably true, as Gamzue alleges, that she rewarded with a royal smile Gascoigne, Sidney, Lyly, Christopher Ockland, and others. (It is doubtful, however, that Sidney expected his literary efforts to be rewarded; like other courtiers he was perennially in need of funds to maintain his retinue and to meet the expenses of his activities in Elizabeth's service.) On the other hand, since Elizabethans were expert tax-evaders, and since the monarch was not provided with sufficient funds to maintain herself, her court, and what Neale terms that "Illustrious Order of Mendicants, the Court and Nobility," as well as to wage the wars her subjects were more intent upon than she, the queen was compelled to economize and to distribute money gingerly. That she provided first for the welfare of the state is not strange (or reprehensible) in view of her steadfast devotion to her people; to a master politician policy always comes before poetry. However, she encouraged drama by her interest probably more than by any large expenditure: she urged (and perhaps indirectly subsidized) nobles to become patrons of dramatic companies, and her will (or her desire for recreation, as the minutes of the privy council put it) effectively thwarted bourgeois magistrates eager to close theaters. Finally, as Daniel recognizes, in creating the climate and prosperity necessary for the flowering of the arts, Elizabeth eclipsed her ancestors and all other living monarchs

> Which wonder at the blessings of thy Crowne,
> Whose Peace more glorious farre than all their warres,
> Have greater powres of admiration showne . . . .
>
> I, who by that most blessed hand sustain'd,
> In quietnes, do eate the bread of rest:
> And by that all-reviving powre obtain'd
> That comfort which my Muse and me hath blest.[12]

Of all Elizabethan patrons the Sidneys and Herberts were by far the most hospitable to literature. Sir Philip Sidney, "the darling of the human race," as one eulogist put it, like Elizabeth, probably encouraged artists more through example than through munificence, although he presumably financed the education of Abraham Fraunce and was evidently the friend of Spenser. If his most recent biographer is to be accepted, he was largely responsible for the new poetry ushered in by *The Shepherd's Calendar,* which, significantly, was dedicated to him. Though this claim is doubtful, since Sidney did not approve of Spenser's archaic diction, and since Spenser was less conservative and traditional than the courtier, he was an intimate of poets and probably stimulated his sister's love of art.[13]

Through her marriage to Henry Herbert, second Earl of Pembroke, Mary Sidney linked her family with the Herberts and thereby aided the establishment of a tradition that extended to Philip, the fourth Earl, who died in 1649. As Countess of Pembroke, Lady Mary received homage usually accorded only a monarch. Typical of the eulogies addressed to her is one by Nashe, to whom invective came more naturally than praise:

Fayre sister of Phoebus, & eloquent secretary to the Muses, most rare Countesse of Pembroke, thou art not to be omitted; whom Artes doe adore as a second Minerva, and our Poets extoll as the Patronesse of their invention; for in thee the Lesbian Sappho with her lirick Harpe is disgraced, & the Laurel Garlande which thy Brother so bravely advaunst on his Launce is still kept greene in the Temple of Pallas. Thou only sacrificest thy soule to contemplation, thou only entertainest emptie handed Homer, & keepest the springs of Castalia from being dryed up.

The countess merited this praise, for on her beautiful Wilton estate she provided a haven for many important poets. There Daniel tutored William Herbert and became an honored member of the household. In a dedication to his pupil Daniel speaks of his own education: "Having beene first incourag'd or fram'd thereunto by your most Worthy and Honourable Mother, receiving the first notion for the formall ordering of those compositions at Wilton, which I must ever acknowledge to have beene my best Schoole, and thereof alwayes am to hold a feeling and gratefull Memory." William Browne was also a member of the household, and Donne a frequent guest. Florio bequeathed his books and manuscripts to the Herberts, and Jonson received from the third earl an annual gift of £20 for the purchase of books. All in all, this was a noble household which showered favors on many of the gifted writers of the late sixteenth and early seventeenth centuries. But, in Miss Thomson's words, "the Sidneys and Herberts established with their poets a gool deal more than the conventional relationship of a patron and his dependant. The great homes were the meeting ground, the mutual interest in literature the bond." [14]

After the Sidneys, the most distinguished family of patrons was that of Francis Russell, second Earl of Bedford (according to Spenser, "that good Earle of rare renowne And noble Patrone of weake povertie"). His daughter Anne married Ambrose Dudley, Earl of Warwick, and his other daughter Margaret married the buccaneer George Clifford, Earl of Cumberland. Both women were praised in Spenser's *Colin Clout's Come Home Again* and in *Four Hymns*. Anne Clifford, who was tutored by Daniel, married first Richard Sackville, Earl of Dorset, and, upon his death, Philip Herbert, thus joining this family with the Herberts. Like her mother she was an intelligent woman well-versed in literature and sympathetic to writers. Lady Anne's uncle Edward, third Earl of Bedford, married Lucy Harington, to whom Goodere had in a sense bequeathed his charge, Drayton. Though Drayton for unknown reasons lost the favor of the countess, Daniel wrote masques in her honor, Donne received from her money to pay his debts before his ordination, and Florio began his translation of Montaigne in her house and completed it with the encouragement and financial assistance of her husband. To her Jonson wrote this tribute:

> Lucy, you brightnesse of our sphere, who are,
>   Life of the Muses day, their morning-starre!
> If workes (not th'authors) their owne grace should looke,
>   Whose poemes would not wish to be your booke? [15]

These were the great patrons of literature in the Elizabethan age. The only other person emulating their generosity was Sidney's uncle, the Earl of Leicester, who, though termed by one commentator "the universal patron," was primarily the friend of historians like Stow and Holinshed and translators like Florio. To him were dedicated, according to Miss Rosenberg, ninety-four books.

As chancellor of Oxford and as an intimate of Elizabeth he was the recipient of many volumes, both of people anxious to curry favor with an important noble and of those whom he encouraged to propagandize his political and religious views. Leicester is best remembered as a friend of Spenser, who, despite a mysterious estrangement (as tiresomely baffling to scholars as the identity of Mr. W. H.), years after the earl's death paid tribute to him in his *Prothalamion:*

> Next whereunto there standes a stately place,
> Where oft I gayned giftes and goodly grace.

In eulogizing the earl, Florio appropriately links the deceased statesman and "the sweetest singer of all our western shepheards": "I account him thrice-fortunate in having such a herauld of his vertues as Spenser; Curteous Lord, Curteous Spenser, I knowe not which hath purchast more fame, either he in deserving so well of so famous a scholler, or so famous a scholler in being so thankfull without hope of requitall to so famous a Lord." [16]

Of the other patrons perhaps the best known is the Earl of Southampton because of his association with the poems of Shakespeare. But so much romantic twaddle surrounds the earl that it is difficult to determine the extent of his patronage. Florio, who benefited from his associations with the Herberts and the Russells, pays tribute to the "most noble, most vertuous, and most Honorable Earle of Southampton, in whose paie and patronage I have lived some yeeres; to whom I owe and vowe the yeeres I have to live." It is also impossible to sift fancy from fact in regard to the patronage of the Earl of Essex (whose wife was Walsingham's daughter and Sidney's widow), but the probabilities are that he was importuned by writers constantly because of his high position, but that with his schemes for self-aggrandizement he had little time or money to ease the plight of authors. Sir Christopher Hatton, who according to legend had danced his way into favor, was the patron, as well as the employer, of such hacks as Churchyard and Rich. That he was probably generous can be inferred from his gift of £3 to Richard Robinson for *A Proceeding in the Harmony of King David's Harp,* but, significantly, he did not give the translator the clerical post he was angling for. Burghley and Walsingham, as one would expect, were associated with nonliterary writers who set out to promote the welfare of the state as well as the views of the two councilors.[17]

Biographers, swept away with zeal for their subjects, have converted almost every important personage of the era into a Maecenas. Yet many dedications were unauthorized. Since writers like merchants were speculators and opportunists, they endeavored to flatter potential patrons into acts of charity, either in the form of a stipend or through appointment to a sinecure. For this reason a dedication to a patron is not prima-facie evidence that a particular author received favor. Second, nobles had not the means to support the swarms of people writing books and soliciting gratuities, and even the best authors did not enjoy sustained patronage from a single family. The peregrinations of writers like Daniel and Florio from one noble house to another clearly indicate a lack of continuity in English patronage, and this inability to relieve authors of economic uncertainty contributed to the debasing flattery and exploitation of new patrons. Third, although writers were certainly not disinterested commentators, their monotonous wails about patronage unquestionably have more validity than the mechanical fawning characteristic of Elizabethan dedications.

That patrons often were not apprised of dedications before publication is graphically illustrated by at least three instances recorded in Robinson's *Eupolemia*. The book he boldly presented to Elizabeth at Richmond in 1595 is fulsome in its praise, but the queen was not to be surprised into parting with her pounds. Nor had Egerton cause to take offense at the flattery contained in the preface to the book Robinson dedicated to him. If we examine the dedication of *A Part of the Harmony of King David's Harp* to Sir Ambrose Dudley, quoted earlier, we might be led to believe that "the good Earl of Warwick" was indeed a generous patron. However, as the bitter pages of the *Eupolemia* inform us, Robinson received nothing and was forced to peddle a hundred copies of the volume in order to pay the printing costs and to make a slight profit. Yet when he presented another translation to Hatton in 1591, he made it appear that Warwick had patronized the earlier volume. In his dedication of *A Second Proceeding in the Harmony of King David's Harp* to Sir John Puckering in 1593, he relates the true story:

Long it is since I began to translate this learned expositor Victorinus Strigelius upon the same harmonie [1582]: wherein had I found so liberall an Alexander to patrocinate and further my first labour, when he [Dudley] favoured better the Harpe & Speare of Achilles, (as in my second translation I had for my Patrone a peerelesse bountiful Pyrhus, the late noble Lorde Chauncellor [Hatton] deceassed: not onely a Patrone of Apollos harpe and muses, but a deere lover and delighter in Davids divine harmonie,) I had I say beene better encouraged long before this, to have brought forth farre greater portion of fruite in these my labours hetherto.

Robinson's relations with these patrons demonstrate the opportunism of Elizabethan authors, including the deceit to which they had recourse in order to alleviate their ever-present need, and should make us wary before accepting dedications as unquestionable proof of patronage. Thus, compilations of books dedicated to an individual are not so conclusive as some scholars appear to believe.[18]

Though his dedication of *The School of Abuse* to Sidney is perhaps the most notorious instance, Gosson was by no means the only Elizabethan to presume upon a nobleman. We are fortunate to have Spenser's statement that Gosson "was for hys labor scorned, if at least it be in the goodnesse of that nature [Sidney's] to scorne," since without it we might have believed that the courtier approved both *The School of Abuse* and *The Ephemerides of Philo*. (Gosson's puritanical conscience evidently had no scruples about creating the impression that Sidney endorsed his books.) Although most authors intuitively recognized the common sense of Spenser's observation to Gabriel Harvey, that it was "follie . . . not to regarde aforehande the inclination and qualitie of him to whome wee dedicate oure Bookes," they took their chances. In fact they had been taking their chances for some time. When Turbervile presented *Epitaphs, Epigrams, Songs, and Sonnets* (1567) to the Countess of Warwick, in his own words, "I made bolde with you in dedication of so unworthy a booke to so worthie a Ladie." When he expanded his book in 1570, he again presumed upon "your Ladishippes pacience": "You accepted that my first offer of honorable and meere curtesie, and I thereby encouraged, blush not to procede to the lyke trade of follie, always hoping for the like acceptance at your hands." In protesting against the translations of bawdy Italian tales Ascham alleges that they were "dedicated over boldlie to vertuous and honorable personages, the easielier to begile simple and innocent wittes." With amusing frankness Brathwaite confirms Ascham's charges:

> Unknowne to you I am, yet knowne I am
> To th'better part of you, your vertuous name;

Which like a precious odour hath infus'd
Your love so much in me, as I have chus'd
Your selfe, to patronize what I have writ,
Whose name I thought had power to shelter it.[19]

An analysis of Greene's writings reveals clearly how exploitative Elizabethan professionals were. Unlike many of his contemporaries Greene was never attached in any capacity to a noble household; moreover, he was on familiar terms with only a few of his many dedicatees. The first part of *Mamillia* (1583) contains a laudatory poem written by Roger Portington, and in the section of this romance entitled "The Anatomy of Flatterers," Greene praises the "liberall bountie & friendly curtesie (whereof without any desert I have tasted)" of Portington's sister, Mary Rogers. The second part of *Mamillia* Greene presented "to the Right Worshipfull, and his especiall friends," Robert Lee and Roger Portington: "You are the Saints to whome in heart I owe most dutiful devotion." He was also an intimate of Thomas Burnaby (or Barnaby), Esquire, who wrote an extravagant eulogy for *Tully's Love* (1589). In 1590 Greene dedicated *Never Too Late* to Burnaby because "in al bounden duetie I have for sundry favors bin affected to your Worship." In the sequel, *Francesco's Fortunes* (1590), we learn that Burnaby "gratefully accepted" the former romance; and Greene, after speaking of his patron's "many friendly, nay fatherly favours," signs his dedication, "Your Worships adopted sonne in all humble dutie to commaund," a valedictory he employs again in *A Quip for an Upstart Courtier* (1592). With these members of the gentry Greene enjoyed a personal relationship, as his unaffected language clearly indicates. From only two noble families did he receive sustained patronage. After dedicating *Penelope's Web* (1587) to the Countesses of Cumberland and Warwick, he presented the Earl of Cumberland with *Pandosto* (1588) and *Greene's Mourning Garment* (1590); and to Sir Robert Carey, who was later to shelter Nashe, he dedicated *Greene's Orpharion* (1589?) and *Greene's Farewell to Folly* (1591). Therefore, it seems probable that only the Portingtons, Burnaby, the Cliffords, and Carey gave tangible encouragement to this prolific hack writer, and for their kindnesses they received a total of ten books.[20]

For the most part Greene gambled with "the incination and qualitie" of patrons. In *Arbasto* (1584) he speaks of "hearing" of Lady Mary Talbot's "exquisite perfection, aswell in outwarde shape, as in vertuous qualities." To the Earl of Essex he writes in *Euphues' Censure to Philautus* (1587):

I thought . . . (having heard of your noble & vertuous resolutions) . . . to present your Lordship wyth this homelie gyfte . . . and shadowed with such bad collours, as might I not excuse my boldnesse, in that blinde men are ever most rash, and honorable men ever the most courteous, I should the more grieve at my inconsidered presumption. . . . if I be favored (as I hope well) my labour hath his reward, and my desire his content.

In *The Spanish Masquerado* (1589) he designates Hugh Offley, sheriff of London, "as a Maecenas, . . . perswaded therunto by the report of a friend, whose opinion I craved, for the choice of a Patrone." "Hearing how" Gervis Clifton "in the prime of [his] youth . . . favoured the study of good letters, as a Maecenas and patron of such vertuous labours," Greene presented him with *Perymedes, the Blacksmith* (1588).[21]

He is "imboldened" to dedicate *Tully's Love* (1589) to Ferdinando Stanley, Lord Strange, and in *Card of Fancy* (1587) he asks Edward de Vere to "take my wel meaning for an excuse of my boldnesse." Greene elaborately excuses his presumption in dedicating *The Royal Exchange* (1590) to Sir John Hart, lord mayor of London, and Richard Gurney and Stephen Soame, sheriffs of London; and ingeniously he reasons that "if any Cittizen or other, gather any principle of worth, or have in-sight for the following of vertue or avoyding of vice, their profits shall be noted to proceed from your honourable and worshipfull dispositions, under whose patronage this booke is shrowded." The tone of the dedications of the first part of *Mamillia* to Lord Darcy and of *The Mirror of Modesty* (1584) to Lady Margaret, Countess of Darby, indicates that again Greene is "presuming" upon his patrons. To men famed for their support of serious writing he excuses his boldness by offering his books as diversion. To the Earl of Leicester in *Planetomachia* (1585) and to Charles Blount, later Lord Mountjoy, in *Greene's Metamorphosis* (1589?), he in effect repeats what he writes to Philip Howard, Earl of Arundell, in *Morando* (1587): "It may bee your Honour passing over many learned workes, will at the last stumble at this fond toy, and laugh at [it]." [22]

In three of his dedications Greene not very subtly exploits patronesses. To Lady Hales, widow of Sir James, he writes in *Menaphon* (1589): "Hearing (madam) of the passions your Ladiship hath uttered a late for the losse of your husband, . . . I thought it my dutie to write this pastorall historie, . . . and when your dumpes were most deepe, then to looke on this little treatise for recreation." In 1592 Greene dedicated *Philomela* to Lady Fitzwaters, a recent widow who is honored in the subtitle of the romance, "Lady Fitzwaters' Nightingale," and whose husband, he reminds her, had given "gracious acceptaunce" to "a small Pamphlet written by an other [Lodge's *Euphues' Censure*], and presented to him by me." Greene gave *A Maiden's Dream*, an elegy upon the death of Sir Christopher Hatton, to the wife of the nobleman's nephew William: "Not for anie privat benefit I ever had of him, which should induce me favorably to flatter his worthie partes, but onely that I shame to let slip with silence the vertues and honors of so worthie a knight." Greene did not forget, however, to remind Lady Elizabeth, "I am your Ladiships poore Countriman, and have long time desired to gratifie your right worshipfull father with something worthie of himselfe." [23]

The results of Greene's bold exploitation of patrons are not known. Only once does he refer, and then ambiguously, to his solicitations. "Having waded," he writes in *Menaphon,* "through the censures of many both Honourable and worshipfull, in committing the credite of my bookes to their honorable opinions, as I have found some of them not onely honourably to patronize my workes, but curteouslie to passe over my unskilfull presumption with silence, so generally I am indebted to all Gentlemen that with favors have overslipt my follies." Since he eagerly ferreted out new patrons during his short unhappy career, returns from patrons were evidently not substantial.[24]

Even less favored was Churchyard, the patriarch of sixteenth-century hacks, who was writing before Greene was born and who outlived him by twelve years. During the late 1570's and early 1580's Churchyard was in the employ of Sir Christopher Hatton, probably as a personal agent or spy. To this nobleman, whom he later termed his most generous benefactor, he dedicated three books, the last of which appeared about 1580. Upon his death in 1591, he composed an epitaph, printed in *A Reviving of the Dead,* and later he dedicated one poem in *Churchyard's Challenge* (1593) to Sir William Hatton. A former member of the Earl of Surrey's household, Churchyard availed himself of this connection in two dedications to

Lord Charles Howard; and to Sir George Carey, whom he met during the Irish campaigns, and to members of his family he presented four works. Because for years he vainly sought a pension for his military labors, he dedicated three books to Elizabeth herself and two to Sir John Wolley, her Latin secretary.[25]

In addition to these five patrons, Churchyard presented works to at least twenty-nine other persons, most of whom were soldiers or their widows. Books dealing with military campaigns or the plight of soldiers in an ungrateful and "effeminate" age, he addressed to Drew Drury, Sir John Skidmore, Edward Dymock, Sir Michael Blount, John Savage, Sir Henry Knevet, Sir John Russell. To the widows of two military men, Sir John Brocket and Sir Walter Wawller, he presented the appropriately lugubrious *A Farewell to the World* and *A Doleful Discourse of a Great Lord and a Lady*. Renowned soldiers like Ralegh and Essex received works of broader interest: *A Spark of Friendship* (1588), an essay on friendship based upon classical writers, and *A Musical Consort of Heavenly Harmony* (1595), a typical Churchyardian miscellany which discusses the decline of charity and hospitality in England's "Iron Age." [26]

More so than Greene, because his need was greater, Churchyard seized upon occasions, festive or solemn, for dedications of his numerous writings. "The gladnes" men felt when Egerton was appointed lord keeper of the great seal on May 8, 1596, "called up my muse that seldom sleepth, to awaken the world with some verses, that vertuous men may consider of. They are but the invention of time, practise of pen, suffrance of old custome, and the boldnes of a writer, that often salutes men of great worth with bookes and blessednes, in the first entrie of their worldly honor." Whether Churchyard was greeted with "Literae petaces?" we do not know. (Like Robinson, he evidently sought a clerkship; three years earlier he had dedicated a poem to the wife of Sir John Puckering, Egerton's predecessor.) When Sir George Carey became second Lord Hunsdon in 1596, Churchyard celebrated the occasion with *A Pleasant Discourse of Court and War*. He also capitalized upon Sir Edward Seymour's appointment as lord lieutenant of Somerset and Wiltshire on May 28, 1602, in his dedication of *A True Discourse Historical of Succeeding Governors in the Netherlands,* a work written jointly with Robinson. Churchyard was equally prompt in producing epitaphs of famous people. He presented *The Epitaph of Sir Philip Sidney* to the courtier's widow, *A Sad and Solemn Funeral . . . of Sir Francis Knowles* (1596) to Knowles's son-in-law, Thomas Lord Delaware, and *Churchyard's Goodwill* (1604), an epitaph upon the death of Whitgift, to the archbishop's successor, Dr. John Bancroft. In addition, Churchyard published collections of elegies in *A Reviving of the Dead* (1591) and *A Feast Full of Sad Cheer* (1592); most of these had probably been sent in manuscript to the families of the deceased, or perhaps the poet gave copies of the collected elegies to widows and relatives. Regardless of the means of transmission it is certain that Churchyard's muse did not waken to lament without an expectation of reward. The products of the Elizabethan epitaph factory were like all manufactured goods — for sale.[27]

The "muse that seldom sleepth" produced much unreadable verse but little remuneration. Though he had carefully selected Walsingham, recently ambassador to Flanders, as patron of *A Lamentable and Pitiful Description of the Woeful Wars in Flanders* (1578), Churchyard informs Thomas Wilson that "my work neither found free passage nor acces to [Walsingham's] noble judgement." Churchyard laments to Ralegh that few "have either lent me anie porcion of preferment (or procured me but a peece of anie certaine living.)" The exceptions were, he continues, Sir Christopher Hatton, "who got me two great Seales (besides common courtesies manie) to shifte withall a season. And furthermore, your selfe 6. yeres past bestowed good speaches to the Q. Majestie in my behalfe, by the which I got some comfortable recreation, to quicken my spirites & keepe me in breath." Then Churchyard makes a significant admission:

I have sixteene severall bookes printed presently to bee bought (albeit they are but trifles) dedicated in sundrie seasons to severall men off good and great credite, but to be plaine not one among them all, from the first day of my labour and studies, to this present yeere and hower, hath anie waye preferred my sutes, amended my state, or given mee anie countenaunce.

In other words almost one-half of his dedicatees never so much as acknowledged his presentations.[28]

Miss Sheavyn accuses Churchyard of lacking "self-respect," and specifically cites this foreword to Ralegh as "an instance of moral debasement." But such judgments are neither humane nor relevant. Churchyard was no more crass than Spenser, Jonson, Greene, Nashe, or the courtiers who loved Elizabeth — but her money more. Indeed, this plodding poet, in his own words, "unfurnished both of heavenly gifts & worldly good fortune," had a stubborn streak of integrity. When he writes in *Churchyard's Charge,* "If I could gaine mountaines of golde, to flatter any one in Printyng an untrothe, I would rather wishe my handes were of, then take in hande sutche a matter," he is melodramatic but honest after his kind. For his dedications have a kind of dignity and restraint rare in an age of verbal extravagance. But such were the economics of publications, and such was his lack of "worldly good fortune," that he was compelled to capitalize upon every opportunity for patronage. "The poor can't afford morals." Or, to let Churchyard speak for himself,

> For he that wants shall hardly gette,
> Except he fishe with finer nette:
> Then either rime or reason knitts,
> This worlde yeelds not to pleasaunt witts,
> To basest mynds sometymes it bends,
> For all the happs blinde Fortune sends:
> Doeth light on those she favours mitche,
> Some men you see can nere be ritche.[29]

In addition to the promotional techniques utilized by Greene and Churchyard, another common scheme was the use of multiple dedications, the most famous instance of which is Spenser's addition of sixteen sonnets to the second printing of *The Faerie Queene,* and the most infamous example of which are the ninety-three dedications in Geoffrey Whitney's *The Choice of Emblems* (1586). *Churchyard's Challenge* (1593) contains twenty dedications. Weever arranges his *Epigrams in the Oldest Cut and Newest Fashion* (1599) in seven groupings, termed weeks, and dedicates each section to a different patron. (According to D'Israeli, an eighteenth-century Italian work had a dedicatory epsitle for each day of the year!) Chapman's *Iliad* is prefaced with sixteen dedications, and Markham's *Cavelarice, or, The English Horseman* has, in addition to a dedicatory preface, dedications for each of its eight divisions. But it is superfluous to cite instances of a device utilized by hack and genius, and familiar both in England and in foreign countries. Perhaps the most significant point about multiple dedications is their frequency after 1590 — still another indication that patronage was inadequate to cope with the new conditions of bookmaking. In view of the circumstances authors can hardly in fairness be censured for their reluctance to put all their eggs in one basket.[30]

Of all the exploitative tricks probably the most damaging to the integrity of writers was what Dekker, who apparently coined the term, described as falconry. According to Dekker's account of authorial cony-catching, the falconer either patched up a book by cutting passages from various works or bought up "any old Booke (especially a Sermon, or any other matter of Divinity) that lies for wast paper." The former he printed at his own expense with the assistance of a henchman called a "mongrel"; to the latter he simply added "a new-printed Epistle." Next the falconer and his aide-in-mischief consulted a herald for the names of knights and gentlemen living in a certain district and printed "so many Epistles as they [had] names; the epistles Dedicatory being all one, and vary in nothing but in the titles of their patrons." Some falconers carried with them "an Alphabet of letters . . . being able to print any mans name (for a Dedication) on the suddaine." [31]

Though Dekker is the only author of the period to mention the trick, critics have frequently referred to this fraudulent practice without citing many concrete instances. That the deception was fairly common is clear from Erasmus' record of a conversation with Grocin concerning the dedication of *Hecuba* to Archbishop Warham in 1506. Grocin informed Erasmus that Warham suspected that he had "already dedicated the book to some one else. This surprised me. How, I asked, could the archbishop get such an idea into his head? Grocin laughed his sardonic laugh. 'Because it is what you people do', he said; meaning that it was usual with folk of the literary kidney." [32]

Yet, despite the research of modern bibliographers and the exactness of their descriptions of books, few examples of the same issue of a volume with different dedications have been turned up. One of the earliest is Walter Bailey's *A Short Discourse of Three Kinds of Peppers* (1588), a little tract obviously prepared and printed by an amateur as a New Year's gift to his friends. In the dedication there are blanks for salutation and signature, so that Bailey could personalize his book by insertions in his own autograph. Here there was no duplicity. Cunningham notes two copies of Rich's *Opinion Defied* (1613) in the British Museum with dedications to Prince Charles and Sir Thomas Ridgeway, and Wilson has discovered three copies of Ralph Crane's *The Works of Mercy* (1621) with separate dedications. Later in the seventeenth century Thomas Jordan, like a true falconer, left blank the top of the dedication page and inserted, as the occasion arose, the name of the dedicatee by means of a small hand press he carried with him. Mead has found that five copies of Jordan's *Death Dissected* (1649), a reissue of *A Buckler against the Fear of Death* (1640), were dedicated to five patrons. These examples by no means prove that falconry was a widespread evil in the sixteenth and seventeenth centuries; but, combined with the other tactics to which authors resorted, it increased the suspicions of patrons and debased the reputation of the literary profession.[33]

Examination of the preferments and monetary rewards given to authors demonstrates that patrons were neither so miserly as thwarted writers alleged nor generous enough to provide continuous security for individual artists and widespread encouragement of the arts in general. To the credit, and critical acumen, of patrons is the fact that the greatest writers of the age were the most favored. Hacks like Greene and Churchyard had difficulties in obtaining sustained patronage or even stipends from occasional patrons. As pathetic as the struggles of hacks to obtain a livelihood are, it is hardly fair to censure patrons for not encouraging mediocrity. Except for poets, creative writers fared worse than translators, historians, and chroniclers. "Utility" was as much the allegiance of patrons as of merchants and Puritans; like other Elizabethans they too distrusted entertainment in prose. Unfortunately for authors patronage was deemed a responsibility, an obligation almost of citizenship, only by a small number of the nobility; the merchant class for the most part did not construe as an obligation of wealth support of the literary profession.

Of the important artists Spenser probably received the least support from patronage. Yet he obtained his fateful secretaryship with Lord Grey de Wilton through the efforts of the Earl of Leicester and Sidney, whose father was Grey's predecessor. His business rather than his poetic skill undoubtedly led to his wealth and political preferment during his long years in Ireland. It was not until 1591 that Elizabeth awarded her greatest poet an annual pension of £50. Daniel, on the other hand, had one sinecure after another bestowed upon him: tutor of William Herbert and Anne Clifford and groom of the privy chamber in Queen Anne's household, for which office he received £50 annually. In 1608 he retired to a farm in Wiltshire, the gift of the Earl of Hertford. In his early life Drayton was subsidized by Goodere and the Countess of Bedford, and Aston's aid enabled him to undertake his monumental poetical geography. In addition, Prince Henry gave Drayton an annuity of £10 for at least one year. The prince bestowed upon Joshua Sylvester, translator of Du Bartas, an annuity of £20, which was paid in 1608 and 1609, rewarded Thomas Coryat's *Crudities* with a gift of £10, and reportedly promised Chapman £100.[34]

The recipient of the most munificent favors from patrons was unquestionably Jonson, who, according to Aubrey, "was well payd for love or fere of his raling in verse or prose, or both." Though the Earl of Rutland resented the poet's presence at the table with his wife (Sidney's daughter), Esmé Stuart, Lord d'Aubigny, had Jonson as a house guest for five years; and the Countess of Bedford, the Earl of Pembroke, William Cavendish, the Duke of Newcastle, and Lucius Cary, Viscount Falkland, were his benefactors. It was from the crown, however, that Jonson's major support came. In 1616 James granted him a pension of 100 marks (£66 13s. 4d.) annually. Years later, in 1629, dissatisfied with this pension, Jonson wrote to Charles I,

> Please your majesty to make
> Of your grace, for goodness sake,
> These your father's marks, your pounds.

In the following year the king obliged. In addition Jonson had received a gift from Charles of £100 in 1629. Though it is impossible to ascertain precise amounts in all cases, Jonson clearly had little cause to lament aristocratic and royal generosity.[35]

However, it is an important fact that among creative artists only Jonson and Daniel obtained continuous support from patrons — and then through the assistance of a number of persons. After his estrangement from the Countess of Bedford, Drayton had to shift for himself. Upon Prince Henry's death Sylvester had difficulties in supporting himself. As for the others, most duplicated the experience of Nashe, who for a year or two received gratuities from the Careys.

On the whole, utilitarian writers and translators were better provided for. Florio was aided by many important patrons of the era and was given a sinecure paying £100 annually by Queen Anne. Elizabeth herself wished Camden, the most famous of her historians, "eased of the charge of living" and "fixed on Westminster . . . to be granted by writing for life." The privy council recommended to Archbishop Whitgift the preferment of the Reverend Richard Hakluyt, who "hath bestowed his tyme and taken very great paynes in matter of navigacion and dyscoveryes, a labor of great desert and use." In 1563 Dr. John Dee, mathematician and astrologer, requested Cecil to "procure for him the learned leisure of which his country and the republic of letters shall reap the fruit"; Dee never lacked for Elizabeth's favor. Thomas Harriot, another mathematician, received aid from Ralegh and later a pension of £120 from Henry Percy, Earl of Northumberland. John Sadler, translator of Vegetius Renatus' *The Four Books . . . of Martial Policy* (1572), notes in his preface to the Earl of Bedford, "Nowe manye yeares latelye passed, [I] have received a liberall annuitye or stipende of your honoure." In his will Archbishop Parker provided for "an antiquary in his house, who wrote this history, *De Antiquitate Britannicae ecclesiae,* a prebend worth 30£ per annum, and procured for him 300£." [36]

The majority of writers did not obtain sinecures or pensions from individuals or from the state. Although they fondly hoped for something more substantial, upon the presentation of a volume to a patron they accepted, not always gratefully, a monetary gift. Churchyard received 10s. from Robert Nowell, to whom he dedicated *A Warning to the Wise* (1580), but it is possible that Churchyard's personal plea of poverty rather than his account of the 1580 earthquake earned the fee, since in Nowell's notebook appears the following entry: "Too one Thoms Church yeard being in some distres the xiiith of October 1580 — x^s." Peele received £3 in June 1593, upon the presentation of a congratulatory poem to the Earl of

Northumberland. According to this nobleman's account books, a writer named Naylor received 30s., and "Mr. Davyes, the writer," was given 40s. in 1607. Since Davies was the tutor of the earl's son Percy, this may have been compensation for services rendered. On the basis of Nathaniel Field's preface to *A Woman Is a Weathercock* (1612), in which he refuses to dedicate his play to anybody "because forty shillings I care not for! and above few or none will bestow on these matters," it has been assumed that £2 was the usual fee for a published drama. However, in the absence of additional corroboration, we cannot safely generalize from Field's statement. Prince Henry, probably because of his affluence and his interest in literature, generally paid writers from £3 to £5 for a dedication, but his generosity was exceptional.[37]

The only detailed record of gifts from patrons appears in Richard Robinson's *Eupolemia,* one of the most significant literary documents of the period. For his many translations and modernizations of older English books Robinson averaged slightly less than £1 per volume. For thirty-one books, first and subsequent editions, he received from patrons a total of £24 6s. 4d. The average return was roughly 15s. 8d. for each volume. If we eliminate reprints, his income was £20 4d. from twenty books. For the dedications of eleven reimpressions he obtained only £4 6s. On the basis of Robinson's experience, though he was but a hack translator, we can probably conclude that the ordinary writer for the most part fared no better. When, for instance, we recall that sixteen of Churchyard's books brought no return (and undoubtedly other authors suffered a similar fate), our view that £1 was the average stipend paid for a dedication is again reinforced.

Since Robinson's account of patronage is unique, and therefore of significance in any discussion of the Elizabethan literary profession, it is included here in tabular form, arranged according to the size of the gift to the indigent translator.

ROBINSON'S PATRONS

Sir Edward Manners, Earl of Rutland	£3		
Sir Christopher Hatton, lord keeper of the great seal	£3		
Philip (£2) and Sir Henry Sidney (10s.) (1579)	£2	10s.	
*Edmund, Henry, and Elizabeth Uvedale	£2	10s.	
Edmund Uvedale	£2		
Sir William Allen, leatherseller, lord mayor of London	£2		
Sir John Puckering, lord keeper of the great seal (£1), and Lady Jane Puckering (6s. 8d.)	£1	6s.	8d.
Lord Arthur Grey, governor of Ireland (10s.), Sir Henry Sidney (6s. 8d.), and Thomas Smith, haberdasher and custodian of the port of London (6s.) (1582)	£1	2s.	8d.
Sir Edward Seymour, Earl of Hertford	£1		
*John Miller and Leathersellers' Company	£1		
Lady Margaret Douglas, Countess of Lennox		13s.	4d.
Sir William Winter, surveyor of the navy		12s.	8d.
David Lewis, judge of the high court of the admiralty		12s.	
Simon Roe, master (2s. 6d.), and Leathersellers' Company (7s. 6d.)		10s.	
Alexander Nowell, Dean of St. Paul's		10s.	
Sir George Barne, haberdasher and lord mayor of London (1587)		10s.	
Gabriel Goodman, Dean of Westminster (1583)		8s.	
Thomas Smith (1583)		5s.	
*Sir George Barne (1590)		5s.	
*Sir Cuthbert Buckle, vintner and lord mayor of London, and Peter Banning and Peter Haughton, sheriffs		5s.	

*Gabriel Goodman (1590)	2s.
*Gabriel Goodman (1593)	2s.
Anthony Watson, Bishop of Chichester	2s.

I have arranged patrons according to size of their gifts. When a work was dedicated jointly to several people, I have noted the amounts given by each individual in parentheses. Only the position held by the dedicatee at the time of Robinson's presentation is indicated. Asterisks indicate a second or later edition. Years are included in parentheses when a patron made more than one gift to Robinson.

Upon examination of this list it is at once clear that for the most part Robinson's gifts came from nobles who were well-known patrons in the era. (It must be remembered, however, that he was spurned by Sir Ambrose Dudley, Elizabeth, and Egerton.) The Uvedales, who on two occasions rewarded the translator, were evidently of the Dorsetshire gentry. Sir William Allen, a devoted public servant and a wealthy leatherseller, was not distinguished as a patron; his gift, rather than a tribute to Robinson's skill in translating Patrizzi's *A Moral Method of Civil Policy* (1576), was probably a reward for the writer's twelve years of service in Allen's household. Perhaps more revealing are the gifts from the new nobility and the clergy. Sir George Barne and Sir Cuthbert Buckle, for instance, were not overly generous; of course they may have been angered because Robinson was attempting to capitalize upon their recent mayoralty elections. Yet, if Robinson's experience was typical, as it probably was, the impassioned cries of Elizabethan authors against "upstarts" were in part justified, for this new class did not support the arts on a scale appropriate to its wealth. The chart indicates another significant fact: the clergymen of Protestant England either lacked the artistic taste or, more probably, the affluence of Catholic prelates during the early part of Henry VIII's reign. Though Robinson spent years englishing Strigel's paraphrases of the Psalms and other religious writings, Dr. Bancroft refused one of his translations, and other clergymen were far from munificent. Thus, another source of patronage was closed to Elizabethan professionals. On two occasions the Leathersellers' Company was willing to reward modestly one of its members; the gift of £1, coming in 1600 in the period of Robinson's destitution, was no doubt welcome because for years Robinson had received little but rebuffs from patrons.[38]

On the basis of Robinson's returns and in view of the preceding analysis, four tentative conclusions may be reached: (1) the average Elizabethan author (especially the hack) rarely received more than a stipend of £1 from a patron; (2) apparently only a small group of people (well-known nobles and ladies for the most part as well as a few merchants and even fewer ecclesiastics) supported the literary art with any degree of largesse; (3) competition for the support of this small group was keen; (4) since patrons rewarded reprints even less bountifully than new books, authors had to come into print much too frequently for their own good.

Because authors were anything but businessmen and because patronage was acceptable (and economical) so far as stationers were concerned, writers were destined for almost two more centuries to seek the "honorable good favour and furtherance" of nobles and wealthy citizens, as Francis Thynne phrases it, "to add oyle to the emptie lampe of my muse, for mayntenance of the light therof, which without the comfortable heate of your honorable patronage will soone be extinguished." Toward the conclusion of a long career and after the publication of numerous works, Peacham writes: "I have (I confesse) published things of mine owne heretofore, but I never gained one halfe-penny by any Dedication that ever I made, save *splendida promissa,* (and as Plutarch saith) *Byssina verba.*"

To someone who says that "the Dedication will bee worth a great matter, either in present reward of money, or preferment by your Patrones Letter, or other meanes," Peacham replies:

Let me tell thee, whosoever thou art, if now adaies (such are these times) thou gettest but as much as will pay for the binding and strings, thou art well enough, the rest thou shalt have in promises of great matters; perhaps you shall be willed to come another time, but one occasion or other, will so fall out, that come never so often, you loose but your labour, your great Patrone is not stirring, he is abroad at Dinner, he is busie with such a Lord; to bee short, you and your labour are forgotten.

Fifty years after Churchyard made his complaint to Ralegh the situation was unchanged. Patrons did not — indeed they could not — give "present reward of money, or preferment." [39]

Even when an author was fairly certain that he would receive no stipend, he frequently composed a dedication to an important personage not only to protect himself against Momus and Zoilus, the traditional enemies of writers, but also to promote his own work by a technique which we would call in modern advertising jargon the testimonial device. Readers had no means of knowing whether a dedication was authorized, but they could not but be impressed by the association of a nobleman with a book. Thomas Howell in a dedication to the Countess of Pembroke admits as much:

If the Reader hereof, behold your name in the fyrst leafe, he will deeme the whole Booke the more fruitfull, and the framer thereof the more skilfull: but if he shall once perceyve your Honor to be Patronesse to this labour, he will eyther love it, bicause he doth honor you, or wil not dare to reproch it, bicause he perceyveth you are as ready, and knoweth you are as able to defend it, as eyther Ajax was to garde Tewcer, or Pallas to guyde Ulisses.

If patrons were not fond of this device, perhaps a few impoverished writers gained some small benefits. Seemingly they were unaware that exploitation and mendicancy lowered the prestige of the profession.[40]

Although Spenser had lamented the decline of patronage as early as 1579, it was not until the end of the century that raucous voices were heard castigating the system and, like Dekker's, protesting the loss of self-respect in humbling oneself before a Maecenas. With candor Hall in his *Virgidemiarum* (1598) deplores the financial dependency as well as the author's self-debasement through sycophantic dedications,

> When grand Maecenas casts a glavering eye,
> On the cold present of a Poesie:
> And least he might more frankly take then give,
> Gropes for a french crowne in his emptie sleeve . . .
> Nor can I crouch, and writhe my fauning tayle
> To some great Patron, for my best availe.

Prior to 1598, however, what criticism authors dared voice had been restrained. The anonymous author of *The Institution of a Gentleman* (2nd ed., 1568) recognized from a moral viewpoint the evils of flattery in dedications, "whereby such men have falne into a double abuse: thone in geving unto noble men such presentes as are unfit for their persons, in the other they abused themselves: for of al coloured things flatery is sonest espied." In *The Adventures of Brusanus* (1592) Rich deplores the tendencies of authors "to glorifie the parties whome they have chosen to be patrons of their workes, with manye strained wordes and far sought for phrases," but, it should be added, he is writing to his cousin. Lodge, in *A Fig for Momus* (1595), protests against meager stipends:

> But now, these frugall patrons, who begin
> To skantle learning with a servile pay,
> Make Poets count their negligence, no sinne.

But these are mild attacks and peripheral criticisms of patronage.[41]

Nashe, as one would expect, was more forthright, and he set the tone for the tirades of Hall, Middleton, Dekker, and others. Appropriately in *A Knight's Conjuring* (1607) Dekker invokes the specter of his predecessor: "For Nash inveyed bitterly (as he had wont to do) against dry-fisted patrons, accusing them of his untimely death, because if they had given his muse that cherishment which shee most worthily deserved, hee had fed to his dying day on fat capons, burnt sack and suger, and not so desperately have ventur'de his life, and shortend his dayes by keeping company with pickle herrings." But Dekker's account omits one important fact: like that of most Elizabethans (and of Dekker himself) Nashe's attitude toward patronage was equivocal. On the one hand he loathed toadying, but he also recognized that without the support of patrons a writer's financial returns were precarious. Thus, his books contained violent denunciations mixed with affected sycophancy.[42]

The fawning appears in the dedication of *Astrophel and Stella* (quoted above), in which Nashe lauds the Countess of Pembroke with a servile extravagance worthy of the mountebanks he condemns. In *Pierce Penniless* (1592) he admonishes noblemen and gentlemen to have their deeds celebrated by poets rather than by illiterate literary fakirs. Then he lays bare his motivation: "If any Mecoenas binde me to him by his bounty, or extend some rough liberalitie to mee worth the speaking of, I will doo him as much honour as any Poet of my beardlesse yeeres shall in England." Aware that he has demeaned himself, Nashe wriggles to regain his self-respect by adding a threat: "If I bee evill intreated, or sent away with a Flea in mine eare, let him looke that I will raile on him soundly: not for an houre or a day, whiles the injury is fresh in my memory, but in some elaborate, pollished Poem, which I will leave to the world when I am dead, to be a living Image to all ages, of his beggerly parsimony and ignoble illiberaltie." Toward the conclusion of *Pierce Penniless* he returns to the subject of patronage in the form of a conversation with himself about his book. Pierce should not be "daintie" and refuse a patron if he can find one. But "where is he?" And if one finds a patron, "cap and thankes is all our Courtiers payment: wherefore, I would counsell my frends to be more considerate in their Dedications, and not cast away so many months labour on a clown that knowes not how to use a Scholer." Then, with gusto Nashe describes a meeting of a silken fop and a threadbare author: the glib praise of the book, the promise of reward within a few days, and the fop's subsequent refusal to see the writer. "These are the common courses of the world," Nashe concludes, "which everie man privatlie murmurs at, but none dares openlie upbraid, bicause all Artists for the most part are base minded." [43]

Despite Nashe's willingness to state publicly what "base minded" writers muttered among themselves, he did not intrepidly (and unrealistically) spurn the patronage of the Careys, who for a year or more cultivated him. He penned to Lady Carey one of the most stilted and mannered dedications ever written:

Excellent accomplisht Court-glorifying Lady, give mee leave, with the sportive Sea Purposes, preludiatelie a little to play before the storme of my Teares: to make my prayer ere I proceede to my sacrifice. Loe, for an oblation to the ritch burnisht shrine of your vertue, a handfull of Jerusalems mummianizd earth, (in a few sheetes of wast paper enwrapped,) I heere (humiliate) offer up at your feete. More embellished should my present bee, were my abilitie more abundant.

(An unlettered citizen-author like Robinson penned nothing worse than this.) And, to the Earl of Southampton he writes contritely, in *The Unfortunate Traveler* (1594): "A new brain, a new wit, a new stile, a new soule will I get mee, to canonize your name to posteritie, if in this my first attempt I be not taxed of presumption." That for his "presumption" he evidently received nothing, since the dedication does not appear in the second edition, is not so important as Nashe's humbling himself in order to gain favor. Though he wobbled in his attitude toward patronage, he evidently murmured (chiefly in private) so often and so vociferously that to Dekker he became a spokesman against patrons.[44]

About 1600 writers attacked patronage on three grounds: the servile language of dedicatory epistles placed an author in a humiliating relation to a patron; patrons, particularly the *nouveaux riches,* were criticized for their stinginess, condescension, and indifference to art; a few voices were raised against the system itself. As one would anticipate, more attention was directed to the first two charges than to the last, as evidenced in Nashe's criticisms. Furthermore, the language of prefaces and the characters of patrons were personal and specific evils, and Elizabethans were adept in dramatizing such matters but slow in comprehending the general problem.

More violently than Rowlands, whose refusal to employ the clichés of dedications is quoted earlier, Davies cries, "Away with Patronage, a plague upon't":

> Call for no aid where none is to be found;
> *Protect my Booke*: such Bookes O fates confound.
> *To shew my gratefull minde*: That's stinking stale;
> Yet in new 'Pistles such geare's set to sale.
> The poore mans present to the Emperor;
> O that in 'Pistles keepes a stinking sturre.

PATRONAGE

And not the Guift, but givers poore good will:
This, this, (O this) my vexed Soule doth kill!
This is a Pill (in deed) to give more stooles
Than Mouthes will fill of forty such fine-fooles.

Dekker chooses to dedicate *News for Gravesend* to "Syr Nicholas *Nemo*, alias Nobody":

Shall I creepe (like a drownde Ratte) into the warme bos-ome, (my Benefique Patron!) with a piece of some olde mustie Sentence in my mouth, stolne out of *Lycosthenes Apothegmes,* and so accost thee? Out upont! the fashion of such Dedications is more stale than kissing. No, no, suffer me (good Nobody) to dive (like a White-Friars Puncke) into thy familiar & solid acquaintance at the first dash: And in stead of Worshipfull Syr, come upon thee with honest Jew, how doest? [45]

The same bawdy-house language appears in Middleton's description of Sir Christopher Clutchfist, "knighted at a very hard pennyworth, neither for eating musk-melons, anchovies, or caviare, but for a costlier exploit and a hun-dred-pound feat of arms." To him the author "wisheth the decrease of his lands and the increase of his legs, that his calves may hang down like gamashoes." This is the man who uses ribbons for shoelaces, gives the parchment of books to his tailor, and saves the gilding to decorate a pair of spurs. "Such are the miserable conceits they gather of you, because you never give the poor Muse-suckers a penny." Favorite epithets for these patrons are "leaden Mydas," "Maecenasses" (Nashe's pun), "Golden-Asse" — not very original appellations in a wordmongering age. Dekker writes of patrons "with cold hands and hot livers: they give nothing, and yet have red cheekes for anger, when anything is given to them." [46]

Rowlands perceives that the author's servility before patrons benefited neither himself nor his art. No poet can have a "freeborne Muse," he charges, so long as he humbles before boors for money.

> Our best and worthy witts being true divine,
> Will not be brib'd, to wright a lying lyne
> For Honours changling, nor for Monyes slave,
> But as they merit, so their worth shall have.

Ten years later Davies makes the same accusation:

> It's the worst way that wit can use his trade,
> For Fee so light, with rich praise Blocks to lade.

Without vehemence but with an essential sanity lacking in many of the attacks upon patronage, Bacon offers this judicious opinion: "Neither is the modern dedication of books and writings, as to patrons, to be commended: for that books (such as are worthy the name of books) ought to have no patrons but truth and reason." But even Bacon had nothing constructive to offer as a substitute for patronage and like all the other commentators avoided reference to the fundamental problem — the economics of publication.[47]

Most poets can never become self-supporting through publication. The Daniels will always need patronage, either from aristocrats like the Herberts or, in modern times, from universities and philanthropic foundations. This function patronage served in the Elizabethan age and, despite the angry criticisms, served it effectively in furnishing security to Daniel, Florio, and Jonson. But Elizabethan patronage was also capricious and erratic, and too often writers had to surrender self-respect to obtain security. Literature could not become a respected profession until it achieved freedom from patronage. Furthermore, no author could expect more than an uncertain livelihood until the economic realities of the printing-press age were faced and met on economic terms.

CHAPTER FIVE

WRITERS AND STATIONERS

Aᴜᴛʜᴏʀs were slow to recognize one of their most formidable enemies — publishers, who are, Mark Twain observes, "not accountable to the laws of heaven or earth in any country." At first, Tudor writers confined their criticisms to such trivialities as misprints and errata and frequently alleged that they were out of the city when their books went through the presses. Later they were wary of unscrupulous stationers who printed any manuscript that chanced to "fall" into their hands, but, as we shall see, authors exaggerated the danger of unauthorized printing. Around 1600, when writers became more vocal, a few like Dekker made snide remarks about the taste and judgment of printers, but they missed, or at any rate failed to state, the main point: authors were without protection in the new commerce of bookmaking. Although in *The Scholar's Purgatory* (1625) George Wither singled out, and called by its proper name, the exploitation of writers by businessmen who became rich while they stayed poor, it was not until late in the seventeenth century that writers as a group abandoned their naiveté and faced up to economic realities: that while the Stationers' Company increased its powers, authors neither controlled their works after the sale of a manuscript nor, except in certain cases, received any moneys besides the initial payment of the stationer.[1]

Writers were in effect paralyzed by ignorance of elementary economics, but stationers faced no such dilemmas, for they were, in McKerrow's words, "merchants pure and simple" who shrewdly grasped the economic and political facts of their society. These men had early perceived the necessity of organization and joint action. From a brotherhood of scriveners eventually had evolved a company of stationers loosely organized and relatively powerless until its incorporation on May 4, 1557. Incorporation served two purposes: politically it enabled the crown, at least theoretically, to control "scandalous, malicious, schismatical, and heretical" printing; economically it conferred upon stationers monopolistic powers to protect their interests. The stationers, masters of *quid pro quo,* exploited the royal fear of subversion and religious deviationism, which to the Tudors was more of a political than religious problem, and in return obtained virtually complete control of the book trade. For the charter granted by Mary enabled the company to control the number of apprentices and printers and thus to regulate practitioners of the art and reduce the excessive number of printers at the time. In addition, stationers were empowered to search printing establishments, seize and confiscate unauthorized books, and imprison resisters. This dubious quasi-legal function gave the company a potent weapon with which to coerce obedience. From the Tudor point of view such conferring of authority was practicable, since printers more effectively than public officials could police the trade and ferret out subversive books and illicit printing establishments. During Elizabeth's reign, especially when Puritan discontent increased and the Jesuit infiltration posed a threat, the company was able to augment its powers. Many of the new regulations, such as restrictions upon the number of copies printed and the enforced distribution of type after each edition, had little direct bearing upon the lot of writers.

But regulations regarding copyright were of paramount importance to professionals. By 1600 printing a book was no longer a one-man operation; it was a complex capitalistic venture that required large financial outlays and elaborate business organization. Rarely was the printer both publisher and bookseller, as Caxton and De Worde had been in the early days of printing. More and more the publisher who advanced the money and guided the undertaking dominated the trade. He hired a printer to produce the book and a bookseller to distribute it. The writer sold his manuscript to the publisher for the best price he could obtain. The stationer then obtained "licence" for publication from the ecclesiastical or other official authorities to whom all manuscripts had to be submitted, and the warden of the company, after ascertaining whether the rights of any other stationer were infringed upon, approved the entry of the manuscript by issuing what may be called a "warrant." Finally, the clerk of the company made the formal entry of the copy in the Hall Book. Upon completion of these formalities the book became the exclusive possession of the stationer. Without consulting the author he was entitled to reprint the book as frequently as sales warranted, to transfer it to another stationer, or not to publish it at all.

Unless an author revised his book, profits from subsequent editions accrued to the stationer, so that when a tract enjoyed a vogue with the public the publisher's coffers were filled but the author's remained bare. Even worse, if a stationer "happened" upon a manuscript and registered it, the writer had no legal recourse. He could only indulge in abusive but futile wordmongering. Wither singles out this abuse for censure: "If he get any written Coppy into his powre, likely to be vendible, whether the Author be willing or no, he will publish it; And it shallbe contrived and named alsoe, according to his owne pleasure: which is the reason, so many good Bookes come forth imperfect, and with foolish titles." [2]

The Elizabethan professionals, then, were in a hopeless economic predicament. They were powerless because unorganized and unprotected either by law or by custom. While stationers effectively enchanced their powers, legal as well as economic, writers were compelled to be lackeys who supplied material for the printing presses without a fair share in the profits. It was not until a century later, in 1711, that authors were granted copyright for a period of fourteen years. Not until that time was it possible for a Pope to assert his independence both of patrons and of publishers. The Elizabethan had to make his peace with patrons and to bargain as best he could with publishers.

Although copyright regulations were chiefly responsible for their economic insecurity, writers, except for the belligerent Wither, who was an author-publisher and therefore a businessman of sorts, were silent on the important subject but vocal in regard to unauthorized publication of manuscripts. Since authors as a whole, including professionals like Nashe, never quite made up their minds whether they were professionals or amateurs, they were perhaps loath to demean themselves by a forthright stand on an economic issue. They could retain their gentlemanly pretensions, however, in assailing printers and publishers who appropriated manuscripts. Since circulation of manuscripts was common practice, the scrivener who made copies for an amateur's friends had only his integrity to restrain him from making additional transcripts for sale to interested purchasers or from transmitting a copy to a stationer. Although the integrity of some scriveners was no doubt adjustable to the laws of supply and demand, it is perhaps surprising that unauthorized publication was not widespread. In an often-quoted passage Nashe avers that his *Terrors of the Night* was providing a profitable business for scriveners:

A long time since hath it line suppressed by mee; untill the urgent importunitie of a kinde frend of mine (to whom I was sundrie waies beholding) wrested a Coppie from me. That Coppie progressed from one scriveners shop to another, & at length grew so common, that it was readie to bee hung out for one of their signes, like a paire of indentures. Whereuppon I thought it as good for mee to reape the frute of my owne labours, as to let some unskilfull pen-man or Noverint-maker startch his ruffe & new spade his beard with the benefite he made of them.

Interestingly, as Pollard has pointed out, Nashe does not entertain the possibility of publication. If scriveners were in truth decorating their shops with his work (a clear indication that demand was great), it is surprising that an enterprising publisher did not exploit the market. Like many of Nashe's allegations, this charge must be accepted cautiously, for, whatever the actual situation, his preface was more advertisement than truth.[3]

In view of the devious tactics of printers like John Wolfe and John Danter, we can hardly maintain that the ethics of Elizabethan printers were simon-pure, nor were those of writers for that matter. Yet, few are the instances of proven appropriations of manuscripts. Copies of Sidney's works evidently circulated in large quantities. In a letter, in 1586, to the courtier's father-in-law, Sir Francis Walsingham, Greville expressed concern that older, uncorrected versions of the *Arcadia* might appear in print. It was not until 1598, twelve years after Sidney's death and four years after the first English edition, that the unauthorized Edinburgh edition appeared — hardly confirmation of the unscrupulousness of Elizabethan publishers. In 1591 Thomas Newman printed *Astrophel and Stella* and Daniel's *Delia* in one volume. Here was a clear case of unauthorized publication which the printer attempted to minimize by having Nashe spew hyperboles upon the Countess of Pembroke. Without condoning Newman's role in this venture, it is perhaps more significant that Nashe, the self-righteous custodian of aesthetic and moral standards, was willing to participate in an illicit enterprise. Whether Thorpe acted on his own initiative in printing sonnets which had been circulating in manuscript as early as 1598, or whether Shakespeare connived in the publication of his poems, we shall probably never know, unless an Olympian Holmes suddenly brushes aside the reams of pages devoted to the subject and unexpectedly sheds light on a riddle that has produced a myriad of speculations, and some ingenious scholarly nightmares, but little verifiable information.

When we turn to less well-known works, it is by no means always certain that purportedly unauthorized publications represented deliberate wrongdoing on the part of stationers. In "An admonicion to the reader," Thomas Cooper relates that for several years he had been gathering "dyvers profytable thinges . . . to adde them to this my chronicle," when he discovered "by reporte that certaine persons, for lukers sake contrarie to honestie, had caused my chronicle to be prynted without my knowlage." He later specifies that "the Edicion of this chronicle set foorth by Marshe and Ceres in the yere of Christe. 1599. is none of myne, but the attempte of certayne persons utterly unlearned." Conspicuously, Cooper does not accuse Marsh and Ceres; rather he implies that they merely printed a manuscript submitted to them by persons who had altered his translation by omitting great sections and by "annexyng an other mans addicions." Cooper was evidently betrayed by unscrupulous friends or, less probably, by a scrivener, that is, if he was in fact betrayed at all. He may simply have been "promoting" a revision of his earlier translation.[4]

Explanations offered by other writers are less convincing than Cooper's. Googe attributes the publication of *Eclogues, Epitaphs, and Sonnets* (1563) to "a very Frende of myne, bearynge as it semed better wyll to my doynges than respectyng the hazarde of my name," who "commytted them all togyther unpolyshed to the handes of the Prynter." Strangely enough, the printer had somehow so delayed matters that the book had not appeared when Googe returned to London and discovered his friend's "deception." At this time the friend

. . . declared the matter wholly unto me: shewynge me, that beynge so farre past, and Paper provyded for the Impression therof: It coulde not withoute great hynderaunce of the poore Printer be nowe revoked. His sodayne tale made me at the fyrst, utterly amazed, and doubting a great while, what was best to be done: at the lengthe agreyng both with Necessytie and his Counsell, I sayde with Martiall. *iam sed poteras tutior esse domi.*

William Percy, "fully determined to have concealed my Sonnets as thing privy to myself," so he avers in his preface to *Caelia* (1594), also discovered his work "secretly committed to the Press and almost finished, before it came to my knowledge." Like Googe he makes "Virtue of Necessity" and coyly beseeches readers "to account of them as of toys and amorous devices." Even more striking is the conclusion of the preface to *The School of Slovenry:* "Yours in print against his will, R. F. Gent. and no more. . . . The truth is, this translation was halfe printed, ere I knew who had it: So that *Quo fata trahunt,* without prevention or correction the fooles bolt must needes be shot. And this is it." It is difficult, however, to accept the explanations of Googe, Percy, and R. F. If it were not possible to stop publication — and there is no convincing evidence that such was the case — these writers had other alternatives: instead of contributing prefaces they could have washed their hands of the whole affair, and they were not obligated to worry about the finances of stationers who were, if these authors are to be credited, appropriating their manuscripts for commercial gain. It is an extraordinary individual who makes a thief into an object of charity. It is perhaps not so extraordinary when we observe that each of these writers by his insistence upon the fact that he had not approved publication had accomplished two goals: he had made clear to readers his gentlemanly indifference to print and at the same time had warded off unfavorable criticism.[5]

In Thomas Blenerhasset's *The Second Part of The Mirror of Magistrates* (1578), the printer's preface informs readers that the author

. . . is now beyond the Seas, and wyl marveile at his returne, to find thys imprinted. For his intent was but to profite and pleasure one private man, as by his Epistle may appeare. But I fynding the copie by chaunce, shewing it unto divers men, both learned and wise: and findyng a booke alredy in print, Entituled, *The first and third part of the Mirrour for Magistrates,* I was moved diversly of divers men, by printyng this latter woorke, to make perfite the former booke.

In his epistle Blenerhasset warns, "According unto the trust reposed in you, keepe these trifles from the view of all men, and as you promysed, let them not raunge out of your private Study." Yet, interestingly, a few lines earlier he evinces the professional's concern with a style comprehensible to a lower-class audience: "I have not thought it convenient to write the complaynts of these men, with so obscure a stile as some other have done, but with so playne an exposition, that he who doth reade them shal not neede to be Oedipus, for every playne Davus shall by reading them, easely understand the Authours drift." One can only conclude that if Blenerhasset was not privy to publication, he had not written for a manuscript audience. Still more peculiar is *The Most Famous and Tragical History of Pelops and Hippodamia* (1587), in which the bookseller Richard Smith prints this verse in his dedication:

> Th'author sure I doe not know,
> Ne whether he be high or low,
> Or now alive, or els be dead:
> But this in few words may be said.
> Hoping your honor accept it will,
> According to the Authours skill.

This is immediately followed by the author's epistle — signed by Matthew Grove.[6]

Richard Jones seemed blessed with friends who entrusted manuscripts to him. In *A New Year's Gift — The Court of Civil Courtesy* (1577) Jones claims that he received the manuscript from "a friende" of Simon Robson, "a Gentleman." In his dedication of *The Schoolmaster* (1583) he informs readers that he "happened on this Pamflet," and, after perusing it, "shewed it also unto some of my freends." He "was by them and others exhorted to publish the same in print." In 1586 Jones dedicated to Walsingham *The English Courtier and the Country Gen-*

tleman, a "litle Dialogue, written by a Gentleman, rather
for pastime, then settled studdy." The author, Jones
writes, "(as a thinge unworthy) is neither content it should
presume to your presence, nor passe among the wise. Notwithstanding, without his leave, I make bolde to adventure
the one and the other." Jones thereupon makes an interesting point: "I crave small praise for my Printing of it,
and hee (being used to loose his labour) desireth nothinge."
This gentleman or would-be gentleman even had the
printer note his disdain of filthy lucre. It is difficult to
believe that Jones alone was responsible for these "unauthorized" printings.[7]

Other stationers use almost identical language. Valen-
tine Simmes asserts in a preface to Tofte's *Laura* (1597):
"What the Gentleman was, that wrote these verses, I know
not . . . but thus much I can say, That as they came into
the hands of a friend of mine by mere fortune; so happened I upon them by as great a chance." The friend
made doubly certain that readers were aware of the true
situation by insertion at the end of the volume of "A
Friend's just Excuse about the Book and Author; in his
Absence": "Without the Author's knowledge, as is before
said by the Printer; this Poem is made thus publicly
known; which, with my best endeavour, the Gentleman
himself, suspecting what is now proved too true, at my
coming up, earnestly intreated me to prevent." Yet, as the
friend unintentionally reveals, the conveniently absent
author was back in London before the book was run
through the presses. Like Googe and Percy he was a generous man. John Danter, "contrarie to the Authours expectation," printed *Greene's Funerals* (1594), the "private
study at idle times" of R. B. (possibly Richard Barnfield).
Danter was somewhat naive if he expected readers to believe that this topical work, designed to cash in on the

Harvey-Nashe quarrel, was the product of gentlemanly ruminations. Unwittingly he himself reveals the hoax at the conclusion of his preface: "Now if the Authors paines, and the Printers labour may be acceptable to thee (Gentle Reader) the one hath his hyer, and the other his desire." A gentleman was not a printer's hack who wrote for "hyer." [8]

The rigmarole surrounding unauthorized publication is perhaps best exposed in *Willoby His Avisa* (1594). When the author left London he asked the printer, "amongst the rest of his frendes," to take charge of "all his bookes till his returne." While "perusing" these books "at leysure," the printer relates, "I found many prety & witty conceites, as I suppose of his owne dooing. One among the rest I fancied so much, that I have ventured so farre upon his frendship, as to publish it without his consent." Later he "christened" the book *"Willoby his Avisa*: because I suppose it was his doing, being written with his owne hande . . . How he will like my bouldnes, both in the publishing, and naming of it, I know not." In later editions the printer supplies more information, which could have come only from the author: "This poeticall fiction was penned by the Author at least for thirtie and five yeeres since, (as it will be proved) and lay in wast papers in his study, . . . and so might have continued still . . . had not I, contrarie to his knowledge, with paine collected it; and (in consideration of the good end, to which it was directed) published it." [9]

Thus consistently, if unconvincingly, the "printer" plays the game according to well-established rules. The stationer happens upon a manuscript or a "friend" thrusts it upon him — or, most curious of all, a writer intrusts his books to a stationer friend. The author, it turns out, is either away from the city or, more conveniently, out of the country. The author is invariably a "gentleman." Unexpectedly he returns to London and "reluctantly" gives consent to publication either out of charity or out of passive acquiescence. Usually the author himself notes these facts in a preface. If he does not, the publisher swears that the gentleman does not write for money.

Skepticism must not lead to the unwarranted conclusion that unauthorized publication did not exist in the sixteenth century. Some books did fall into the hands of printers without knowledge of the authors. Probably *Gorboduc* was printed while Thomas Norton was "farre out of London" and Thomas Sackville "out of England": "One W. G. getting a copie therof at some yongmans hand that lacked a litle money and much discretion . . . put it forth excedingly corrupted." Yet the composer of the preface to the authorized 1570 edition is scarcely indignant; he likens the printing of the play to a "faire maide" who has been ravished by a broker. Daniel, however, berates "the indiscretion of a greedie Printer" (Thomas Newman) who published "the private passions of my youth," his sonnets to Delia, and who thus compelled him "to publish that which I never ment." Webbe wants to be compensated by a friend who is about to publish without permission some of his unpolished verse — "which injury though he meanes to doo me in myrth, yet I hope he wyll make me some suffycient recompence, or els I shall goe neere to watch [match?] hym the like or a worse turn." In *The Pilgrimage to Paradise* Breton accuses Jones of publishing his poetry "without my consent or knowledge," and, according to Thomas Heywood, Shakespeare resented Jaggard's unauthorized printing of *The Passionate Pilgrim* (1599). Bishop Hall, we are told, opposed publication of *Mundus Alter et Idem* because it detracted from his dignity as a clergyman. In the preface to his *Essays* Bacon alleges that because "fragments of my conceites were going to print . . . therefore I helde it best discreation to publish them my selfe as they passed long agoe from my pen, without any further disgrace, then the weakenesse of the Author." [10]

Perhaps Hall was worried about his ecclesiastical dignity; perhaps Bacon knew that "fragments" were about to be printed, yet courageous was the stationer who dared risk the wrath of this important official; probably the *Sonnets* was issued without Shakespeare's consent. Perhaps Edward Blount, a printer, was veracious in his assertion that he was publishing *A Survey of the Great Duke's State of Tuscany* (1605) because "your worke (out of your owne protection) would in the end present it selfe to the generall view." But in none of these cases is the evidence incontrovertible. Though an author apparently had no legal redress if a stationer pilfered his manuscript — Sackville and Norton accepted the surreptitious printing of *Gorboduc* as "remedilesse" — cases of indisputable theft are not common. This is all the more remarkable since the entry of a book in the Stationers' Register transferred ownership to the stationer.[11]

On the basis of the evidence adduced, one is forced to conclude that more often than not unauthorized publications had the silent blessings of the authors concerned. Frequently there was collusion between publisher and writer, and prefaces which explicitly stated that the work was issued without consent constituted titillating advertisements for readers anxious to read books intended (allegedly) for private scrutiny. Finally, the author was able to keep his hands free from the taint of printer's ink and to silence carping critics. The arrangement was convenient for authors concerned with position and fearful of adverse criticism, for publishers interested in sales, for readers eager to peruse literature not intended for publication.

The Printer when I askt a little summe,
Huckt with me for my booke, & came not nere.
Ne could my reason or perswasion,
Move him a whit; though al things now were deere,
    Hath my conceipt no helpe to set it forth?
    Are all things deere, and is wit nothing worth?
                    — Bastard, *Chrestoleros* (1598)

The critical cliché that the Elizabethan author had "distaste (general at the time) for receiving payment from a publisher" Bastard's verses do not support, nor does Nashe's exclamatory candor, "When I doo play my Prizes in Print, Ile be paid for my paines." Only among amateurs like Sidney was "distaste" common, for the late sixteenth century was the age of the professional, not the amateur. Sidney's was a dying gesture of a dying way of life. Spenser expected his works to be rewarded. Although Shakespeare showed little interest in publication, all the evidence points to the conclusion that in handling his plays in the theater he was as practical as Shaw and as well-rewarded. The author (or authors) of the *Parnassus* trilogy, as well as Wither, Birkenhead, Nashe, Greene, Bastard, Dekker, and Peacham — and the list could be extended — reveal no gentlemanly contempt for pay. To expect writers, or any one else for that matter, to be above monetary considerations is to sentimentalize human nature and to minimize stomach pangs as well as to accept literally the ritualistic mouthings of amateurs. Sons of middle-class families had neither inherited means nor lucrative sinecures, to say nothing of a profession; therefore, they could not prance into print with noble disclaimers of interest in compensation. Their poverty scarcely permitted such insincerity.[12]

By the end of the sixteenth century the custom of paying authors (including many of the "amateurs") for manuscripts had been firmly established. Compensation from stationers took one of four forms: a fee, a fee and a specified number of copies of the author's book, a number of copies of the author's book without fee, and employment in a printer's establishment with subsistence and additional remuneration.

But, after these facts have been stated, we are once more confronted with a paucity of concrete data. Although the Stationers' Company had elaborate registers to list financial transactions such as payments of fees, fines, and transfers of books from one stationer to another, no records of payments to authors were kept. The company neither sought laws nor enacted company regulations to formalize relations with authors: publishers were not interested in protecting the rights of authors, and the absence of rules permitted each stationer to bargain and to pay whatever he wished (or whatever the writer would take) for a manuscript. In other words, the Stationers' Company followed sound capitalistic principles: to protect itself from competition it sought and obtained police powers from the state, but in its dealings with authors it adopted and pursued an exploitative laissez-faire policy. Only when piracy had reached such proportions that it endangered the livelihood of publishers, who could no longer exist in the jungle of their own creation, did they come to the aid of writers and seek a copyright law that guaranteed the rights of authors as well as prevented appropriation of books by unscrupulous publishers.

In a prefatory note to Robert Gomersall's *Poems* (1633) John Marriot, with a materialistic frankness generally missing in the public pronouncements of stationers, acknowledges the primacy of the profit motive in his ventures: "To praise the worke, were to set my selfe to sale, since the greater its worth is, the more is my benefit, & not the Authors: He good man may have an Ayery, but I a reall profit. An Ayery one, I terme it, for I judge others by my selfe, who cannot feed by praises." Publishers, of course, like all other capitalists took risks. They had to invest capital in equipment, rent shops, pay laborers their wages, and arrange to sell their wares; and the sale of books depended upon such indeterminable factors as public taste, general economic prosperity, censorship, and sudden disasters like plagues during which people fled London. In addition, there is a great deal of validity to the observation in the petition of the company to parliament in 1643:

Books (except *the sacred Bible*) are not of such generall use and necessity, as some staple Commodities are, which feed and cloathe us, nor are they so perishable, or require change in keeping, some of them being once bought, remain to Childrens Children, and many of them are rarities onely and useful only to a very few, and of no necessity to any, few men bestow more in Books then what they can spare out of their superfluities, and the gain of such as live by selling of Books is not so great, as to raise them to an equality of riches with many others of more sordid and ignoble professions.

There is, however, less validity in the company's claim that "in Pamphlets too there is a great hazard, for scarce one book of three sells well, or proves gainfull to the publisher," since there are at least two convenient (and significant) omissions: any book which went beyond a single impression could more than compensate a publisher for two failures (for later impressions he had only the normal expenses of his printing establishment), and almost all stationers had certain staples which were in constant demand — school texts, prayer books, almanacs, or utilitarian tracts. (The petition of 1643, incidentally, though it requested stricter control of printing, was characteristically silent about authors.)[13]

Despite the risks and uncertainties of a trade that catered

to a fickle public, stationers had advantages not granted to writers. Since only members of the Stationers' Company could register a book, authors sold all rights to the stationers and had no claims upon future printings. How advantageous this arrangement was to publishers is illustrated by the popularity of Greene's *Quip for an Upstart Courtier,* which went through at least six impressions within a year after its publication (1592). If the pamphlet sold for 6*d.* and even if John Wolfe had paid Greene the exceptionally high fee of £5, he probably had a net profit of over £100. Such returns for a single volume were unknown among writers. Second, a neophyte or even an experienced but not overly successful author was sometimes persuaded to accept payment in kind (perhaps twenty or more copies of his book), so that only a small sale was necessary to insure the publisher a nominal profit. Third, when, as occasionally happened, authors (or their friends) subsidized their own writings, publishers had their expenses underwritten and were certain of a profit, since it is doubtful that they undertook printing at cost. Finally, their tightly organized company gave them obvious advantages over authors who were victimized by their lingering desire to take the gentlemanly attitude toward publication, and who were without organization or legal recourses to safeguard their interests. At any rate, most Elizabethan stationers by fair tactics or foul managed to survive the economic risks which they dramatized (and exaggerated) when it served their interests. They could not have remained in business if profits were not to be had.[14]

While no publisher was in business for disinterested love of knowledge, writers have always been anomalies who, for reasons which they have difficulty in articulating, have been willing to accept precarious livelihoods. In the preface to *The Image of Governance* (1541) Elyot observes that some criticize his "studies as vayne and unprofitable, sayinge in derision, that I have nothing wonne therby, but the name onely of a maker of bokes, and that I sette the trees, but the printer eateth the fruites." He acknowledges the accuracy of this charge: "Yf I wold have employed my study about the increace of my private commodity, which I have spent in wrytinge of bokes for others necessity, . . . I shuld have attayned or this tyme to have ben moche more welthy, & in respect of the worlde in a more estimation." Although professionals at the end of the century lacked Elyot's humanistic concern with the general welfare and, like Nashe and Bastard, expected compensation for their manuscripts, they were in a sense idealists, despite their materialistic motivations, since they chose the one profession certain to insure them a starvation diet. Though of necessity they had to imitate Peacham, who desired "a good round summe of a Stationer for thy Coppy," they no doubt envied the amateur's freedom from huckstering stationers and secretly cherished dreams of emulating the withering contempt of a Gascoigne: "And yet some there are who have not spared too reporte that I receyved greate summes of money for the first printing of these Posies, whereby (if it were true) I mighte seeme not onely a craftie Broker for the utteraunce of garishe toyes, but a corrupte Merchaunte for the sale of deceyptfull wares." [15]

As vocal and vituperative as Elizabethans were, there are only a few specific allusions to fees paid by stationers. In *The Return from Parnassus* Danter offers an author "40 shillings and an odde pottle of wine." Wither complains that printers could "hyre for a matter of 40 shillings some needy Ignoramus." J. S., who affected to scorn publication for money, makes it clear that only hacks were awarded (or wanted) such a pittance: "Thus doe our piebald Naturalists, depend upon poore wages, gape after the drunken harvest of forty shillings, and shame the worthy benefactors of Hellicon." Writing in the Restoration, Aubrey reports that Sir John Birkenhead "gott many a fourty shillings (I beleeve) by Pamphlets, such as that of *Col. Pride*, and *The Last Will and Testament of Philip Earle of Pembroke, &c.*" On the basis of these statements many hacks — Wither and J. S. are clear on this point — received a fee of £2 for pamphlets of six or eight, and possibly ten, signatures. However, just as the scholarly tradition that patrons awarded writers usually about £2 is based on inconclusive evidence, so, too, the accepted beliefs about payments to authors by stationers must be modified.[16]

Simple economics will demonstrate that authors of short pamphlets did not always receive 40s. A printer not certain of the sales appeal of a work probably ran off about four hundred or five hundred copies. (Although by an order issued on December 11, 1587, editions, with certain exceptions, were limited to 1250 copies, it seems plausible that, unless the stationer had no doubts as to vendibility, few books achieved that number in the first printing.) If the tract sold at 3d. a copy, the most a stationer could receive from an edition of five hundred copies was £6 5s., and, if, as Willoughby observes, the price of a book is roughly twice the cost of producing it, the stationer's expenses were £3 2s. 6d. To break even he had to sell 250 copies. Since the stationer expected to make a profit, the author was probably fortunate if he received ten or fifteen shillings for his "travail." To pay this fee the stationer had to dispose of forty or fifty additional copies. Even if the book were priced at 6d. and the foregoing figures doubled, it is doubtful that the stationer would have paid the author more than £1. Since no businessman ever operated without a safety margin, and since printing costs could hardly be much reduced, it was the unprotected writers who insured the stationer's profit.[17]

The case of Bastard supports the hypothesis that forty shillings was by no means the usual payment to a writer. In *Chrestoleros* he forthrightly laments:

> And yet the Printer thinkes that he shall leese,
> Which buyes my Epigrams at pence a peece.

In this volume there are 290 epigrams. If Bastard had had his way, he would have received 24*s*. 2*d*.; so that if we make the appropriate insertions in the previously quoted lines,

> The Printer when I askt a little summe [i.e., 24*s*. 2*d*.],
> Huckt with me for my booke, & came not nere,

we can only deduce that Bastard did not receive more than £1. The probabilities are that Bastard's epigrams sold at 6*d*. a copy. For he observes, "Some will give sixe pence for a witty touch," and both Rowlands and Richard Turner testify that at the turn of the century this was the customary price for such collections.[18]

Perhaps when a stationer "came not nere," many a writer in lieu of a fee accepted copies of his book, as Robinson did for his twenty translations. Even the venerable Stow, whose chronicles had intellectual prestige for many decades and were in steady demand because of England's self-awareness, in 1602 received for his *Survey of London* £3 and forty copies and for *Brief Chronicles* £1 and fifty copies. And these were books almost certain of good sales despite the fact that they were enlarged and revised editions of works issued many years earlier. If Stow, who at times had enjoyed the favors of a nobleman like the Earl of Leicester, and who produced laborious compendiums of vendible history, had to be content with such treatment, the unknown author of "trifles," the market for which was always uncertain, had no reason to expect more substantial payments.[19]

Successful writers were accorded better treatment than that given to Bastard or to our hypothetical author, yet they were probably not so well-rewarded as some students have supposed. Because of Nashe's assertion that "glad was the Printer that might bee so blest to pay [Greene] deare for the very dregs of his wit," some commentators have assumed that Greene was a well-paid pamphleteer. (Pollard, for instance, conjectures that Greene received £4 for each pamphlet.) But it must be remembered that Nashe's allegation was in answer to Harvey's devastatingly accurate report of Greene's squalor and poverty at the time of his death. In addition, "deare" is hardly an unambiguous word. Does it mean £2, £3, £5, or £10? Hardly the latter figure, since publishers could scarcely have been so enamored of the dregs of Greene's wit as to wipe out their profit. In the year preceding his death Greene composed six underworld tracts (including *The Defense of Cony-Catching*) which sold for 3*d.* a piece. (One of the characters in *The Defense of Cony-Catching* refers to Greene's earlier exposés, "I have for 3. pence bought a little Pamphlet, that hath taught me to smoke such a couple of knaves as you be.") Assuming that 1250 copies of each of these tracts were printed, it seems highly implausible that Greene received much more than £2 for each pamphlet. If the stationer sold all the copies, he grossed £15 12*s.*, and his expenses were roughly £7 16*s.* If Greene obtained £4 — a sum equal to the stationer's profit — the sixteenth century was indeed a writer's utopia.[20]

It is also significant that in two autobiographical treatments of his own career Greene never refers to payments for his prose works. When Francesco in *Never Too Late* seeks "a means to mittigate the extremitie of his want," he composes comedies. "By this meanes," Greene says of Francesco, "his want was releeved, his credite in his hosts house recovered, his apparell in greater braverie then it was, and his purse well lined with Crownes." In *Groatsworth of Wit,* Roberto meets a traveling player who urges him to write plays, "for which you shall be well paid, if you will take the paines." Soon Roberto is "famozed for an Arch-plaimaking-poet, his purse like the sea somtime sweld, anon like the same sea fell to a low ebbe: yet seldom he wanted, his labors were so well esteemed." Both autobiographical heroes are in agreement as to the rewards to be derived from the stage, which, if we use Henslowe's payments to playwrights in the late 1590's as a guide, probably amounted to £6 for each drama. If Greene had received comparable payments for prose pamphlets, surely his two characters would have churned them out and reported their success. Their silence on this score indicates that for his nondramatic works he received considerably less than £6, in all probability only £2 or £3.[21]

Fees greater than forty shillings were paid, but they were probably rare. We know that the wife of John Dowland, for *The Second Book of Songs or Airs,* received £20 and one-half of whatever the Countess of Bedford decided to give for the dedication. In view of this apparently extraordinary splitting of the sum received from the patroness, the printer Thomas East probably knew, or had good reason to suspect, that the countess had rewarded, or was about to reward, Dowland handsomely; in anticipation of his share of the countess' gifts he was able to increase his payment to the composer's wife. Furthermore, since Dowland's book undoubtedly sold at a high price, and was almost guaranteed a substantial sale among nobles and wealthy merchants, the stationer could afford to be generous. Of one thing we can be sure: East would not have agreed to pay £20 unless he was certain of a profit.[22]

Although evidence relating to fees is admittedly inadequate, we can draw several tentative conclusions. Forty shillings was such a disproportionately high return for a short pamphlet that it was probably paid only under exceptional circumstances, when, for instance, the publisher was confident that there would be subsequent editions, or when the writer's previous works had tangibly demonstrated his popularity. Many a professional must have accepted 20s. or copies instead of money, and those with alcoholic propensities may have settled for Danter's "odde pottle of wine." (Earle's "pot-poet" received "now and then a sixe pence or two in reward of the baser coyne, his Pamphlet.") As McKerrow points out, more than £5 could not have been paid for a pamphlet sold at 6d. a copy, but it appears most unlikely that such a sum was often, if ever, paid. (For his enlarged *Survey of London,* it will be recalled, Stow received only £3.) Finally, while it is true that publishers frequently magnified their economic risks in order to keep down payments to authors, the latter were too desperately in need of cash to hold out for high fees. Hence, stationers were prosperous and authors the not-so-humble poor.[23]

Long before fees became established, publishers, both in England and on the Continent, had given authors a number of copies of their books, one or more for patrons and others to be disposed of in any manner they chose. Payment in kind was commonplace for several centuries. In its 1643 petition to parliament the Stationers' Company admits candidly that the books of many authors "carry no other profit or recompence with them, but the benefit of their Copies; and if this be taken away, many Pieces of great worth and excellence will be strangled in the womb, or never conceived at all for the future." Although the stationers overstated the situation in order to dramatize the hazards of publication, no doubt some books would have been "strangled in the womb" if authors had not agreed to underwrite publication costs by accepting books in place of money. On the other hand, publishers were understandably reluctant to abandon a device that protected their interests. Authors had to concur because frequently there was no other way to have their works printed.[24]

Robinson's manuscript *Eupolemia* contains specific records of payments in kind. He never received a fee from a publisher for any of his translations and depended upon gifts from patrons and upon the sales of the books given to him. Ordinarily he received twenty-six copies from the stationer: one he presented to his patron, the others he sold to friends. In two instances he received more than twenty-six copies. In the following table I have compiled all references to dealings of this kind over a period of almost twenty years. (In three instances I have estimated because Robinson did not list his receipts.)

As the table indicates, the total of £29 11s. 1d. includes estimated receipts of £6 7s. 1d., the accuracy of which cannot of course be verified, but on the basis of known returns these estimates appear to be reasonable. In fact, errors in these estimates are more than compensated for by Robinson's omissions in recording payments. From his notations it is clear that on several occasions he received money but failed to cite the amount. Because of Hatton's gift of £3 for *A Proceeding in the Harmony of King David's Harp*, he writes, "I bestowed very fewe of these Bookes abrode by reason of his liberality which kept mee from trubling my frendes abrode for one whole yeares space afterwardes." These "fewe" sales are unaccounted for. Later he notes,

Books	Copies sold	Number of sheets	Receipts		
A Record of Ancient Histories (1577)	25	21 [a]	£2	10s.	(est.) [b]
Robinson's Ruby (1577)	25	5		10s. 5d.	(est.) [c]
A Dial of Daily Contemplation (1578)	25	10	£1	5s.	
Exposition upon the Twenty-Fifth Psalm (1580)	25	10	£1	5s.	
A Learned and True Assertion of King Arthur (1582)	25	14	£2		
Part of the Harmony of King David's Harp (1582)	100	32	£10 [d]		
The Ancient Order of Prince Arthur (1583)	56 Knights [100] Esquires	12	£4 £3	4s. 6s. 8d.	(est.) [e]
A Second Proceeding in the Harmony of King David's Harp (1593)	25	15½	£2		
A Fourth Proceeding in the Harmony of King David's Harp (1596)	25	7½	£2	10s.	
Total receipts			£29	11s. 1d.	

[a] In this chart I have utilized Robinson's figures as given in the *Eupolemia*, reprinted by Vogt in *SP*, XXI (1924), 629–648. His statements concerning the number of sheets are not always accurate. *A Learned and True Assertion of King Arthur* has twelve sheets rather than fourteen; *Part of the Harmony of King David's Harp* thirty-three rather than thirty-two; *The Ancient Order of Prince Arthur* thirteen rather than twelve. There are no extant copies of the 1577 edition of *A Record of Ancient Histories, Robinson's Ruby,* and *Exposition upon the Twenty-Fifth Psalm.* His descriptions of the other three works are correct.

[b] I have estimated that he sold this translation for 2s. per copy. In 1578 he received 1s. for each copy of *A Dial of Daily Contemplation,* a book slightly less than one-half the size of this one.

[c] Estimated at 5d. per copy.

[d] A copy of this work in the possession of Richard Stonley (1597) was appraised at 6d.; see Hotson, "The Library of Elizabeth's Embezzling Teller," *SB,* II (1949–50), 57.

[e] Since there is no way of determining the number of esquires who purchased copies from Robinson, I have arbitrarily estimated their number at 100. The knights paid 18d. each for their copies, and the esquires 8d.

again without citing the amount, that in 1596 Sir Charles Howard rewarded him generously for a copy of *A Third Proceeding in the Harmony of King David's Harp*. In the same year, for the translation which Egerton refused to patronize, *A Fourth Proceeding in the Harmony of King David's Harp,* a virtuous lady in the city gave him "duble valew therof" — an ambiguous remark probably indicating that he received at least £1 or more, since he was quick to note miserly donations. Another reason for considering these estimates of receipts from book sales conservative is that Robinson charged for his volumes whatever the traffic would bear. For copies of *The Ancient Order of Prince Arthur* he received 18*d.* from knights and 8*d.* from esquires. *A Fourth Proceeding in the Harmony of King David's Harp*, a small work consisting of seven and one-half gatherings, was sold at the unusually high rate of 3*d.* per sheet. (The usual price of sixteenth-century books was two or three sheets a penny.) Thanks probably to his salesmanship, which undoubtedly included references to his desperate struggle to support his wife and daughter, his purchasers often paid exceptionally high prices for his translations.[25]

The importance of Robinson's earnings is not the exact amount of money he received but the deductions we can make about the Elizabethan literary profession. On the basis of his experience it appears that hacks as well as more reputable authors frequently, if not always, earned more from sales of their own works than they received from patrons or publishers. Robinson's gifts from patrons amounted to £23 6*s.* 4*d*; from sales £29 11*s.* 1*d.* and probably more. When Warwick gave the translator "no reward" for *Part of the Harmony of King David's Harp,* he "was therefore driven to make benefit of 100 Bookes within 2 yeares space afterwards to the value of x li sterling." By no stretch of the translator's sometimes winged imagination could he have received £10 from the earl (the largest gift from a patron, it will be recalled, was £3; his average return was slightly less than £1.) Or, note the returns from *The Ancient Order of Prince Arthur*. Thomas Smith, the dedicatee and the president of a London archery society, gave the translator five shillings. But, when Robinson sold the book to the knights and esquires "when they shott . . . at Myles ende greene," he received £4 4s. from knights and an estimated £3 6s. 8d. from esquires. Such a return from a single patron was inconceivable. Or if we take the case of John Stow, who received for *The Survey of London* £3 and forty copies and for *Brief Chronicles* £1 and fifty copies, the historian did not have to sell books at exorbitant prices in order to realize more than his publishers paid him. In view of the small stipends from dedicatees it appears certain that Elizabethan authors by peddling their own books surpassed total receipts from patrons and stationers. In short, salesmanship was an indispensable skill for economic success (and survival) in the Tudor period.[26]

The following dialogue from *The Return from Parnassus* makes this fact clear: "Were thy disappointed selfe possest with such a spirit as inhabiteth my face, thou wouldest never goe fidlinge thy pamphletes from doore to dore like a blinde harper, for breade & cheese, presentinge thy poems like oulde broomes to everie farmer." To the author of the comedy such "fidlinge" involved a serious loss of prestige, since peddling was a mark of the hack. In the midst of a confession that patrons had failed to recognize his merits Churchyard remarks, "I have sixteene severall bookes printed presently to bee bought." Though possibly he refers to the number of his books in the hands of stationers, it seems more probable that, like Robinson, he had to sell his own works. The lack of sales appeal of

Churchyard's pedestrian tracts and more pedestrian poems, as evidenced by the fact that apparently none of his books warranted a second impression, makes it unlikely that booksellers kept on their shelves sixteen slow-moving books, or that publishers paid for his writings. Probably William Fennor had authors in mind in this passage: "Worthy gentlemen, of what degree soever, I suppose this Pamphlet will hap into your hands, before a play begin, with the importunate clamour, of *Buy a new Booke,* by some needy companion, that will be glad to furnish you with worke for a turn'd Teaster." For writers like Robinson and Churchyard and even Stow were needy companions who in their books heralded the New Jerusalem (London) and then had to hawk their books in the new market-place of emergent capitalism.[27]

More ignominious than accepting payment in kind was the subsidization of one's own books. Coryat, after publishing the *Crudities* at his own expense, became a favorite butt of seventeenth-century lampoons. Henry Parrot disdainfully observes, "Tom Coriat solde the Books he made himselfe," and Charles Cotton says, "I will sit down and write my Travels, and like Tom Coriate print them at my own charge." With unconcealed glee and snobbery Nashe accuses Gabriel Harvey of "giving mony to have this his illiterat Pamphlet of Letters printed (wheras others have monie given them to suffer them selves to come in Print)," and then labels Harvey "a manifest briber of Bookesellers and Stationers, to helpe thee to sell away thy bookes (whose impression thou paidst for)." The author of the *Parnassus* comedy has the printer John Danter gloat, "There is many a one that payes me largely for the printing of their inventions." No doubt this fictional character spoke truth.[28]

Not only hacks and falconers paid to have their works

published. John Stell admits that Washington's translation, *The Navigations . . . into Turkey* (1585), was "printed in English at my costes & charges for the general profite & pleasure of the studious, and al such as delight in novelties." Humphrey Barwick caused *A Brief Discourse Concerning the Force and Effect of All Manual Weapons of Fire* (1594?) "at his owne charges . . . to be newly Reprinted." Probably to protect himself from the scandalous gossip surrounding his early poems, Donne, on the eve of his ordination, contemplated issuing them in book form at his own expense. With a great flourish of secretiveness he writes: "It is that I am brought to a necessity of printing my poems, and addressing them to my Lord Chamberlain. This I mean to do forthwith, not for much public view, but at mine own cost, a few copies. I apprehend some incongruities in the resolution, and I know what I shall suffer from many interpretations; but I am at an end of much considering that." It is also conceivable that Harington had *Orlando Furioso* printed privately: "For indeed I suffred some part of the printed copies to go among my frends, & some more perhaps went against my will," just as Daniel wanted his *History of England* reserved for the eyes of certain benefactors: "This Peece of our History, which heere I divulge not, but impart privatly to such Worthy Persons as have favored my indeavors herein." In these last three cases we again detect the hypocrisies of amateurs who abhorred exposure to the gross boors that constituted the reading public, but who were willing to utilize the printing press to serve their own materialistic ends — Harington to gain the favor of the queen, Donne to extract (with decorum) money from some unidentified benefactor, and Daniel to make repayment to those who had favored his writings.[29]

Finally, worse than a subsidy was employment as a

printer's hack: this was the inferno — at least in the eyes of professionals at the close of Elizabeth's reign. For at this time printers like Wolfe and Danter ran factories: they hired writers to english foreign tracts, to produce sensational topical pamphlets, or to prepare a paste book with snippets from various works, a minimum of rewriting, and new prefatory material for the sake of topicality. Working for printers, however, had not always been the occupation of hacks. Erasmus was willing to accept the printer's hire; and Caxton summoned "master John Skelton, late created poet laureate in the university of Oxenford, to oversee and correct this said book, and t'address and expoun' whereas shall be found fault to them that shall require it." Other publishers commissioned works of significance. George Bishop not only paid William Fulke £40 during the nine months required for the composition of *A Defense of the Sincere and True Translations* (1583) but also provided quarters for the author, his two servants, and his horses. Golding undertook Hemmingsen's *A Postill, or Exposition of the Gospels* (1569) at the request of "Lucas Harison and George Byshop Stationers, men well mynded towardes godlinesse and true Religion." In his exile during Mary's reign John Fox was a reader at Basel, and upon his return to England in 1564 he accepted employment in John Day's establishment. Turbervile compiled *The Noble Art of Venery or Hunting* (1575) at the expense of the printer George Barker, who obtained works of foreign writers to aid the translator. One of the most important historical works of the period, *Chronicles of England, Scotland, and Ireland* (1577–1586), was commissioned by Reginald Wolfe. Probably without Wolfe's financial resources this work would not have been written.[30]

The most famous book in the language, the so-called

King James Bible, was in part subsidized by publishers, who paid six revisers thirty shillings each a week for nine months. Although it might be uncharitably argued that in this instance stationers backed a book with an enormous sales potential, at least they rewarded their employees with high salaries in an age when, according to Lodge, a gentleman could live handsomely on an annual income of £40. On the other hand, it is apparent that publishers paid most generously for writings involving the fewest risks — religious books for which there was obvious demand and histories or chronicles for which in a self-conscious and patriotic nation there was certain to be a slow but steady sale.

As stationers strove to cater to a larger reading audience, they employed writers to produce short pamphlets intended to sell in large quantities at a low price. When he composed his fierce attack upon the Jesuit Campion, *A Brief Answer Made unto Two Seditious Pamphlets* (1582), Munday stayed at the "dwelling in Barbicon" of John Charlewood. Later he accepted employment with John Wolfe, who also sought out hacks with the skill of a ferret. Edward Aggas, Anthony Chute, Francesco Marquino, and probably many others now unknown to us supplied Wolfe's factory with French tracts, newsletters, and other trivia. Wolfe's most erudite hack (Nashe notwithstanding) was Gabriel Harvey, who for at least nine months lived with the printer's family and ground out the ephemeral fare his employer specialized in. If Nashe is to be trusted, Harvey fled, owing Wolfe £36. Although he heaped characteristically venomous abuse upon Harvey for selling out to a printer, Nashe himself accepted lodging with Danter and was a paid hack, probably as early as 1593. In *Pierce's Supererogation* Harvey labels Nashe "Danters Maulkin" and claims that the latter "remaineth most humbly, and thrise-affectionately bounden to the Right-honorable Printing-house, for his poore shifts of apparell, and his rich capp of maintenaunce." (There is probably more truth in Middleton's observation than in most modern commentaries upon the fliting of the two men: their railing, according to Middleton, "was but the running a tilt of wits in booksellers' shops on both sides of John of Paul's churchyard.)" [31]

Unquestionably publishers traded upon the chronic poverty of writers. When Harvey turned out tracts for Wolfe, he was a Cambridge outcast and poverty-ridden. Despite the occasional patronage of the Careys, Nashe was perpetually in trouble with his creditors. A character in *The Return from Parnassus*, who echoes Harvey's remarks about Nashe and Danter, acknowledges that he remains "thrise humblie & most affectionatlie bounde to the right honorable printing house for my poore shiftes of apparell." Ingenioso, who appears to be a dramatic representation of Nashe, swears that "if poverty presse not too much; Ile correct no presse but the presse of the people"; and Judicio comments: "Would it not grieve any good spirritt to sit a whole moneth nitting over a lousy beggarly Pamphlet, and like a needy Phisitian to stand whole yeares tooting and tumbling the filth that falleth from so many draughty inventions as daily swarme in our printing house?" Little wonder that writers' sensibilities were lacerated when they were driven to produce "filth." Despite the pretensions they entertained of acting the role of gentlemen after graduation from the universities, they frequently found themselves in positions not unlike those of domestics. For not only did they produce the publisher's trivia, they had to live in his house. [32]

Though professionals had ample grounds for attacking the miserly payments of stationers and the degrading conditions imposed upon them by a trade interested primarily in promoting its own interests, criticism, even in the years of self-assertion at the end of the century, was restrained. In fact, authors were powerless to battle the Stationers' Company; they were unable to bite publicly the hand that did not feed them. Publishers were not fools; they had no intention of printing diatribes denouncing their greed. Hence, one searches in vain for scathing indictments or acute analyses of the economic problems of authorship. Chettle, more like a moralist than an author, vouches that in the golden past no printer "would set finger to a lascivious line," but in 1592, when he wrote, only "ballad-singers" are in demand. In a personal letter to William Cotton in 1595 Nashe writes that printers seek "the coppy of my L. of essex voyage & the ballet of the thre score & foure knights" and show no interest in serious works. "Only mr Harrington of late," Nashe continues, "hath sett up sutch filthy stinking jakes in pouls churchyard, that the stationers wold give any mony for a cover for it." Like many other authors, then and now, Rich complains that "the Printer himselfe, to make his booke the more vendible, doth rather desire a glorious Title, than a good Booke." Until Wither and John Taylor ventured into the printing business themselves, stationers effectively stifled authors and ran their trade as they saw fit.[33]

Although stationers frequently took advantage of authors, they were by no means unmitigated villains. For by the end of the sixteenth century they had created a prosperous business, which in turn had produced a new literary profession. Without a sound business organization to manufacture and distribute books, aspiring middle-class writers would never have had the opportunity to write; at best they would have been scriveners transcribing manuscripts for wealthy amateurs. Though Churchyard, Rich, Robinson, Dekker, Greene, and many others never wallowed in luxury because of literary remuneration, they could have found neither audience nor prestige (such as they had) without stationers. Fees paid to writers were small (smaller than many historians have supposed), because publishers were zealous in protecting themselves and their capital from real (and imaginary) risks. Stationers could do little about the high cost of their commodity in relation to the prices of foods and other necessities. If the prices of books had been reduced, probably neither publisher nor writer would have benefited markedly. Furthermore, large numbers of book purchasers are possible only when living standards are high enough to support them. Such was not the case in the Elizabethan age. Finally, authors were in part responsible for their plight: many stubbornly affected amateurism and feigned indifference to the economics of publication — yet, like Dr. Johnson, they wrote for money or its equivalent in preferment. Much too frequently they dreamed of Parnassus — without the pungent odors of presses, materialistic stationers, stalls crudely decorated in order to sell literary wares, and indifferent customers.

CHAPTER SIX

CENSORSHIP

O<small>N</small> September 27, 1579, the London populace, gluttonous for gory spectacle, flocked to the scaffold. They were not to be disappointed: the show was a good one. John Stubbes had intrepidly but tactlessly voiced in *The Discovery of a Gaping Gulf* the disgust and fear with which many Englishmen, including Sidney, viewed Elizabeth's prolonged flirtation with connubial bliss — her erratic relationship with the Duke of Alençon, who in addition to being a Catholic was a Frenchman. On this day Stubbes, the publisher William Page, and the printer Hugh Singleton were to receive punishment for trespassing upon the province of majesty. For a moment the drama almost collapsed before it began, when Singleton for mysterious reasons (probably influential friends intervened successfully) was suddenly spared physical torture and compelled only to humble himself before the spectators. But the throng was not to be cheated of a spectacle. Stubbes and Page were, if witnesses are to be trusted, patriotic English-

[171]

men. Although John Harington reports what one would expect, that Stubbes swooned when his hand was severed, the eminent historian William Camden, who was also a spectator, declares that after the rash author lost his right hand, he doffed his hat with his left hand, and exclaimed in stentorian tones, "God save the Queen!" Though disagreeing with Camden as to Stubbes's behavior, Harington records that Page lifted his stump and said to the crowd, "I have left there a true Englishman's hand." With that he went from the scaffold, in Harington's words, "very stoutlie, and with great corradge." [1]

Whatever the facts about this notorious incident, some modern writers, unimpressed by what would appear to be the overly zealous patriotism of the two contemporary witnesses, have made the loss of the right hand a symbol of Tudor censorship and its inhuman repressiveness. Miss Sheavyn, for example, asserts that "in the sixteenth century, when the function of government in relation to literary production was mainly to pounce upon possible offenders, it was rare good fortune for the writer to succeed in eluding its grip." There is no doubt that the authorities, sometimes with genuine zeal but often with no more energy than the issuance of awesome proclamations demanded, attempted to ferret out recusant authors, yet many Puritans, with the open protection of Leicester and Walsingham, expressed their views in tracts and in sermons. Stubbes lost his hand, but "Martin Marprelate" successfully evaded the government and the established church. The Star Chamber punished a defendant because a personal letter contained infamous matter; that the letter had not been published, as the accused pleaded, mattered not at all. Yet the abuse of Burghley in Spenser's *Mother Hubbard's Tale* resulted only in the recall of the edition. Only when the Elizabethan settlement was under direct attack, or the government considered its existence imperiled, as, for instance, during the Jesuit mission in the 1580's, did authorities impose the death penalty.[2]

Equally subject to modification is the point made by another commentator: "Gascoigne, who experienced more than most the keen edge of criticism and interference, was so cowed by his experiences with the *Posies* that thereafter he wrote only didactic poetry, the *Glasse of Governement,* the *Steele Glas,* and other slighter poems in the same vein, or didactic prose like the *Droome of Doomes Day* or *A Delicate Diet for daintiemouthde Droonkardes."* Here, in addition to presuming to read Gascoigne's mind and to articulate his unexpressed fears, J. W. Saunders states that the ever-present threat of governmental censorship forced Gascoigne to write innocuous didactic works. But two points are overlooked: the *Posies* apparently contained material, despite its obscurity for modern critics, of a libelous nature; and, more important, Gascoigne, an amateur who took up literature to further his own social and political aspirations, with or without "interference" was compelled to write what he assumed would gain him favor. So too must the allegation that "the printed-book poets were, if anything, even more at the mercy of the middle-class authorities who regulated the London book-stalls than their colleagues of the public theatres" be qualified. For, just as puritanical magistrates failed to close permanently the "sin-infected" theaters of London, so they failed to change stationers from businessmen into moralists.[3]

It is scarcely consistent with the facts or the complexities inherent in any discussion of censorship to lay all blame upon the government, to create a picture of writers shaking in their boots and composing inoffensive material, or to dogmatize as to the extent the fear of governmental reprisal motivated writers. Finally, despite the lurid pictures of some modern critics, censorship in Tudor England was not ever-vigilant and ruthlessly consistent. Frequently censors dozed, often they were obtuse, sometimes they were lazy, and occasionally, like lawyers, their palms were greased with angels. This was Elizabethan England, not the mythical-real terrain of Kafka and Orwell, where only blacks and whites are evident and neutral shades are nonexistent.

If, instead of resorting to melodramatic oversimplifications one recalls the observation of one of the great Elizabethan scholars, E. A. Arber — "All our preconceptions to the contrary notwithstanding, the Press in England in the reign of Queen Elizabeth was probably the freest in Europe; as free indeed as the political situation at this time would admit of" — one begins to see Elizabethan censorship in perspective. Censorship cannot in fairness be judged in absolute terms. Relatively speaking, Englishmen had more liberty of expression than people in other lands, just as they had a government which, though a monarchy, differed from foreign governments in its responsiveness to the populace. During the forty-five years of Elizabeth's reign, moreover, the amount of freedom granted her subjects varied considerably. In the 1560's and 1570's Elizabeth suppressed unorthodox religious treatises and books directly attacking her person, but she willingly accepted recantations and, characteristically, avoided extreme punishments. At the time when it appeared that the queen had succeeded in solidifying her nation, in making effective the Elizabethan settlement, and in contributing to the economic prosperity of her subjects, new dangers threatened. There were Catholic Mary in Scotland, the militant Jesuits, strengthened by the excommunication of Elizabeth, and the deteriorating relations with Spain. Stubbes was among the first to suffer from the renewed vigilance of the government. In the 1580's recusants, especially Catholics, were punished with a severity without parallel in Elizabeth's reign. Even after the great triumph of 1588 the government did not abandon its controls or curtail the activities of its informers. Not only was there the prospect of renewed war with Spain but also the threat of Essex and the problem of succession. Subjects feared to express themselves freely in personal correspondence. In a letter to Robert Sidney in 1595 Rowland Whytes discusses the queen's anger because *A Conference about the Next Succession to the Crown of England* was dedicated to the Earl of Essex, and adds in a postscript: "To wryte of these Things are dangerous in so perillous a Tyme but I hope yt wilbe no Offence to impart unto you Thactions of this Place." [4]

The sixteenth-century climate of opinion, however, sanctioned neither democracy nor democratic aspirations. Discipline in the state and in the church was almost unanimously accepted. Certainly one of the cardinal aims of Tudor policy was to reestablish discipline in the state; and Elizabeth, despite her artful vacillation, pursued this policy throughout her reign and for the most part received the cooperation of her subjects: like all great politicians she subtly molded public opinion by never directly flouting it. Discipline within the church was also accepted, although one sect steadfastly resisted the strictures of another. Puritans in spite of their assaults upon the episcopacy were not modern democrats; like many other minority groups they were more intolerant than their adversaries. Catholics, Anglicans, and Puritans were in complete agreement in their willingness to ban objectionable literature; they differed only in what they considered objectionable. Catholics banned the writings of heretics; they encouraged Henry VIII to support their warfare against biblical translations and paraphrases when they perceived the inadequacy of clerical edicts. With less rigidity and less consistency Anglicans were ready to suppress the writings of Catholics and Puritans. Puritans joined Anglicans in attacking the books of papists. Only because they lacked power were Puritans unable to suppress nonpuritanical books. More fiercely than Anglicans they inveighed against imaginative literature, perhaps because they perceived the dangers to religion in the increasing secularism of professional writers.

In addition to prelates and Puritans other Elizabethans accepted censorship of books, and in many instances implored the government to take sterner measures against nonconformists and against purveyors of filth. In *The Dial of Princes* (1557) Sir Thomas North evows that "manye bookes deserve to be broken and burnte," since readers "learne not how they oughte to flye vice, but rather what way they may with more pleasour embrace it." After citing classical precedents for burning books, Becon, in *The Book of Matrimony* (1564), warns Englishmen of "the day of judgement" because they "banishe not, nor burn not, but rather Print, publishe, set forth and sell baudy balades and filthy bookes unto the corruption of the reders." The humanist-teacher of Elizabeth, Roger Ascham, was more serve in his attitude toward printed material than his pupil and indeed than many Anglican bishops. His impassioned attack upon translations of Italian books borders on hysteria despite its sincere concern (and fallacious logic) for the state and his countrymen:

It is pitie, that those, which have authoritie and charge, to allow and dissalow bookes to be printed, be no more circumspect herein, than they are. Ten Sermons at Paules Crosse do not so much good for movyng men to trewe doctrine, as one of those bookes do harme, with inticing men to ill living. Yea, I say farder, those bookes, tend not so moch to corrupt honest livyng, as they do, to subvert trewe Religion. Mo Papistes be made, by your mery bookes of Italie, than by your earnest bookes of Lovain. And bicause our great Phisicians, do winke at the matter, and make no counte of this sore, I, . . . though I have no authoritie to amend the sore my selfe, yet I will declare my good will, to discover the sore to others.

As every student of the Elizabethan stage knows, London magistrates, not all of whom were Puritans, glared at the theaters with righteous wrath and charged that morals were undermined and licentiousness encouraged by stage spectacles. If they had had their way, the dramatic glories of the age would never have appeared on the boards. Similarly, William Vaughan, in *The Golden Grove* (1600), concludes "that many of our English rimers and ballet-makers deserve for their baudy sonnets, and amorous allurements, to bee banished, or severely punished." Eleven years later, in *The Spirit of Detraction*, he is still "intreating your further vigilancy in rooting out those vaine Vines, which according to the nature of ill weedes will in time over-grow your pruned plants." [5]

Though Gosson assailed the theater and Lodge defended it, fundamentally their views were not so divergent as they thought. Lodge abhors "those poets that savor of ribaldry," and "will with the zealous admit the expullcion of such enormities." Where Gosson, however, shows no mercy to offenders, Lodge proposes to "correct" abuses "with advise" from wise statesmen. In his discussion of the lewd matter in such authors as Ovid and Martial, Webbe concedes, "If they be prohibited from the tender and unconstant wits of children and young mindes, I thinke it not without good reason." F. S. observes that "filthy and unchast Pamphlets, (whereof the World is too full) are fitter to be burned as corrupters of Youths." Thomas Heywood, the dramatist of the bourgeoisie, "could wish that such as are condemned for their licentiousness, might by a generall consent bee quite excluded our society." Nashe maintains that "amisse it were not, if these which meddle with the Arte they knowe not were bequethed to Bridwell, there to learne a new occupation." An anonymous poet, in *Certain Elegies, Done by Sundry Excellent Wits* (1612), after enumerating the excrescences of artistic mountebanks, concludes tersely and dogmatically, "Burne em all." [6]

Clearly, then, public opinion accepted discipline and religious and political orthodoxy. (Even those who departed from governmental orthodoxy feared that diversity of viewpoint led to choas; their own deviations they rationalized with ease.) Except for a solitary voice now and then no one deplored the penalties imposed upon a Page or a Stubbes. In fact, Elizabeth's subjects frequently revealed more lust for blood than their ruler, nor were the sensibilities of artists offended by the brutalities of the age. Spenser, for example, has a revealing scene in *The Faerie Queene*. As Prince Arthur, the ideal knight and the epitome of justice, and Artegall approach the castle of Mercilla, who embodies the virtues of Elizabeth herself, they come upon a grisly scene.

> There as they entred at the Scriene, they saw
>   Some one, whose tongue was for his trespasse vyle
>   Nayld to a post, adjudged so by law:
>   For that therewith he falsely did revyle,
>   And foule blaspheme that Queene for forged guyle,
>   Both with bold speaches, which he blazed had,
>   And with lewd poems, which he did compyle;
>   For the bold title of a Poet bad
> He on himselfe had ta'en, and rayling rymes had sprad.

Thus there he stood, whylest high over his head,
  There written was the purport of his sin,
  In cyphers strange, that few could rightly read,
  BON FONT: but *bon* that once had written bin,
  Was raced out, and *Mal* was now put in.
  So now *Malfont* was plainely to be red;
  Eyther for th'evill, which he did therein,
  Or that he likened was to a welhed
Of evill words, and wicked sclaunders by him shed.

The knights do not cringe or waste sympathy upon the poet-railler: as in Dante's world, the punishment fits the crime. Without comment they pass by "unto the presence of that gratious Queene." Mercilla is no less "gratious" for punishing those who place national safety and God-enjoined order in jeopardy. In doing so she has fulfilled the responsibilities of majesty.[7]

In truth, Elizabeth was more enlightened and humane than her poetic counterpart. Though personal allusions consistently provoked her wrath, diversity of opinion, personal aberrations, and licentiousness (the *bête noire* of puritanism, and few Elizabethans were not tainted with puritanism) she tended to disregard except in moments of peril to her government and her countrymen. It is true that what Puckering said to parliament in 1593 about freedom of speech conveyed in essence Elizabeth's attitude toward freedom of the press:

Her Majesty granteth you liberal but not licentious speech; liberty, therefore, but with due limitation. For even as there can be no good consultation where all freedom of advice is barred, so will there be no good conclusion where every man may speak what he listeth, without fit observation of persons, matters, times, places and other needful circumstances. It shall be meet therefore that each man of you contain his speech within the bounds of loyalty and good discretion.

It is therefore true that Elizabeth uttered no noble sentiments about liberty — historically, in fact, she was buttressing a dying way of life — nor did she espouse liberalism, partly because of her conservatism and partly because of the perils her nation faced at the end of the century. But her actions as well as her refusals to act were often more effective than high-sounding platitudes. While fanatics were ready to fetter England with their dogmatisms, Elizabeth, sometimes almost alone, trod the middle way and thereby protected her people's freedom. As Allen observes, "Had Parsons had his way and England become subject to a Spanish Catholic, had Travers succeeded in getting his 'discipline' established, there would have been far less freedom in England than there was under Elizabeth." [8]

Almost as important as political considerations were the activities of pressure groups to preserve what they claimed to be public morality or to protect their own self-interests under cloak of the national welfare; the economic realities of publication, the publisher's fears and his decisions as to marketable and unmarketable subject matter; the author's economic dependency, the sources of his income, and the patrons to whom he catered.

Censorship without legal support appears in every society, either exerted collectively through public opinion or through organized groups. In 1591 the traders with Russia, alarmed lest their trade be curtailed, forced the recall of Dr. Giles Fletcher's *Of the Russe Commonwealth.* Merchants protested successfully against Nashe's scathing but medieval criticisms in *Christ's Tears over Jerusalem.* Intrenched economic interests commanded such influence with a government in desperate need of resources to maintain ships and soldiers that their desires became orders, and criticism was frequently silenced. Their verbal demands we know nothing of; in a compact society like the

Elizabethan a word to a highly placed official, or to an influential member of the Stationers' Company, undoubtedly stopped publication of certain offensive manuscripts.

In addition to official censors and self-appointed censors the government had a formidable ally in the Stationers' Company. By the proclamations of 1557 and 1586 the company became in effect an agency of the crown, when it was empowered to seize and destroy the presses of members who printed contrary to edict. Since printing was a business venture, and a rapidly expanding one at that, and since the trade depended for its survival upon profits, stationers could "interpret" the various restrictions upon printing in the light either of national interest or of self-interest. That the latter was often decisive is hardly surprising. While the authorities were calling in unsold copies of John Hayward's *Henry IV*, John Wolfe was running off a second impression. No doubt, since, by his own declaration, "never any book was better sould or more desired that ever be printed," Wolfe realized enough from the sale of five hundred or six hundred copies of the first edition to pay the fine without personal sacrifice. Other stationers had similar experiences. The unwritten rules of an acquisitive society militated against official regulation. Publishers, after all, were little different from sea captains who cheated the royal coffers, nobles who winked at (perhaps even subsidized) recusant literature, or merchants who were only honest when their customers' eyes were sharp. On the other hand, fear of confiscation of books, loss of presses and type, or a transfer of a royal monopoly may have led some stationers to reject potentially dangerous pamphlets. It is impossible to determine with any accuracy what writers and what books were rejected because printers refused to risk governmental interference.[9]

The lack of substantial compensation for authorship and the consequent reliance upon nobles and wealthy patrons for stipends as well as sinecures constituted another type of control over writers. So long as they were dependent upon subsidies, they frequently paid lip service to the opinions and biases of Maecenas. Like Faustus, many amateurs were not averse to selling their souls for the sake of advancement in the church, the universities, or the government. Professionals like Greene, Nashe, and Dekker were not slow to humble themselves and to pour heaven-shattering praise upon nobles or wealthy merchants who might reward them. Authors were not necessarily hypocritical; many probably subscribed to the views of the upper classes either out of sincere conviction or because of their desire to rise socially. Regardless of their motivation and their sincerity, the important point is this: patronage unquestionably had a more direct effect upon authors in inducing conformity of opinion than had the laws promulgated by the Tudors.

Elizabethan censorship can be evaluated only within the historical context, which is a complex of legal, social, and economic restraints. Similarly, the tendency to impose twentieth-century standards upon a past age must be avoided, since it is easy to spotlight the weaknesses of the past and to gloss over the inconsistencies of modern English-speaking nations in the regulation of printed matter. The Tudor ogre is a twentieth-century notion which not only ignores the realities of our era but also fails to account for the greatness of Elizabethan literature in spite of voluntary and involuntary censorship. All societies impose upon intellectual, political, and artistic endeavors boundaries either explicitly formulated in law or, more frequently, collectively asserted through the unconscious assumptions of a people. These assumptions —

the climate of opinion — are unquestionably more co-
ercive and binding than laws. Finally, most Elizabethans,
like most other people in all ages and in all societies, accepted censorship with its curbs upon freedom and without
discernible tension or embarrassment lived with it.

Some, however, read what they wished despite awesome
(but repetitious) proclamations and solemn warnings of
punishments, and rationalized their conduct. The Puritan
was not disturbed when he placed God above Caesar and
read forbidden translations of the Bible. He let his conscience be his guide. So did the Catholic. Similarly, others
justified their violations of laws. This is not to suggest
that regulations were blatantly and universally ignored:
most Elizabethan readers were probably compliant because
they shared the beliefs and the fears of their rulers. But
violations are of significance since they point up the
cleavage between theory and practice and demonstrate
the fallacy of the myth that when Tudors decreed subjects obeyed.

For twenty or thirty years printing was a novelty, a toy
for wealthy patrons; there were no compelling reasons to
regulate the trade. Printing gradually became a business
which sold its wares to all classes, and, since its growth
coincided with the split in Christianity, it was no longer
a harmless activity; it posed an immediate threat to religious uniformity. Hence, only a few years after Luther
pounded on the doors in Wittenberg, in 1524, the English
church began to promulgate regulations of the trade: new
books had to be approved by religious authorities, booksellers were forbidden to handle Luther's tracts, and foreign books could be imported only with the consent of
Cardinal Wolsey and the Bishop of London. Although the
church acted quickly to exert its authority over the press,
controls did not bring automatic compliance. As Reed

points out, "Nothing more clearly shows the triumph of the heretical writers than the licence issued by the good Tunstall to his friend More in 1527, permitting him to have heretical books and even ballads or trifles, 'nugae,' in order that he might reply to and refute them. It was a confession of the defeat of the repressive methods." The church, however, did not publicly acknowledge defeat. But by 1529, only five years after its first proclamation, the church turned to Henry VIII and, without awareness of the permanent effects of its action, began to surrender its powers to secular authority. After this date proclamations controlling the activities of stationers bore the royal signature, and offenders appeared before nonecclesiastical courts. This transfer of authority did not drastically alter the situation. In 1534 a church convocation again requested the king to ban the circulation of unorthodox tracts, and Henry issued the Act of 1534, providing for supervision of the printing trade and prohibiting the importation of heretical writings. In 1538 the government enacted the most comprehensive code of censorship up to that time, and it transferred to the privy council and other appointed officials the power to censor books. In 1546 a royal proclamation specifically banned the works of Tyndale, Coverdale, Wycliffe, and other nonconformists, and ordered their books confiscated. By this time Henry's fiats had become repetitious.[10]

During Edward's brief reign old proclamations were rephrased and the authority of the state reasserted. Catholic books were repeatedly censured, and the king's library at Westminster was purged of "superstitious books." In 1549 the privy council ordered "that from hensforth no prenter sholde prente or putt to vente any Englisshe booke butt suche as sholde first be examined by Mr. Secretary Peter, Mr. Secretary Smith, and Mr. Cicill, or the one of them, and allowed by the same, undre payne, &c." This was but a restatement of provisions in the Act of 1538. These repetitions suggest that smugglers and unimportant booksellers were not the only ones who foiled the government's attempts to regulate the distribution of books, and that many Englishmen did not shed their religion like old clothes and complacently assume the quick-changing garb of majesty.[11]

Spurred by her sincere devotion to Catholicism and by her earnest desire to lead England back into the fold of the church universal, Mary had no patience with what must have seemed to her the halfhearted measures of her family. With a heavy hand and a fanaticism unrepresentative of the Tudors and her countrymen she wanted to put claws into the censorship laws. In 1553 she decreed that books were to be printed only upon royal authorization. (She forgot that in 1538 her father and in 1549 her brother had issued similar decrees.) Two years later she issued a "new" proclamation, listing once more books which had been objectionable since 1524. (Rather than upon English precedents, she probably drew upon the first Catholic index of 1544.) She commanded "that no person or persons . . . from henceforth presume to brynge or conveye . . . into this realme, any bokes, wrytynges or workes, . . . conteynynge false doctryne, contrarye, and agaynste the catholique fayth, and the doctryne of the catholyque Churche." Not satisfied with all-inclusive legal statements of this kind, she granted the power of enforcement "to all Bisshoppes and Ordinaries, and all Justices of peace." When two years later, in 1557, Mary permitted the incorporation of the Stationers' Company and added printers to her ferrets, clerics, justices great and small, and businessmen were united in a frenzied search for subversive literature. In numbers there may be strength, but not always success. By January 1558, Mary was compelled to empower yet another commission to search out and seize heretical books. Later in the year, in what proved to be a dying gesture of this defender of the faith, she decreed that any one possessing or reading forbidden books "shall . . . be reputed and taken for a rebel and shall without further delay be executed for that offense according to the order of martial law." By this act she accomplished little except to contribute to the unpleasant epithet with which her name is associated.[12]

Mary's less devout but more politically astute half-sister dealt with censorship in an early proclamation. Though she censured printers who "for covetousnes cheifly regard not what they print, so thei may have gaine," fundamentally Elizabeth lacked a novel approach to the problem. Borrowing from the edicts of her forebears,

The Quenes majestie straytly chargethe and commaundethe, that no manner of person shall print any manner of boke or paper, of what sort, nature, or in what language soever it be, excepte the same be first licenced by her majestie by expresse wordes in writynge, or by .vi. of her privy counsel, or be perused and licensed by the archbysshops of Cantorbury and Yorke, the bishop of London, the chauncelours of both unyversities, the bishop beyng ordinary, and the Archdeacon also of the place where any suche shalbe printed, or by two of them, wherof the ordinary of the place to be alwaies one. . . . And bycause many pampheletes, playes and balletes, be often times printed, . . . Her Majestie likewise commaundeth, that no manner of person shall enterprise to print any such, except the same be to him lycenced by suche her Majesties commyssioners or .iii. of them, as be appoynted in the citye of London to here, and determine divers causes ecclesiasticall, tending to the execution of certayne statutes, made last parliament for unyformitye of order in religion.

Unless the three ecclesiastical members of the commission objected, older works on religion and government could be reprinted without license. Finally, the act provided that the names of licensers should appear at the conclusion of every book "for a testimonie of the alowance thereof." Thus, Elizabeth laid down the old-new tenets of censorship for her reign.[13]

Like previous attempts the decree of 1559 did not check the distribution and sale of unauthorized works. (Few books of the period, for example, contain the names of licensers.) In June 1566, when the privy council was concerned about the activities of Puritans, new regulations for the reform of "disorders" in the printing trade were issued, and penalties became more severe. But criticism was not muted. Seven years later *An Admonition to Parliament* was specifically singled out for confiscation. Equally futile were the government's renewed attempts to prohibit the smuggling of heretical books printed abroad. Speaking in the Star Chamber on November 28, 1567, the lord keeper noted the circulation of seditious books; though he was no advocate of "bloody laws," he deemed it better "for a man to be twice whipped than once hanged." In 1569, 1570, and 1573, the throne ordered this bootlegging of books ended, but it continued on a vast scale throughout Elizabeth's reign. A. C. Southern estimates that, before 1580, twenty thousand recusant books were smuggled into England and clandestinely distributed, and that slightly over one hundred Catholic tracts were printed between 1559 and 1583. This was an illicit traffic of sizable proportions.[14]

In addition, though the Tudors had banned unauthorized presses, recusants were able either to employ English stationers or to smuggle in their own presses from abroad. By his own admission the famous Jesuit Parsons maintained two presses in England from 1580 to 1582, on which were printed five tracts. In condemning the works of Henrick Niclas on October 3, 1580, the privy council implied that his books were being printed in England. Lawrence Vaux's *A Catechism of Christian Doctrine Necessary for Children* (1583) was printed in Antwerp and probably in England. Thomas Gybson narrowly escaped hanging at Bury St. Edmund in 1584 for binding sheets of tracts written by Robert Browne and Robert Harrison and printed in Middleburg. The probabilities are that as more information is uncovered we shall find that many works of recusants were printed surreptitiously in England. One can only conclude that the language of censorship was stronger than the vigilance exercised by officials who had unlimited powers to search and seize.[15]

It would appear that, except in times of national crisis, Elizabeth had no serious intention of punishing offenders to the full extent of the law. Stubbes she allowed to be mutilated because he offended her person — and was brazen enough to express in public what she knew only too well. For the most part she was no more anxious to punish subversive writers than she was to consent to the death penalty for Mary of Scotland. The nonconformist authors of *An Admonition to Parliament,* John Field and Thomas Wilcox, were confined in Newgate, but after six months the privy council was so "gladd of the good conformitie" of the prisoners that they were intrusted to Archdeacon Molines until "they might have more occasion to procure her Majesties pardon." Robert Browne was released from prison on the security of Burghley for his good behavior; eventually Browne recanted. Burghley, in 1587, requested Stubbes to write the "official" reply to one of Cardinal Allen's tracts, and Walsingham utilized the talents of Thomas Cartwright, despite his trenchant criticisms of the established church.[16]

Toward Catholics, however, the government showed

less mercy. The Jesuit mission in the 1580's, supported by foreign financial assistance and motivated by desires which any ruler would deem traitorous, was countered with a violence unknown in England since the days of Mary. The scaffolds which in 1577 Holinshed, how accurately we cannot know, reported rotting from lack of use were in these years gory with the blood of booksellers and authors. This is the period in which Norton, co-author of *Gorboduc,* became infamous as "Mr. Norton the Rackmaster," because he was said to have boasted that he had stretched a priest a foot longer than God had made him. In 1581, the Queen, taking note of the new situation and the threat to English sovereignty, condemned writing "containing any false seditious and slanderous matter to the defamation of the Queen's Majesty that now is, or to the encouraging . . . of any insurrection or rebellion within this realm," and further decreed that "every such offence shall be deemed felony, and the offenders therein . . . shall suffer such pains of death and forfeiture as in case of feloney is used, without any benefit of clergy or sanctuary." Here Elizabeth's language is reminiscent of Mary's in 1558, but the provocations to a ruler whose natural tendency was to procrastinate and compromise were great. It was rumored that books like *A Treatise of Schism,* presumably written by Gregory Martin, "exhorted the Queen's Gentlewomen to act the like against the Queen as Judith had done with Applause and Commendations against Holofernes." The printer of this tract was hanged at Tyburn on January 11, 1584. (About the same time Elias Thacker and John Copping were hanged at Bury St. Edmunds for distributing the works of Browne and Harrison.) In the following year Thomas Alfield, who had imported Cardinal Allen's *True and Modest Defence of English Catholics,* and Thomas Websley, a dyer who had helped to distribute the tracts, received the same punishment.[17]

Elizabeth's last major attempt to regulate the press was the Star Chamber decree of 1586. This order compelled all printers to record the number of presses in their establishments, permitted printing only in London, except for the presses at Oxford and Cambridge, strictly forbade secret presses with the penalty that press and type were to be destroyed and the printer imprisoned for a year, granted the warden of the Stationers' Company power to seize secret presses, and banned new presses until the present number was reduced. No books were to be printed without the approval of the Archbishop of Canterbury or the Bishop of London, or deputies appointed by them. Punishment for failure to heed the licensing system was six months' imprisonment. This was, according to Siebert, "the most comprehensive regulation of the press of the entire Tudor period, continuing in effect until 1637." Yet, essentially, it reassembled and restated earlier regulations, and its promulgation conclusively reveals the failures of the government to impose its will upon its subjects.[18]

The Act of 1586 was destined to work no miracles. Two years later Archbishop Whitgift, unable to cope personally with the gigantic problems of licensing, delegated his authority to subordinates, who frequently showed no more zeal than their superiors in scrutinizing books for heretical and seditious material. Samuel Harsnett, for instance, licensed Hayward's *Henry IV*, which evoked a storm in 1599 and led to the imprisonment of its author. (Though Harsnett's excuses were lame, his carelessness was only unusual in that this time it got him into trouble.) If censors napped, so did magistrates. In 1588 and 1589 the authorities were not able to capture "Martin," who must have been known to many of his associates in the Puritan movement. "Martin" and his henchmen scampered all over England, ingeniously disassembling their press and transporting it from one hiding place to another, mysteriously finding the necessary supplies for another pamphlet attacking the episcopacy. That in 1599 the ecclesiastics ordered burned, in Elizabeth's greatest bonfire of books, a number of satires and ribald works is the most concrete evidence that the new code was no more successful than earlier ones.[19]

This survey of sixteenth-century regulations of the press makes it clear that Tudor censorship had only nominal success. Whether the monarch was a zealot like Mary, entranced with visions of herself as a savior of England, or an adroit defender of religion for political reasons like Elizabeth, many Englishmen refused to adjust their religious views to royal decrees. The writings of heretics and nonconformists found audiences. Unauthorized ballads, romances, and bawdy books were not without readers. The church shrieked of eternal damnation, the state promised the gallows at Tyburn, but Englishmen were a stubborn lot.

On the other hand, only rarely did an Elizabethan oppose this control either on principle or on point of law. William Monson, judge of the Common Pleas, and a Mr. Dalton protested against the force of the statute under which Stubbes lost his right hand. For their intrepidity they were imprisoned and compelled to apologize to the queen. Martyrs and victims of the state's repressiveness never questioned the state's authority or proposed a concept of liberty that sanctioned and protected diversity of viewpoint. On the contrary, Stubbes reputedly praised the queen, and More jested on the scaffold without questioning the legality of his punishment. According to Holinshed, the executioner observed to the Duke of Norfolk, who had just placed his head on the block, "My lord, your head lieth not well." To this courteous recognition of position in a tragedy of manners, "I will make it lie well, saith he, and therewith lifting up his bodie he laid his necke even upon the blocke." [20]

For the most part the same immunity to criticism extended to royal advisors. Elizabeth pronounced the *Copy of a Letter Written by a Master of Art to His Friend in London* (more generally known as *Leicester's Commonwealth*) "malicious, false and scandalous." Criticism of her intimates was generally construed as an affront upon her person. In a letter to Walsingham, Norton termed seditious a book in which he was referred to as "Mr. Norton the Rackmaster." Not only monarchy, religion, and persons of great position were in effect sacrosanct, but also the established institutions of the realm were not to be subjected to abuse, direct or indirect. After the publication of *Three Proper and Witty Familiar Letters,* Gabriel Harvey "was advised by certaine honourable, and divers worshipfull persons, to interpreate my intention in more expresse terms: and thereupon discoursed everie particularitie, by way of Articles or Positions, in a large Apology of my duetiful, and entier affection to that flourishing Universitie [Cambridge], my deere Mother." [21]

Because of the government's religious predispositions it was permissible to caricature papists and Puritans as traitors, hypocrites, lechers, or what have you. Nor was action taken against what might be called the Elizabethan literature of social protest, which monotonously intoned, either from a moralistic or a secular bias, against evils which Chaucer had satirized two centuries earlier. But these criticisms were phrased in general terms, names were not cited, and ordinarily qualifications were stated. Especially was this true in the case of lawyers. In *The Defense of Cony-Catching* Greene cautiously takes the edge off his criticisms:

Doo not the Lawyers make long Pleaes, stand upon their demurres, and have their quirks and quiddities to make his poore Client a Cony? I speake not generally, for so they be the ministers of justice, and the Patrons of the poore mens right, but particularly of such as hold gaines their God, and esteeme more of coyne then of conscience.

In the same year a character in Lodge's *Euphues' Shadow* observes that lawyers "are miserable, for they get with care, they thrive by contention, they are all in the quantity not in qualitie, you know the predicaments, Philamis, I may not preach further." Such caution is comprehensible when one recalls that many of Elizabeth's advisors were lawyers and members of the Inns. Under the circumstances unqualified disparagement of the legal profession was, to put it mildly, injudicious, as Jonson learned when his *Poetaster* was published in 1602.[22]

Merchants were also quick to protest against objectionable views. Probably with the assistance of London magistrates, most of whom were successful businessmen, they compelled Nashe to soften his indictment of merchants in *Christ's Tears over Jerusalem*. With his customary sound and fury Nashe had termed English merchants more avaricious than usurers:

Is it not a common proverbe amongst us, when any man hath cosend or gone beyonde us, to say, Hee hath playde the Merchant with us? But Merchants, they turne it another way, and say, He hath playd the Gentleman with them. . . . The Merchant eates up the Gentleman, the Gentleman eates up the Yeoman, and all three do nothing but exclaime one upon another.

In the second edition this passage was altered and made

innocuous through qualifications and the substitution of "usurer" for "Merchant."

Many good men, many good magistrats are there in this City, diverse godly & wise counsellers hath she to provide for her peace, them no part of any reproofe of mine concerneth, how ever it may be otherwise thought. Other wicked livers in it questionlesse there be, which want no ill gotten goods, nor ill mindes to the common wealth. Verie good it were, when they are revealed, they had plague bills set upon their doores, to make them more noted and detestable. . . . the Usurer eateth up the Gentleman, and the Gentleman the yeoman, and all three being devoured one of another, do nothing but complaine one upon another.[23]

As Ralegh points out in the preface to his *History of the World,* to comment on recent history was to court punishment:

Howsoever, I know that it will be said by many, that I might have been more pleasing to the reader, if I had written the story of mine own times, having been permitted to draw water as near the well-head as another. To this I answer, that whosoever in writing a moderne history, shall follow truth too near the heels, it may happily strike out his teeth. There is no mistress or guide that hath led her followers and servants into greater miseries. He that goes after her too far off, loseth her sight, and loseth himself; and he that walks after her at a middle distance, I know not whether I should call that kind of course temper or baseness.

Though Ralegh was intrepid and sometimes rash, he also knew when to be cautious. For every Elizabethan knew of Stubbes's topicality and of the long history of imprisonments (or worse) for those who dared to write adversely on current happenings. One of the first nonreligious works censored during Elizabeth's reign was apparently a broadside, in 1561, which contained portraits of the queen and the king of Sweden side by side: "an Allowance to have

hir self joyned, as it wer, in Mariadg with the sayd Kyng."
In 1568 John Alde and his associates were committed to
prison because they had issued an eight-page pamphlet
concerning the Duke of Alençon. Though a queen's
marital arrangements were hardly a personal matter, especially after Mary's alliance with the detested Philip, Elizabeth consistently refused to sanction printed speculations
and gratuitous advice. Toward the conclusion of her reign
she showed similar abhorrence of public discussion of the
succession. Here too a matter of obvious national importance was peremptorily dealt with. Essex, for example,
was in constant difficulty because his friends and occasionally his enemies persisted in advancing his claims to
the throne. Hayward's dedication of *Henry IV* (1599) to
the ambitious earl infuriated the queen. According to
Wolfe, Essex said nothing when he read Hayward's dedication, but such an evasion was foolhardy when the subject
of the books was the usurpation of Henry IV. Earlier in
her reign Elizabeth, or her advisors, suppressed the implied
criticism of her Irish policy in the first edition of Holinshed's *Chronicles* as well as John Stow's account of the
Earl of Leicester in the second edition. (Leicester was at
the time out of favor because of his reckless expenditures
and highhanded conduct during the campaigns in the Low
Countries.) Hot-tempered Sir John Smith, who spoke his
mind regardless of circumstances only to find himself in
prison, castigated unnamed military commanders in *Certain Discourses Concerning Weapons* (1590); the book was
immediately called in.[24]

That Smith's libelous remarks were not tolerated is to
be expected. Though Gascoigne's allusions in *The Adventures of F. J.* elude scholarly sleuths, they were clear
enough to Elizabethans to get him into trouble. If Green-
law's argument is correct that the 1580 version of *Mother*

Hubbard's Tale was called in — his "evidence" seems more like conjecture than proof — Spenser's animal imagery did not camouflage his criticisms, and there can be little doubt, in view of contemporary references, that the 1592 edition of this satire was called in. In the late 1590's, when satires and epigrams began to pour from the presses, and when a previously unknown candor and salaciousness characterized many books, for the first time in the Elizabethan era authorities resorted to wholesale confiscation. A few years earlier with impunity Harvey and Nashe had heaped abuse on each other. In 1599 the Archbishop of Canterbury and the Bishop of London ordered that "all Nasshes bookes and Doctor Harvyes books be taken wheresoever they maye be found and that none of theire bookes bee ever printed hereafter." The two prelates also ordered burned Marston's *The Metamorphosis of Pygmalion's Image*, Guilpin's *Ski-aletheia, All Ovid's Elegies,* which included translations by Marlowe and elegies by Sir John Davies, *The Book against Women,* and the translation of Margaret of Navarre's *The Fifteen Joys of Marriage.* In addition, they directed "that noe Satyres or Epigrams be printed hereafter." The order also consigned to the flames Hall's *Vir-gidemiarum* and Thomas Cutwode's *Caltha Poetarum,* but both were exempted in the decree of June 4. The latter order called in all copies of *Willoby His Avisa,* first published in 1594; if the ingenious interpreters are correct, it contains a veiled attack upon the Essex-Southampton faction and a defense of Ralegh's coterie. Through this extraordinary bonfire the prelates endeavored to discourage libelous writings and to halt the output of indecent works. Sir Roderick, in *The Return from Parnassus,* shakes his head approvingly, because now "an old knight may have his wench in a corner without any Satyres or Epigrams." [25]

It is significant that the authorities did not confiscate

books except on religious or political grounds until the end of the sixteenth century. Yet, as one examines the titles of the books destroyed in 1599, one immediately is aware that the prelates were not hostile toward art: their purpose was to curb topical and libelous utterances characteristic of many books in the last decade of the century. If the church-men failed to accomplish their purpose, they at least did not like fanatics consign to the flames indiscriminately. In fact, the 1599 conflagration furnishes complete proof that literature was not tampered with in Elizabethan England, and that, as McKerrow pointed out long ago, not a single major literary work was censored in the era. Not many periods, it need scarcely be added, can make such a claim.

Another interesting fact about the bonfire of 1599 is the myopia evident in censors who swooped down on essentially unimportant works like the diatribes of Nashe and Harvey but overlooked the implications of Marlowe's plays. Fortunately for posterity, censors have generally been more concerned with the words than with the implications of subject matter. Sir Henry Herbert, master of the revels from 1623 to 1663, illustrates the point. In justifying his proposal to extend his powers to include books as well as stage plays, he observes:

> The designe is, that all prophaneness, of oathes, ribaldry, and matters reflecting upon piety, and the present government may bee obliterated, before there bee any action in a publique Theatre.
> The like equities there is, that all Ballads, songs and poems of that nature, should pass the same examinacion . . . because such things presently fly all over the Kingdom, to the Debauching and poisoning the younger sort of people, unles corrected and regulated.

Apparently Sir Henry thought that he was protecting the nation's youth when he altered "by Jesu" to "believe me," "by heaven" to "by these hilts," "by the just gods" to "by all that's good," or "the gods" to "my hopes." [26]

Since Puritans and their sympathizers lacked power during Elizabeth's era, indecency did not become a major issue in censorship. The puritanical magistrates were thwarted in their attempts to ban plays and to close theaters because of licentiousness. The officers of the Stationers' Company, according to Greg, stigmatized certain books and ballads as lewd, "though their standards of propriety seem rather uncertain." In his preface to *Tamburlaine* Richard Jones acknowledges that he has "(purposely) omitted and left out some fond and frivolous Jestures." Richard Field did not immediately enter Harington's *The Metamorphosis of Ajax* (1595) in the Stationers' Register because he feared the charge of indecency, and the author himself was so concerned about the reception of his discourse on privies that he implored Lady Russell to intervene with Burghley. Yet, with the exception of references to indecent ballads in the Stationers' Register, only in the fire of 1599 were licentious works burned, and their authors received slight punishment. So long as Elizabeth ruled, authors exercised self-restraint, a trait conspicuously absent during the reign of James, and middle-class morality did not make itself felt in literature or in the theater.[27]

The idealist may argue that, since the government had unlimited power to check freedom of expression and was not unwilling to exercise its power, Elizabethan authors lived in fear of repression and studiously avoided controversial matters. True, the separatist, the Catholic, and the critic of the government lived in fear — perhaps even the satirist after 1599. But it is doubtful that the literateur was any more worried in the sixteenth century than he is in the twentieth century. Miss Sheavyn calls attention to Spenser's letter to Ralegh, in which the poet speaks of selecting the age of Arthur as "furthest from the danger of envy, and suspicion of the present time . . . for avoiding of jealous opinions and misconstructions." "We are led to wonder," she continues, "whether English Literature may not have been deprived, by a suspicious Government, of a great epic based upon contemporary national history." But this idea assumes that a topical poem has greater immediacy than an allegory like *The Faerie Queene,* and that Spenser's genius was like Shaw's. To have Spenser's knights and ladies cavorting in Tudor England is to convert a romance into a farce and to impugne the artistic choice of genius. Furthermore, Spenser through his calculated choice achieved imaginative freedom such as he could not have had if he had confined himself to the contemporary scene. It is too facile to assume that external restrictions necessarily damage art. Geniuses like Shakespeare and Mozart achieved greatness within the forms and norms of their societies, and unfettered ages like our own do not produce more geniuses because of the relative absence of legal restraints.[28]

Although the greatest of Elizabethans once wrote of "arte made tung-tide by authoritie," few writers commented directly on censorship. Possibly they remained silent out of fear, but most authors were not seriously affected by the edicts and proclamations. Nashe comes close to attacking censorship in his ridicule of the traders who sought and obtained the suppression of Giles Fletcher's *Of the Russe Commonwealth*:

Out steps me an infant squib of the Innes of Court, that hath not halfe greased his dining cappe, or scarce warmed his Lawyers cushion, and he, to approve hymselfe an extravagant statesman, catcheth hold of a rush, and absolutely concludeth, it is meant of the Emperour of Ruscia, and that it will utterly marre the traffike into that country if all the Pamphlets bee not called in and suppressed, wherein that libelling word is mentioned.

Yet he seems more amused by the absurdity of the incident than alarmed about the principle of freedom of the press.[29]

Only the irascible moralist obsessed with man's depravity, Marston, explicitly assails censorship. While Mecho perjures himself, while Furia sells her sister to a brothel, while Crossus makes his wife "a stale," and while "fat-paunch'd Milo" corrupts innocents, Marston argues, no one intervenes. But

> . . . my satyrick vaine
> Shall muzled be, not daring out to straine
> His tearing paw? No gloomy Juvenall,
> Though to thy fortunes I disastrous fall.

It is doubtful that Marston is protesting anything more than libel laws which forbade his giving English names to Mecho and the others. Laws may have thwarted Marston's desire for specificity (and his neurotic needs) but certainly did not materially dampen his moral ardor. One does not feel that Marston was at all concerned with censorship as a principle; he was even unwilling to recognize the decency and kindness of regulations protecting erring mortals from righteous fanatics.[30]

Despite Shakespeare's comment, Marston's embittered protest, or the possibly unprinted criticisms of other objectors, this survey does not indicate that Elizabethan censorship seriously affected the quality, diversity, or subject matter of literature. And the statement is perhaps more than personal opinion; it is capable of empirical proof. No other period in England can boast of Shakespeare, Marlowe, Jonson, Chapman, and Webster in drama; Spenser,

Sidney, Daniel, Donne, and Drayton in poetry; Hooker, Hakluyt, Florio, and Bacon in prose. Nor was the Elizabethan a drab age of uniformity. To place Marlowe next to Spenser, Hooker next to Bacon, Daniel next to Jonson (or Marston), Sidney next to Donne, is to see sharply the diversity of viewpoint. Or, if we glance at the lesser figures, we find combustible personalities like Nashe, Harvey, and Marston; competent, if not inspired, narrators of tales like Greene, Lodge, and Deloney; amateurs of poetic talent like Ralegh and Dyer; and authors of pleasant trifles like Gascoigne and Breton. Individualism is conspicuously present in Elizabethan literature.

It is difficult to believe that the age would have been more golden if art had been less tongue-tied by authority. With impunity Elizabethans diagnosed human nature, man's bestiality, the tragedy of life, and the social ills of a materialistic society. As psychologists and analysts they have had few peers in literary history. In spite of Marston's lament, the state did not interfere. Second, one must not forget the nature of writers. Revolutionaries they may be in literary techniques and daring in their experimentation, but they are often either conservative politically and orthodox religiously or nonpolitical and nonreligious. With the possible exception of Marlowe, almost all Elizabethan authors, geniuses as well as hacks, fit into these categories. Hence, they rarely came in conflict with the proclamations of the government. Finally, and perhaps most important, Elizabeth, who was only as severe as events compelled her to be, never emulated modern dictators in proscribing a stereotyped literature glorifying an English hero. She was not a humorless, semiliterate, inhuman ogre; she was an enlightened Renaissance queen. Marlovian supermen with their infantile aggressiveness and lust sputtered and gesticulated, trampled upon and butchered men like swine, and then, like their creator, vanished in an irridescent cloud of words. The Cheshire cat grinned, and with humanity and passion went about her business not only of solidifying her people and bringing prosperity and peace to her beloved England but also of providing an environment hospitable to literature. Though Elizabeth laid the foundations of a great empire, her memory is freshest in a literature which outlives marble and gilded monuments.

CHAPTER SEVEN

THE ELIZABETHAN GRUB STREET:
"PENNIE KNAVES"

Throughout this study I have frequently mentioned authors now known only to specialists in sixteenth-century literary history, men who struggled with the specter of poverty, who, like Dekker's falconers, resorted to any type of chicanery to get on in the literary profession, who sought out patrons and accepted their bounty or their sarcasm (Literae petaces?), who catered (or, if viewed harshly, pandered) to the tastes of the mass audience. These were the men who came from the provinces to the city — Greene from Norwich, Richard Robinson from Newark-on-Trent, Churchyard from Shrewsbury — because only in London were there publishers and readers anxious to purchase and peruse their writings. Here they congregated and "dined" (when lucky) on Rhine wine and pickled herring. Here was the beginning of Grub Street.

Grub Street was unknown in earlier days when literature was an aristocratic diversion and books were transcribed by hand. After the printing press inaugurated mechanical reproduction of books, scribes gave way to printers, and printers eventually to publishers who organized and financed a rapidly expanding business. The growth of this new industry paralleled a similar expansion in trade and commerce. In fact, emergent capitalism produced a literate populace and thereby contributed the customers the printing trade required for its growth. This growth, in turn, depended upon human mechanics willing to grind out the fare businessmen needed for profit and readers for entertainment and information. Thus, Grub Street was born — born of the dreams of middle-class young men desirous of fame and position but born also of economic forces destined to wipe out feudal paternalism and to create impersonal slums as well as to provide opportunities for self-improvement unknown under the rigid medieval order and to usher in a more broadly based literature, simultaneously aristocratic and bourgeois, that was to become one of the wonders of the modern world.

Because the greatest writers of the age frequented Grub Street only briefly, if at all — poets finding employment in noble households or in governmental service, Shakespeare becoming an entrepreneur and, comparatively speaking, a wealthy man — I shall once more discuss the lesser talents of the period, the men afflicted with the literary virus but without literary genius. Second-rate they may have been, but their struggles and even their devious tactics are on the one hand frequently poignant and on the other hand revelatory of the somewhat sordid foundations upon which publication rested in the Elizabethan era.

Some of the hacks were educated (Greene, Nashe, and Lodge, for example), and one (Gabriel Harvey) was a Cambridge don gone awry. More were graduates of the grammar schools with as much Latin and Greek as Shakespeare brought to his dramatic art. Some were free members of livery companies (Robinson, Munday, and Deloney) who sought more than their parents' occupations offered. Others, like Rich and Churchyard, were soldiers, veterans of the wars in Ireland and the Low Countries. Their origins and background are of interest but not of paramount importance, for the difficulties of getting on in the literary profession created a democratic camaraderie. Thus, the sheltered and aristocratically reared Drayton became a frequent collaborator with the draper Munday in the leveling employment of Henslowe. That vigorous spokesman for standards in literature, Nashe, found himself defending Churchyard's mediocrity against Harvey's criticisms. Lodge, a university graduate and later a physician, corrected the manuscript of *The Adventures of Don Simonides* by the grammar school graduate and soldier, Rich.

Munday, Churchyard, Greene, Nashe, and Harvey manufactured news reports of domestic and foreign happenings. They and countless unknowns were among the first journalists in an age which had not yet invented the newspaper. The well-born Arthur Golding was no less quick to exploit the 1580 earthquake than the humble Churchyard and other anonymous hacks. Greene converted earlier semifactual accounts of roguery into racy, entertaining stories which proved that, if crime did not pay, it was at any rate interesting. This master of arts was succeeded by Rowlands, Dekker, Anthony Nixon, Samuel Rid, and the anonymous author of *Ratsey's Ghost,* all of whom were skillful in idiomatic prose as well as in the art of appropriating from Greene's tracts. Lyly and Nashe as well as Munday became hacks of the episcopacy in the Marprelate fracas. In turning out light verse, topical, sentimental, patriotic, and moralistic, Breton, a member of the gentry, rivaled commoners

THE ELIZABETHAN PROFESSIONAL WRITER

like Churchyard, Deloney, and Richard Turner. The last
three, however, had no aversion to becoming balladmongers. Golding and Greene prepared translations commissioned by printers; Munday made an industry of englishing romances; and poor Robinson spent a quarter of
a century peddling his translations. Sir Thomas Cockaine,
Turbervile, and Ascham compiled manuals on hunting,
archery, and similar sports; later Gervase Markham made
a business of books on the care of horses, so much so that
the Stationers' Company in 1617 attempted to put an end
to his equestrian treatises. Robert Record, the eminent
mathematician and Tudor scientist, sought to enlighten
Tudor readers through translations and publication of useful scientific information. Thomas Hill, "who never tasted
of the learned Lake, but rather always rudely taught,"
posed as an expert on such subjects as gardening, grafting
and planting, palmestry, the interpretation of dreams, phys-
iognomy, astrology, alchemy, and medications. Thus,
humanist educators soon gave way to the charlatans with
nostrums for all ailments, and amateurs permitted the
hacks to take over the book stalls in St. Paul's Churchyard.[1]

What is a hack? As a term of opprobrium we understand
it, howbeit more vaguely than we are sometimes aware, as
an author who produces a marketable commodity chiefly
for monetary considerations. Among the hacks have appeared not only those disinterred from obscurity by literary
historians but also writers of genius like Skelton, Holinshed, Dryden, Dr. Johnson, and Whitman. Literature has
been stingy with its rewards and publication easy only for
the rare individual. In addition, except for the anomalous
aesthete practically every writer examines the market.
Shakespeare did not impose his art upon his audience with
reckless disregard of public taste, nor did Molière, Dr.
Johnson, Henry James, or Ernest Hemingway. On the

other hand they did not pander. Many an Elizabethan, driven in his economic need to employment in a printer's shop, produced what his master decreed; but, if he failed to rise above such pedestrian work, the failure was his, not the printer's. The journalistic mentality perceives only the ephemeral in the ephemeral. The important point is not the materialistic motivation but the vision and the art with which an author handles marketable material.

So, too, it is not enough to dismiss hacks because of the speed with which they composed their works. Few literary geniuses have emulated Flaubert's fastidiousness. Yet the academicians who wrote and witnessed the *Parnassus* plays imply that unpolished works are inferior: "But to the pointe, for the husbanding of my witt, I put it out to interest, and make it returne twoo Pamphlets a weeke." And Nashe endeavors to protect himself and *Pierce Penniless* from censure by a candid admission of hasty composition: "And let him not (whatsoever he be) measure the weight of my words by this booke, where I write . . . as fast as my hand can trot." Unfortunately, such was Nashe's need that his hand trotted throughout his brief career, yet it is doubtful that leisure (and economic security) would have enabled him to discipline his energies and to discover a literary form adequate for his turbulent personality. Similarly, Greene's effort to excuse his writing because of economic pressures does not withstand scrutiny. Hacks of less talent than these are no worse in their impromptu pieces than in their other writings: Churchyard's lame poetry and his stumbling prose remained lame and stumbling regardless of circumstances, Whetstone was no less mediocre in his hastily penned epitaphs than in his other works, and Rich attempted to compensate for his paucity of ideas and art by his productivity. In addition, since journalism was not a recognized profession in Elizabethan days, readers and

particularly critics often judged what we would call newspaper reports according to the standards of literature. This
is manifestly unfair to a work like Churchyard's *A Warning for the Wise,* a factual (and platitudinously moral) account of an earthquake on April 6, 1580; the title page was
dated "1580. April 8." [2]

Neither marketability nor haste explains or defines the
hack. But the tendency to compose small volumes of a
few signatures — the penny and threepenny literature of
the day — does mark off the Elizabethan hack from the
creative artist. When one glances at the list of books written by Churchyard, neatly set down in *Churchyard's Challenge,* one is immediately impressed by the prolificness of
this ex-soldier. Examination of the actual works reveals
that he wrote many brief tracts. *The Epitaph of Sir Philip
Sidney* (1587), *The Honor of the Law* (1596), and *The
Fortunate Farewell* (1599), for example, contain only one
signature; *A Reviving of the Dead* (1591), *Churchyard's
Goodwill, and Sad and Heavy Verses* (1604) have two; *A
Feast Full of Sad Cheer* (1592) and *A Handful of Glad-
some Verses* (1592) have three. In addition, his miscellanies
are collections of short works, some of which had been
printed earlier and others of which had apparently been
sent in manuscript to the people eulogized or to the families of the deceased. Breton, though he had more talent
than Churchyard, also tended to publish small volumes of
prose and poetry. A brief description of the seasons and
the holidays and a compact collection of model letters for
all occasions characterize his output. And Greene's productivity in the final year of his life (six cony-catching pamphlets, *A Maiden's Dream, A Quip for an Upstart Courtier,
Groatsworth of Wit,* and *The Repentance of Robert
Greene*) is not quite so impressive when one is aware that
the longest of these works contains but seven signatures,

and that in the underworld tracts and in *A Quip for an Upstart Courtier* he sometimes borrowed extensively from earlier writers.

Authors needed money, and even the pittance received for a brief pamphlet relieved their distress. Second, the mass audience which they and their publishers catered to sought information or entertainment in small doses. Munday's observation — "a Booke growing too bigge in quantitie, is Profitable neither to the minde nor the purse: for that men are now so wise and the world so hard, as they love not to buy pleasure at unreasonable price" — says briefly all that need be said. The mass audience had neither money nor taste for weighty tomes; in their idle moments they wanted pithy tales and condensed versions of history. Actually this audience corresponds to the modern magazine audience, for the tracts we have been describing are of about the same length as the average magazine article. Third, most Elizabethan hacks (and this is not untrue of many of the greater writers) were incapable of developing and sustaining a plot and presented history in calendar form. Their books consist of small units, episodes and anecdotes being tied together by the subject matter itself or by employment of a narrator in the fashion of the Italian *novella*.[3]

More so than the geniuses of the age the hacks reveal a facile versatility. While Spenser and Daniel endeavored to perfect their poetic art, a writer like Munday was a reporter, poet, translator of popular romances, dramatist, composer of entertainments for livery companies, and successor to Stow. Churchyard, too, turned out prose or poetry at a moment's notice; he was a reporter of military experiences, author of *Shore's Tragedy*, epitapher, translator, composer of entertainments for Elizabeth, and commemorator of any occasion that promised favor. Though he eschewed poetry, Rich was a prolific writer on military subjects, translator of romances, historian (or reporter) of Irish affairs, author of courtesy books, and a tiresome moralist. That these men failed to excel in any one of their diverse roles is scarcely surprising. That they undertook so many is comprehensible from an economic point of view. They attempted to exploit sensational occurrences, occasions of rejoicing and sorrow, the euphuistic fad, and the widespread interest in romances; and they were attracted by the returns to be realized either from nobles who entertained Elizabeth on her progresses or from livery companies which spent money lavishly in the annual celebrations of the lord mayor's installation. Like most other Elizabethans they were not specialists; all kinds of activities interested them equally, and usually they had no more talent for one type of writing than for another.

If all other tests were inconclusive, Elizabethan hacks could be identified by their flagrant pilferings from the writings of others. As modern scholarship has revealed, many authors stole others' feathers in wholesale fashion. To imitate was an accepted artistic practice, but to plunder the works of another writer was as reprehensible then as now. No one objected to the fact that Shakespeare converted Greene's *Pandosto* and Lodge's *Rosalind* into dramatic masterpieces, but contemporaries had little esteem for Dekker, who pieced together his underworld exposés from the writings of Greene, Rowlands, Markham, Harman, Awdeley, and *Mihil Mumchance,* or for Nixon, who composed his books with scissors and paste.

Finally, hack writers were (and are) primarily entertainers and journalists. Greene's prefatory remarks to his *Planetomachia* — "The minde wearied with weightie affaires, seeketh as soone to be recreated with some pithie conceipts, as with any deepe contemplations: & rather with sleight devises to procure mirth, then with sollemme shewes to foster melancholie" — was in effect echoed by Churchyard, Breton, Munday, and many others. The honest hack, like Richard Turner, frankly acknowledges his limitations: "Pardon my branches that buds but in Sommer with the Mulberie, for I am one of those Poets that came to Homers bason, to lap up that he dooth cast off. It sufficeth me to be a water bough, not a top bud, so I may be of the same roote." Most hacks, content to give the public what it wanted in the quantities it wanted, stuck to tested formulas: Munday translated old romances; Robinson modernized Leland's translation of the *Gesta Romanorum;* Churchyard, Greene, and Chettle utilized such medieval devices as the dream; Deloney drew upon jest-books; Churchyard retained the alliteration of an older prose; and all confused truisms and moralisms with profundity. Popular literature usually dresses up the old in contemporary attire, and this factitious topicality presumably satisfies its audience. As a practical printer John Danter observes in *Greene's Funerals*: "Gentlemen, fine wits are quickened with one cup of pure wine, where many woulde make them dull; And this small Pamphlet may recreate your mindes, when large Volumes would but cloy and weary you." Thus, the writer has "his hyer" and the reader "his desire." [4]

Elizabethan Grub Street took a frankly commercial attitude toward publication. Although Munday wrote *Zelauto* (1580) while he was "Servaunt to the Right Honourable the Earle of Oxenford," and dedicated the romance to him, he was not so sheltered or so rewarded by De Vere that he posed as an amateur. On the contrary, in a preface to the reader he candidly discusses the saleability of his work: "The Printer (you will say) hath painted it full of Pictures, to make it be bought the better: and I say the matter is more meritorious, and therefore you should buy it the sooner. So, if you wyll be ruled by the Printer and me, you shall at no tyme want any of the Bookes." Thus, despite its effusive dedication *Zelauto* is a commercial work — and further testimony that Elizabethans were not content to depend solely upon a patron's generosity.[5]

Authors of sixteenth-century handbooks early learned to publicize their wares by detailed descriptions of published and forthcoming books. (For some reason commentators have persistently assigned the incorporation of advertising matter into books to the middle of the seventeenth century.) In the preface to the second book of *The Pathway to Knowledge* (1551) Richard Record lists seven books as "shortly to be set forth," and then goes on to cite "sundrye woorkes partely ended, And partely to bee ended." This is apparently the first instance of advertising in English books.[6]

Both in *The Profitable Art of Gardening* (1568) and *The Contemplation of Mankind* (1571), Thomas Hill surpasses Record in detailing the contents of published and unpublished volumes. Advertisements occupy ten pages in *The Contemplation of Mankind*. Hill divides his books into three categories: "The Bookes and Treatises of mine sundrie tymes printed"; "The bookes of mine in a readinesse to be imprinted, and resting with the Printers"; and "The Bookes which remain with me fully ended, and neare brought to an ende." In the first group he cites nine titles and presumably some of the descriptive material appearing on title pages, including names of printers, numbers of editions, and dates of editions. In the second group he lists five works, including titles and names of printers. In the final category are nine books, six of which, Hill informs us, are "in a readinesse to the Printing." As for the other three works "Such minded to have a private Copie written out . . . let them resort unto Maister Barkers shoppe, or

Mayster Walleyes in Paules Church yarde, and there they shall understande of the Authour, with whome they may common, when the worke is fully brought to an ende." [7]

Although John Hester, alchemist and distiller, never catalogued his translations of medical treatises, he apparently was the first to utilize another form of advertisement: at the conclusion of his books he invariably reminded readers that medications were available at his chemist's shop. Sometimes his advertisements are more detailed and sales-alluring, like this one: "For the receiptes in this Booke specified, as also for many other rare thynges mentioned els where: if any be disposed to use them, let them repaire to my house at Poules Wharfe, where they shall either finde them readie made, or me at reasonable warnyng readie to make them simply and plainly without sophistication." In view of the small returns from publication it is no wonder that Hester promoted his trade with the insistence of modern advertising agencies. [8]

Whetstone, or his printer, was probably the first non-scientific writer to ape Hill's technique. On the verso of the title page of *The Enemy to Unthriftness* (1586) appears this statement:

The Printer to the Reader.
To the intent, that the variable humors of men, (which delight as much in chaynge as they differ in opinion) may be satisfied with the varitie of M. Whetstone's workes and writings: I have therefore not (here) thought it amisse to set downe the severall tytles of his severall workes alredy printed and compiled.

Thereupon he cites thirteen books by Whetstone. But it is doubtful that the printer's only interest was to impress readers with "the varitie of M. Whetstone's workes and writings." For *The Enemy to Unthriftness* consists of the sheets of *A Mirror for Magistrates of Cities* (1584) with a new title page. In short, Whetstone's writings had not been selling, and the stationer wanted to clear his shelves of the 1584 volume and other books.[9]

Probably because Churchyard, like Richard Robinson, was compelled to accept payments in kind and to sell his own writings, *Churchyard's Challenge* (1593) contains a list of thirty-one titles under the heading "The bookes that I can call to memorie alreadie Printed." At the conclusion of the preface he publicizes future publications:

> My next booke shalbe the last booke of the Worthines of Wales.
>
> And my last booke called my *Ultimum Vale*, shalbe (if it please God) twelve long tales for Christmas, dedicated to twelve honorable Lords.

Many years earlier Churchyard had begun to announce future books. In his dedicatory preface to an anonymous translation of Ovid's *De Tristibus* (1st ed., 1572?, 3rd ed., 1580) he elaborately describes his *Chips* (1575) and the impending second part, which apparently was never printed. He alludes to the printing of *Churchyard's Challenge* in *Churchyard's Charge* (1580), *Churchyard's Chance* (1580), and *A Feast Full of Sad Cheer* (1592). Evidently Churchyard had to wait thirteen years before the *Challenge* was printed.

At the conclusion of *A Brief and True Report of the Execution of Certain Traitors* (1582), Munday, a vigorous promoter of his own books, writes: "Let this suffise thee (gentle Reader) at this time: and if thou desirest to be more acquainted with their Romish and Sathanicall juglinges, read my *English Romaine lyfe,* which so soone as it can be printed, shall be set foorth." Irritated by the (valid) criticism that in *A Watchword to England* (1584) he had rehashed the *Chronicles* and Fox, Munday swears that in the second part "I will (God giving me leave) set them downe such matters, as they shall not say hath beene borrowed from any, but absolute and sufficient of it selfe." In even more extravagant language he goes on to promise "my *Court of Conscience,* which I dare awarraunt thee to be such a Booke, as thou hast not read the lyke in all thy life, as well for the circumstaunces of the matter, as the woorthinesse of the whole in generall." In *The Third and Last Part of Palmerin of England* (1602) he observes that "as for my last part of *Primaleon* of *Greece,* and the third and last part of *Palmerin d'Oliva,* both them I confesse to have in mine owne custodie, and as I perceive your willingnesse to entertaine, so shall I bee ready to hasten them for you." [10]

Like Churchyard and Munday, Greene constantly advertised his books. He promises a second part of his first romance *Mamillia,* and, indeed, at the conclusion of the second part pledges a third installment, a pledge evidently unfulfilled. He later promises continuations of *Morando, Penelope's Web, Perymedes, the Blacksmith,* and *Never Too Late.* In *Perymedes, the Blacksmith* he urges his readers to look for *Orpharion* at the next term. In *A Disputation between a He Cony-Catcher and a She Cony-Catcher,* Nan refers to Greene's impending "blacke Booke," which, we are informed in *The Black Book's Messenger,* "I had many daies since finished, had not sickenes hindered my intent." One reason for ascribing the anonymous *Defense of Cony-Catching* to Greene is the publicity given by this avowed "enemy" to a new exposé to be entitled *"The repentance of a Conny-catcher."* In *The Black Book's Messenger* Greene observes, "I had thought to have joyned with this Treatise, a pithy discourse of the Repentance of a Conny-catcher lately executed out of Newgate, yet . . . I altered my opinion." [11]

Stationers often produced title pages which spelled out

the contents and the readers to whom various books appealed, and they frequently tacked up title pages to poles near their shops. But it was commercially minded authors who began to compose the blurbs that are part of modern book production.

To capture a middle-class audience without great means to purchase books and, perhaps more important, without the sophisticated literary knowledge of coteries or of university graduates, hacks wisely, both from an economic and literary viewpoint, adapted their style to the taste of their readers. When Greene, for instance, began to grind out threepenny fare for "Al Yoong Gentlmen, Marchants, citizens, apprentices, yeomen, and plaine countrey farmers," he stripped his prose of euphuistic mannerisms, excessive alliteration, rhetorical figures, and allusions to fashionable animal lore. In *The Second Part of Cony-Catching* he replies to those who objected that he "shewed no eloquent phrases, nor fine figurative conveiance in my first booke [of cony-catching] as I had done in other of my workes." To these writers rhetorical figures and tropes were embellishments savoring too much of university pedantry and upper middle-class pretentiousness. The military historian, Thomas Styward, claims that he has "attired" *The Pathway to Martial Discipline* (1581) "for the campe, and not for the Carpet, for the Souldier, and not for the Rhetorician." Another soldier-author, Henry Roberts (or Robarts), advises his patron, "Looke not for curious phrases, as flowing from the muse of learned CICERO, nor bewtified with fine inckhorne tearmes." In a collection of model letters Markham is as contemptuous of inflated style as his title, *Hobson's Horse-Load of Letters,* is disdainful of affectations in the epistolary art: "Here are no farre fetcht Phrases to pusle and amaze the people, nor any so rude and barbarous to distaste the nobler spirits, but an even & common language spoken usually, and understood of every body." [12]

The choice of a mean or plain style by hack writers was not so novel as they supposed. When Greene in his defense of his "new" style in his underworld exposés observes that "a certaine decorum is to bee kept in everie thing," he is uttering a rhetorical cliché. In their desire to propagate the best that was known and thought humanists discarded Ciceronianism, the language of the university, for a simple, colloquial style. Elyot, for instance, notes in *The Image of Governance* (1541) that it is his intent, "with more exact diligence," to "conforme the style therof with the phrase of our englishe, desiringe more to make it playne to all readers, than to flourishe it with over moch eloquence." Like the humanist the Puritan had no traffic with eloquence: the word of the deity was not to be obscured by verbalisms but rendered clear and simple in diction comprehensible to all readers regardless of social status and formal education. Gosson, despite some lapses into euphuism, esteems "rude Macedon," who is "taught too call a spade, a spade without any glossing" and who "useth no going about the bushe." For, he concludes with typical puritanical oversimplification, "hee that tempers his speeche with art, smootheth his style with a double tongue, shall quickly have infinite swarmes of freendes, but angle with poyson, and doe much hurt." [13]

In short, humanists, Puritans, compilers of utilitarian treatises, and authors of penny literature, some because of a genuine desire to bring enlightenment to the English people and others because of their materialistic needs, were striving in their various ways to establish and make respectable a language purged of Ciceronian eloquence, upstart (and foreign) affectations, and pedantic crabbedness. Theirs was to be the language of the future, not the euphuistic circumlocutions of university wits, not the dandyism of Elizabeth's courtiers, not the strained academese of Gabriel Harvey and Mulcaster, not even the majestic periods of Hooker. Despite its colloquialisms, which undoubtedly appear more picturesque in the eyes of modern readers than of contemporaries, the prose of Grub Street was often naked, colorless, and much too frequently careless. In fact, the leveling out process which we too quickly attribute to modern journalism began to reveal itself in the sixteenth century.

Unlike moderns, Elizabethans were preoccupied with style. Early critics like Puttenham and Webbe anglicized classical rhetoric and discussed minutely oratorical devices. That critics were preoccupied with tropes and figures we should expect, but that soldiers and citizens rarely failed to allude to diction perhaps surprises. In a society in which education seldom managed to go beyond techniques and schoolmasters beat into their charges rhetorical precepts, the neophyte author was almost compelled to comment upon his own art or lack of it. Hence, Elizabethan literature reveals a self-consciousness about style and diction that appears incongruous in light of an almost childish conception of syntax and structure and an almost universal inability to compose in paragraph units.

The writings of Rich are filled with allusions to style and to his lack of skill in composition — a lack which interfered not at all with his unending production of pamphlets. In one of his early books, *A ... Dialogue between Mercury and an English Soldier* (1574), he professes to be overcome by his own audacity: "When I called to my remembraunce my own ignorance in the knowledge of wryting, & the slender sence of that I had wrytten, it utterly discouraged me, so that I was at a controversie in my selfe, what I might do." In *Alarm to England* he at one moment excuses his "simplicitie and trayning up, which hath not bene so much with my penne, but more with my pike, nor in the scholes amongest learned clarkes, but rather in the fieldes amongst unlettered companions, or as some will terme them, amongst a companie of rusticke souldiours." At the next moment he assails "the delicacie of our readers at this time, that there are none may be alowed of to write, but such as have bene trained at schoole with Pallas, or at the least have bene fostered up with the Muses," and advises "anxious Coxcombes" not "to reade in homely style of matters, more behooveful and necessarie, then eyther curiouse or fyled." Thirty years later, in *A Short Survey of Ireland* (1609), he still harps on the same theme: "I am no scholler. . . . what am I then? I am a Souldier, a professed Souldier, better practised in my pike then in my penne." And in *The Honesty of This Age* (1614) he once more castigates the learned and lauds his own honesty — "I speake plainly, and I meane honestly, and although my wordes be not imbroydered with high morality, I care not, for I leave that to Schollers, Maisters of Art and Methode" — as he assumes that honesty is but a question of style.[14]

This assumption, in fact, was common among hacks. Richard Johnson makes his unembellished style synonymous with his personal integrity: "His simple truth shewes he is without deceyt, and his plaine speech proves, he flatters not. He can not boast of Art, nor claime the priviledge of scholasticall cunning." Robert Pricket, like Rich a soldier by profession, versifies his freedom from servile hypocrisy:

> I cannot smooth with flatteries filed phrase,
> Wherein doth stand a Poets gilded prayse.
> A warlike pike is made a Souldiers pen,
> Wherewith is writ the deeds of worthy men.

This assumption obviously rests upon two fallacies: that

integrity belonged only to the humble, who, not unlike Deloney's heroes, fearlessly stated the truth and did not cringe like sycophantic courtiers before majesty; and that the schools taught cunning and deceit. John Shute proudly described himself as "a simple souldior better practised abrode in martiall matters, then furnished at home with cunnyng of the scoole," and Robert Barret, another soldier, freely admits that his discourses "be but rough, & not polished with schoole termes, yet happily not so barraine, but you may reape some good fruit from them." In short, Elizabethan hacks, like so many other members of the middle class, distrusted (and perhaps feared) intellectuals, partly because of their pride in their own success without the assistance of education and partly because of their own insecurity as self-trained men. Yet, though they scorned artists, or pretended to do so, they were more ambivalent than they realized and often rationalized their own feelings of inadequacy.[15]

Perhaps custodians of taste drove hacks to self-defense and exaggerated claims on behalf of their books. Stanyhurst, whose translation of Vergil's *Aeneid* should have earned him a high place in the unwritten Elizabethan *Dunciad*, pours pedantic contempt upon uneducated "rythmours":

Good God, what a frie of such wooden rythmours doth swarme in Stacioners shops, who never instructed in anie Grammar schoole, not attayning to the parings of the Latine or Greeke tongue, yet lyke blinde bayards rushe on forwarde, fostring their vaine conceits with such overweening sillie follies, as they recke not to bee condemned of the learned for ignorant, so they bee commended of the ignorant for learned.

Nashe is no less severe in his castigation of "unlearned Idiots" and "brainless Bussards" who "are every quarter bigge wyth one Pamphlet or other." Men "exquisitly furnished with learning shroude themselves in obscuritie, whereas they that are voide of all knowledge, endevour continually to publish theyr follie." Of course, both Stany-hurst and Nashe are justified in their endeavors to main-tain artistic standards; yet both fail to distinguish the role and function of ephemeral journalism. The uneducated as well as learned men like Ralegh and Gabriel Harvey were avid readers of reports of discoveries and voyages not note-worthy for their artistry but acceptable as journalism.[16]

Since commemoration of important occasions — victo-ries in war, marriages, death, installations in great offices — was accepted literary practice of classical authors and of such sixteenth-century writers as Skelton, Gascoigne, Spen-ser, Daniel, and Donne, it is hardly surprising that hacks with or without commissions (usually the latter) exploited whatever appeared exploitable and bastardized commem-orative literature. Peele, for instance, produced mediocre verse on several occasions. In *The Device of the Pageant* (1585) and *Descensus Astraeae* (1591) he celebrates the in-stallations of lord mayors of London. In 1589 he published *A Farewell to Sir John Norris and Sir Francis Drake,* in which he precedes an acknowledged old poem with a topi-cal dedication and a prefatory poem alluding to the feats of the two commanders. *Polyhymnia* (1590) describes thir-teen pairs of lords and gentlemen who participated in a triumph at tilt on November 17 last, and *The Honor of the Garter* (1593) the induction of the Earl of Northumber-land into the order. If Peele's commemorative poetry is pedestrian, the verse and prose of hacks are often despic-able but no less crassly exploitative. While Peele perhaps received a stipend in advance in some instances, Church-yard, perhaps the Elizabethan master of occasional composi-tions, had failed to write his way into favor — despite the "sixteene severall bookes printed presently to be bought

. . . . dedicated in sundrie seasons to severall men off good and great credite." [17]

New Year's was a gala holiday in the sixteenth century, the occasion on which Tudor subjects gave generously to their monarch and received often only miserly tokens in return. Very early in the century writers began to capitalize upon New Year's festivities. Erasmus presented at least three translations to patrons on these occasions. The author of *The Dietary of Ghostly Health* (1520) was probably the first Englishman to reward his friends with a new book: "In the begynnynge of this newe yere / my good systers whan I consyder and se many frendes gyve tokens of custome one to another . . . dyvers of you have gyven tokens unto me. Wherfore havynge nothynge redy to gyve unto you agayne / I purpose in my mynde to prepare one token for you all / to profyte eche of you." [18]

The author of *The Dietary of Ghostly Health* was undoubtedly an amateur who sought a novel way of bestowing greetings and gifts upon his intimates. His example was followed by Walter Bailey, who in three successive years printed at his own expense little tracts on health as New Year's gifts, *A Brief Treatise Touching the Preservation of the Eyesight* (1586), *A Brief Discourse of Certain Baths or Medical Waters in the County of Warwick* (1587), and *A Short Discourse of the Three Kinds of Peppers in Common Use* (1588). Bailey had the stationer leave spaces for names, appropriate pronouns, and the author's signature. The Huntington Library copy of the 1588 volume is inscribed to Egerton and reads as follows (passages in script are italicized):

As in former yeeres at this season I have been alwaies careful to shew my affection towards *you* by offering som present appertaining to the preservation of your health: so at this time, in token of a good and prosperous newe yeere, (God grant you many) I have emboldened my selfe to exhibite *unto you* in our vulgar toong, this short discourse of the three kindes of Peppers.

Unlike Bailey, who apparently sought nothing for himself, Gascoigne was not without ulterior designs in his presentation of *The Grief of Joy* to Elizabeth:

I right humbly beseeche youre heighnes to accept this Nifle for a newyeres gyfte and therewithall to pardon the boldnes of your servaunt who eftsones presumethe (by contemplation) to kysse your delicate and most honorable handes and vowethe willingly to purchase the continewance of youre comfort, by any deathe, or perill, whiche occasion maie present for accomplishment of any least service acceptable to so worthie a *Queene* Whome God preserve, this first of January, 1577 and ever. Amen.

For Gascoigne, whose career as a soldier had not profited him much in material goods, had presented *The Tale of Hermetes, the Hermit* to the queen on the preceding New Year's Day; and he hoped that an unbending monarch would bend slightly on this holiday.[19]

It was probably Churchyard who decided to make New Year's Day into a business holiday for hacks. With his usual frankness he acknowledges his motivation:

> Then thought I to beginne the yere:
> On New yeres daie with some device,
> And though that many men be nice.
> And blushe to make an honest shifte,
> I sent eche Lorde a Newe yeres gifte:
> Such treasure as I had that tyme,
> A laughyng verse, a merrie ryme.

For those ready to criticize he is ready with an answer.

> Some thinke this is a cravyng guise,
> Tushe holde your peace, world waxeth wise
> A dulled horse that will not sturre,
> Must be remembred with a spurre:

And where there serves ne spurre nor wand,
A man must needs lead horse in hande.
So I was forste on causes greate,
To see in fire where laye the heate:
And warme their witts that cold did waxe,
But thrust the fire into the Flax.

For the rich with coffers "faste lockt" should "helpe the poore at every tide." In keeping with his own resolution, on New Year's day in 1580 he honored the Earl of Surrey with *Churchyard's Charge* and Thomas Bromley with *Churchyard's Chance,* which also contains a poem entitled "A New Year's Gift to the Earl of Ormond." But though he "did good will discharge,"

. . . nothyng did retourne to me,
That I could either feele or see.

No wonder he finds that the "golden worlde is tournd to brasse." Sixteen years later, in *A Pleasant Discourse of Court and Wars* (1596), Churchyard, now broken in health and as indigent as ever, sends another volume at the first of the year to Sir George Carey:

Loe knights, how plaine poore poets shifts,
In scrambling world to scowre the coast,
With rimes, and sends such new yeers gifts,
From sicke mans couch to court in poast:
Where this may make a merry hed,
To smile before he goes to bed.

Yet the impoverished bleakness of Churchyard's existence was dramatically altered late in 1593, as he tells us in *A Pleasant Conceit,* "which pleasant conceite I have presumed (this Newe-yeeres day) to present to your Majestie, in signe and token that your gracious goodnesse towardes me oftentimes (and cheefely now for my pencyon) shal never goe out of my remembrance, with all dutifull services, belonging to a loyall subject." [20]

Though there is nothing specific to indicate it in the text, perhaps Spenser intended *Daphnaïda* as a New Year's present to the Marquise of Northampton, for his dedication is dated January 1, 1591. If so, he was one of the few important writers in Elizabeth's era who made use of the holiday in this fashion. Ordinarily, except for amateurs like Bailey, it was the Churchyards and the balladmongers who capitalized on the occasion. The latter, as one would expect, were fond of having their half-penny sheets available at New Year's time. In 1570, for instance, appeared "an newe yeres gyfte intituled the schole of honeste lyf," "a newe yeres gyfte or a newe Christe crosse Roo called purge the old lavyn that yt may be nowe doo," and "a newe yeres gyfte to the Rebellious persons in the north parties of Englonde." Though I have identified just under sixty books and ballads which were intended as New Year's greetings, undoubtedly the practice was more widespread than this number indicates. For otherwise the ridicule of a character in *The Return from Parnassus* is pointless:

I had almoste forgotten the cheife pointe I cald thee out for: new years day approcheth, and wheras other gallants bestowe Jewells upon there Mistrisses (as I have done whilome), I now count it base to do as the common people doe; I will bestow upon them the precious stons of my witt, a diamonde of Invention, that shall be above all value & esteeme.[21]

In the absence of newspaper obituaries and in view of the classical precedent that men of renown were to be immortalized in poetry upon death, elegies and epitaphs were as numerous as sonnets in the sixteenth century, as evidenced by Googe's miscellany, *Eclogues, Epitaphs, and Sonnets* (1563). "Epitaphers and position Poets have wee more than a good many," Nashe observes, "that swarme like Crowes to a dead carcas." Their effusions appeared as ballads and were hawked on the streets almost as soon as a great man died. Contemptuously A. H. writes of this desecration of nobility.

> What steeled patience could behold those Dawes
> Praevaricate the Muses sacred Lawes,
> And blabber forth his Funerall, in Rimes,
> I needs must say, much like these wretched Times?
> To heare the noselesse Ballad-woman raise
> Her snuffling throat to His ill-penned praise:
> Or the ofte beaten fellow make his mone,
> Who in the streets is wont to reade *Pope Jone*.

Frequently these ballads were tacked to walls and became the Elizabethan equivalent of modern news releases. "These bastard rimers," Puttenham complains, "make long and tedious discourses and write them in large tables to be hanged up in Churches and chauncells over the tombes of great men and others, which be so exceeding long as one must have halfe a dayes leasure to reade one of them." He has also found elegies "upon many honorable tombes of these late times erected, which doe rather disgrace then honour either the matter or maker." [22]

The epitaphers were censured with characteristic Elizabethan fury by the upholders of standards in art. Nashe compares them to crows. Guilpin charges that "puling Elegies / Slaunder the Muses." Hall, without charity, abuses "the veriest Lacklatines, and the most Unalphabeticall raggabashes that ever bred lowse" who "cannot make two rimes in their mothers tongue in two houres, and yet these shake-ragges live by other mens trenchers, filling all the tavernes in the town with Epithalamiums, Elegies, and Epitaphes." More penetratingly than other critics Wither details the evils of the epitaph factory — the crassness of the producers who regurgitated elegies, their perversion of an ancient form through indiscriminate praise written solely for profit and often in a tavern, and their hounding of widows and heirs:

> I have no Muses that will serve the turne,
> At every Triumph; and rejoyce or mourne,
> Upon a minutes warning for their hire;
> If with old Sherry they themselves inspire.
> I am not of a temper, like to those
> That can provide an houres sad talke in Prose,
> For any Funerall; and then goe Dine,
> And choke my griefe, with Sugar-plums and Wine.
> I cannot at the Claret sit and laugh,
> And then halfe tipsie, write an Epitaph. . . .
> I cannot for reward adorne the Hearse,
> Of some old rotten Miser, with my Verse:
> Nor like the Poetasters of the Time;
> Goe howle a dolefull Elegie in Ryme,
> For every Lord or Ladiship that dies:
> And then perplex their Heires, to Patronize
> That muddy Poesie. Oh! how I scorne,
> Those raptures, which are free, and nobly borne,
> Should Fidler-like, for entertainment scrape
> At strangers windowes: and goe play the Ape,
> In counterfeiting Passion, when there's none.
> Or in good earnest, foolishly bemoane
> (In hope of cursed bounty) their just death;
> Who, (living) merit not, a minutes breath
> To keep their Fame alive, unles to blow,
> Some Trumpet which their black disgrace may show.[23]

Although Whetstone, a prolific epitapher, denies interest in compensation — "Not fed with hope rewardes thereby to get" — the unusual haste with which he and other authors came into print makes mockery of his statement. Lodge entered his epitaph to his mother in the Stationers' Register on December 23, 1579, a week in advance of her death. This is perhaps the most notorious instance of the carcass-seeking crow. At least the anonymous author of the elegy in praise of Hatton (*A Lamentable Discourse of the Death of . . . Sir Christopher Hatton*) did not enter his poem until four days after the nobleman's death. John Taylor's *Great Britain's Greatest Woe, or an Elegiacal Lamenting* was entered on the day following Prince Henry's death, the earliest of seventeen different works. So far as we know, no Elizabethan equaled Elkanah Settle, who, D'Israeli informs us, "had latterly one standard *Elegy* and one *Epithalamium,* printed off with blanks, which by ingeniously filling up with the printed names of any great person who died or was married, no one who was going out of life or was entering into it could pass scotfree." On the other hand, Hall alleges that "these shake-ragges live by other mens trenshers," and we know, through Professor Williams' research, that in Richard Johnson's *Anglorum Lacrimae* (1603), an epitaph to Elizabeth, all but 49 of the 480 lines are lifted from Thomas Rogers' *Celestial Elegies of the Goddess and the Muses* (1598) — a "bare-faced" robbery if ever there was one.[24]

Despite Whetstone's protestations, repetitions in his elegies indicate that he manufactured rather than created his epitaphs. For example, the dedicatory material in *A Remembrance of . . . Sir James Dyer* (1582) reappears in *A Mirror of True Honor . . . Lord Francis [Russell], Earl of Bedford* (1585):

I have made a weak remembraunce of a fewe of the pretious vertues, which governed the good Lord Dyer, late cheefe Justice of the Common Pleas, which I humblie laie before your Lordship [Sir Thomas Bromley's] searching judgement, no better garnished then Diamonds set in Brasse (sig. A3).

I have made a weake remembraunce, of many sounde vertues which governed, the thrise noble Earle your Grandfather, and the most valiant Lorde your noble father, who although they

as it were at one tyme, accompanied each other unto heaven.
Yet the world, while there is any worlde, shalbe possessed with
their illustrus deedes, which I humbly present unto your Lordship, noe better garnished, then Dyamonds set in Bras (sig.
A2v).

Or we discover that stanzas in *A Remembrance of . . .
Lord Thomas* [*Radcliffe*], *Late Earl of Sussex* (1583) are
closely followed in *A Mirror of True Honor:*

Whylom of Macedon, the mighty King,
By Homer pend, Achylles life did reade,
Who forthwith wisht, his owne renowne to ring
Homer alive, and Alexander dead:
Desire of Fame, Contempt of life so bread,
And trueth to say, mans life is but a breath.
When Fame outlives, Envie, Time, and Death (sig. A3).

What is become of Caesars Equipage,
Of Pompeys Rule, of Alexanders Raigne:
Of Samsons Strength, of Salamon the sage,
Of Tullies skil, of Mydas golden gayn:
Of them, and al, this only doth remayn:
They liv'd like Gods, and leave as men did take.
And for their pompes, have large accompts to make (sig. B3).

Let Curtius be, example for the rest,
A gaping Gulfe, who chose to be his hearse.
Desire of Fame so burned in his brest,
The Macedon, that through the world did pearce,
Reading Achilles Fame in Homers vearse.
Forthwith did wish his noble actes to spread,
Homer alive, and Alexander dead (sig. B1).

What did become of Caesars clyming head?
Of Pompeis rule, and Alexanders raigne?
I light account, so soone as they were dead,
Yet they whose mindes, a world could not containe,
With much a doe: a seemely Tombe did gaine.
Their conquestes great, returnde and waxed lesse,
For nought may stand, but what gods hand doth bles (sig. C1).

[229]

And these three lines appear verbatim in both elegies:

His purple robe, doth shew his honor sound,
his armed sworde, the mettle of his hart,
his forward leg in S. George garter bound (sigs. A3v, B1v).

Although these repetitions by no means account for the bulk of the lines in the two poems, certainly Whetstone composed *A Mirror of True Honor* with the two earlier works in front of him.[25]

If Whetstone made composition simpler by such repetitions, Churchyard, too honest perhaps to lift from his own writings, nevertheless made a business of composing epitaphs to famous personages. *The Epitaph of Sir Philip Sidney* was perhaps the earliest of his elegiac compositions to appear in print. He later published two collections of epitaphs, *A Reviving of the Dead* (1591) and *A Feast Full of Sad Cheer* (1592), which contain eleven poems. Since the former volume includes elegies to Henry VIII and Edward VI, Churchyard probably began to compose elegies early in his career and to deliver manuscript poems to widows and heirs. Later he gathered his copies of the poems and published collections. Some such explanation plausibly explains the appearance in the same volume of epitaphs to Henry VIII and Hatton, who had died in 1591. (There is also the possibility that some of these epitaphs had been printed earlier.) In 1596 he printed *A Sad and Solemn Funeral of . . . Sir Francis Knowles,* and his epitaph on the death of Whitgift, *Churchyard's Goodwill, Sad and Heavy Verses* (1604), was his last published work. Thus, Churchyard produced "sad and solemn" verses and New Year's trifles in his unending pursuit of a livelihood.

In view of the pilfering of Johnson, the repetitiveness of Whetstone, the factory-like productions of Churchyard, as well as the inappropriate (and sometimes offensive) display of funereal ballads, the harsh criticism of epitaphers is understandable, since they blithely resorted to any type of skulduggery in order to exploit the deceased as well as the public. On the other hand, these epitaphers did not create the market for obituaries: the public knew what it wanted, and the *nouveaux riches,* who spent a lifetime and frequently a fortune in emulating the nobility, eagerly paid for eulogies. In addition, the dogmatism of Hall notwithstanding, many an epitapher was neither alcoholic nor insincere; he frequently "felt" grief, and at the same time appreciated the market for his product as well as the preferment a noble or a wealthy family might grant him.

There may be some doubt as to the number of falconers, those mountebanks who pasted dedications in stolen books and conducted a literary swindle, but there is no doubt whatever as to the number of literary conycatchers. Johnson's flagrant thefts from Rogers qualify him for admission into the society of dishonest hack writers who, not content to borrow a phrase or two from another writer, composed books by lifting entire sections from other volumes. Greene castigates "scabd Jades" whose writings were "either distild out of ballets or borrowed of Theological poets." Drayton attacks "these yonkers" who "strut the stage with reperfumed wordes." Donne, after deploring those poets "who write to Lords, rewards to get," insists that

> . . . hee is worst, who (beggarly) doth chaw
> Others wits fruits, and in his ravenous maw
> Rankly digested, doth those things out-spue,
> As his owne things; and they are his owne, 'tis true,
> For if one eate my meate, though it be knowne
> The meate was mine, th'excrement is his owne.

Despite bitter attacks such as these the traffic continued unabated.[26]

This literary underworld was inevitable under the circumstances. To earn a few shillings hacks had to produce books at a rate that precluded original composition. They soon learned the art of rewriting other people's books or, if they were without scruples, of cutting out sections from various books and pasting them together. Scissors-and-paste books were by no means uncommon after hacks began to exploit the marketplace.

Analysis of Samuel Rid's *Art of Juggling* (1610) reveals that except for a few passages he appropriated wholesale from Reginald Scot's *Discovery of Witchcraft* (1574) and from *Mihil Mumchance* (1597), a tract probably issued by a printer in order to take advantage of the popularity of Greene's cony-catching tracts. (*Mihil Mumchance* is for the most part a verbatim reprint of apparently the first Elizabethan underworld exposé, *A Manifest Detection . . . of Dice Play*.) The extent of Rid's pilfering is all too clear when the pamphlet is dissected:

RID	SOURCES
Magical tricks, sigs. B3–C4	Scot, pp. 321–328, 330
Dice tricks, sigs. C4–D1	*Mihil Mumchance*, sigs. B4v–C1 *Manifest Detection*, pp. 15–19
Card tricks, sigs. D1–D1v	Scot, p. 332
Card tricks, sigs. D1–D2v	*Mihil Mumchance*, sigs. C4v–D1 *Manifest Detection*, pp. 23–25
Legerdemain, sigs. D2v–D3v	Scot, pp. 332–334
Other magical tricks, sigs. E1–E4	Scot, pp. 309, 338–340, 343, 346–351
Alchemy, sigs. F1–F3v	Scot, pp. 356–359, 368–369
Charms, sigs. F3v–F4v	Scot, pp. 242–249, 265–266

It is apparent that only a few pages in Rid's book are unaccounted for: the discussion of Egyptians (sigs. B1v–

B2v), a card trick (sigs. D3v–D4), and an additional alchemy trick (sigs. E4v–F1). Undoubtedly future research will pinpoint these passages and demonstrate that what Rid labels his "first fruits" is but the fruits of others.[27]

Pilfering of this sort was not the practice only of unknowns like Rid. Greene borrowed from his predecessors frequently, and in *A Notable Discovery of Cosenage* stole large sections from *A Manifest Detection . . . of Dice Play*. Nashe, despite his vociferous contempt for "hackneys," did not hesitate to plunder from other writers. Lodge made such artful use of many books, especially in *Catharos, The Devil Conjured,* and *Wit's Misery,* that Alice Walker comes to the conclusion that "Lodge, even more than the majority of his contemporaries, succumbed to this labour-saving method of book-production." (Miss Walker is accurate except for her assertion that Lodge was worse than fellow hacks.) Rowlands in *Greene's Ghost Haunting Cony-Catchers* stole from Greene's tracts and Nashe's *Summer's Last Will and Testament;* in *The Letting of Humour's Blood* (1604?) he drew heavily upon Lodge's *Wit's Misery.* Deloney borrowed and reworked material from jest-books, the popular *Life and Pranks of Long Meg of Westminster,* Thomas Fortescue's *The Forest,* Stephen Batman's *The Doom Warning All Men to the Judgment,* and Thomas Johnson's *Cornucopiae.*[28]

Equally flagrant were the borrowings of Dekker in his underworld tracts, *The Bellman of London* (1608) and *Lanthorn and Candlelight* (1609). To the revelations of his predecessors he added little. When he composed *The Bellman of London,* he sat at his desk surrounded by four tracts of Greene (*A Notable Discovery of Cosenage, The Second Part of Cony-Catching, The Third Part of Cony-Catching,* and *The Defense of Cony-Catching*), Awdeley's *Fraternity of Vagabonds* (1565), Harman's

Caveat to Common Curseters (1567), *Mihil Mumchance* (1597), and Rowlands' *Greene's Ghost Haunting Cony-Catching*. From these tracts, most of which were secondary sources because of their indebtedness to earlier books, he lifted here and there, arranging material to suit his purposes and rewriting passages when necessary. The result of his efforts is the following conglomeration:

DEKKER'S *The Bellman of London*

	DEKKER	SOURCES
Upright Man	pp. 92–93	Harman, pp. 31–35
Ruffler	p. 94	Harman, pp. 29–31
Angler, Rogue, etc.	pp. 94–100	Harman, pp. 35–47
Quire Bird	pp. 100–101	Awdeley, p. 4
Abraham Man, Whipjack, Counterfeit Crank	pp. 101–103	Harman, pp. 47–51
Dummerer	p. 103	Harman, pp. 57–59
Jackman, Patricio	pp. 103–104	Awdeley, pp. 5–6 Harman, p. 60
Irish Toil	pp. 104–105	Awdeley, p. 5
Swigman	p. 105	Awdeley, p. 5
Kinchin Co., Mort, Dells, Doxies	pp. 105–107	Harman, pp. 73–76
Walking Mort, Autem Mort	pp. 107–109	Harman, pp. 67–68
Bawdy Basket	p. 109	Harman, p. 65
Demanders of Glimmers	pp. 109–110	Harman, pp. 61 f.
Haunts of beggars	pp. 110–111	Harman, pp. 77–78
Cheating Law	pp. 116–124	*Mihil Mumchance*, title page, sigs. B1v–B2, B3–C2
Barnard's Law	pp. 124–132	Greene, *Notable Discovery*, pp. 17–20, 26–31
Vincent's Law	pp. 132–136	Greene, *Second Part*, pp. 19–22
Black Art	pp. 136–138	Greene, *Second Part*, pp. 54–55

Curbing Law	pp. 138–140	Greene, *Second Part*, pp. 47–49
Prigging Law	pp. 141–145	Greene, *Second Part*, pp. 13–16
Lifting Law	pp. 145–147	Greene, *Second Part*, pp. 44–46, 47
(1) Batfowlers	pp. 147–148	Rowlands, p. 19
(2) Tale of a lifter	p. 148	Awdeley, p. 10, or *Mihil Mumchance*, sig. D2
(3) Tale of a rogue	pp. 148–149	Rowlands, pp. 19–20
High Law	pp. 150–151	Greene, *Notable Discovery*, p. 38
Sacking Law	pp. 152–154	Greene, *Notable Discovery*, pp. 38–39, 41–42
Figging Law	pp. 154–161	Greene, *Notable Discovery*, p. 39; *Second Part*, pp. 30–37
Five Jumps at Leapfrog		
(1) Horse-coursing	p. 162	Rowlands, pp. 14–15
(2) Carrying stones	pp. 162–164	Greene, *Defense of Cony-Catching*, pp. 38–39; Rowlands, pp. 22–24
(3) Fawning	pp. 164–165	Greene, *Third Part*, pp. 29–31
(4) Fool-taking	pp. 165–166	Greene, *Third Part*, pp. 27–29, 31–33
(5) Spoon-meat	pp. 166–167	Rowlands, pp. 20–21

In one respect this chart gives a misleading impression of Dekker's book, since it reveals neither his picturesque vocabulary and vigorous prose nor the clever framework for his rogue material. On the other hand, the chart makes glaringly clear how easy it was to yark up a pamphlet in a night and a day. Interestingly, Dekker extensively reworked the prose of all his sources except that of Greene, most successful of Elizabethan hacks until Dekker eclipsed him.[29]

As this examination of Dekker demonstrates, Greene's cony-catching exposé were the delight of hack writers. Rowlands, Rid, Nixon, the anonymous author of *The Life and Death of Gabriel Ratsey* and *Ratsey's Ghost,* and Luke Hutton in *The Black Dog of Newgate* grabbed passages everywhere. In fact, it is hardly an exaggeration to allege that chronicles of the underworld for forty years after his death were warmed over snips and snatches from Greene. (Since some of Greene's material came from Awdeley, Harman, and *A Manifest Detection . . . of Dice Play,* "revelations" in the 1630's are often traceable to books written about seventy-five years earlier.) Naturally each writer claimed inside knowledge, much as Greene had done in 1591 and 1592, but the supposedly inside knowledge came from the pages of books.

In these later exploitations of Greene's pamphlets an interesting fact emerges: only on rare occasions did more than one writer appropriate identical material. For the most part, as though aware of what their fellow hacks were pilfering, Greene's successors respected the thefts of others. But perhaps in final analysis this fact should not surprise us too much, since authors of underworld tracts, not unlike scholars, evidently collected all books pertaining to their subject before they began to write, and kept them at hand for easy reference. Or perhaps there may even be honor among thieves.

The usefulness of Greene's books to his successors is apparent in the following examination of *The Second Part of Cony-Catching,* from which four authors, Dekker, Rowlands, and the anonymous authors of *The Life and Death of Gabriel Ratsey, Ratsey's Ghost,* and *Mihil Mumchance,* borrowed enough material to "compose" six tracts.

GREENE, *The Second Part of Cony-Catching* [30]

GREENE	BORROWINGS
pp. 3–4 Cant of Black Art, Curbing Law, Vincent's Law, Lifting Law, Prigging Law	Dekker, *Bellman*, III, 137, 139, 132, 146, 141 (identical terminology and cant)
pp. 13–16 Prigging Law	Dekker, *Bellman*, III, 141–145 (verbatim except for one omission)
pp. 19–22 Vincent's Law	Dekker, *Bellman*, III, 132–136 (verbatim except for addition of abuses in tennis and shooting)
p. 25 "seeking with the Orators *Benevolentiam captare*"	*Ratsey's Ghost*, sig. D4 (similar phrasing)
p. 25 "I thinke he would with *Batillius* hang himself"	*Life and Death of Gabriel Ratsey*, sig. C1 (verbatim)
p. 27 "the Conny-catchers . . . were brought to the place of judgement, and there like valiant youthes, they thrust twelve men into a corner, who found them guiltlesse"	*Ibid.*, sig. E2 (almost verbatim)
p. 28 "*Miserere mei*, had like to have beene my best mattins . . . and that is the next neighbour to the gallows"	*Ibid.*, sig. A3v (almost verbatim)
pp. 30–36 Figging Law	Dekker, *Bellman*, III, 154–161 (verbatim, but rearranged)
	Dekker, *Jests to Make You Merry*, II, 326–329 (similar material)

GREENE, *The Second Part of Cony-Catching* [30]

GREENE	BORROWINGS
p. 34 Nips and foists of city and country	Rowlands, p. 18 (paraphrased)
p. 34 "An Eagles eie to spy out a purchase, . . . and then a Lions heart, not to feare what the end will bee"	*Life and Death of Gabriel Ratsey*, sig. A4 (almost verbatim)
p. 37 "although they be by the great discretion of the Judges . . . to beare fruit fit for the gallows"	*Ibid.*, sig. B1v (verbatim)
pp. 37–39 Cony-catcher's trick	Rowlands, pp. 15–16 (freely adapted)
p. 39 "which stroke such a quandary . . . small beere next his heart"	*Life and Death of Gabriel Ratsey*, sig. A4v (verbatim)
pp. 39–40 How to lift a purse	Rowlands, pp. 17–18 (freely adapted)
pp. 44–46 Lifting Law	Dekker, *Bellman*, III, 145–147 (close rendering) Dekker, *Jests to Make You Merry*, II, 312–314 (similar tricks)
pp. 46–47 Theft of articles from scrivener's shop	Rowlands, pp. 18–19 (freely rendered)
p. 47 Brokers	*Mihil Mumchance*, sig. D4v (adapted) Dekker, *Bellman*, III, 149–150 (freely adapted)
pp. 47–49 Curbing Law	Dekker, *Bellman*, III, 138–140 (verbatim)
pp. 51–53 Curber cozens maid	*Life and Death of Gabriel Ratsey*, sigs. A3v–B1 (similar tale)

p. 53 "Late it grew, and the morning began to wax grey, . . . I refer to them that have greeved at the like losse" | *Ibid.,* sig. B3 (almost verbatim)

pp. 54–55 Black Art | Dekker, *Bellman,* III, 136–138 (verbatim)

pp. 57–59 Tale of a tinker | *Life and Death of Gabriel Ratsey,* sigs. D2v–D3 (almost verbatim)

It is one of the ironies of Grub Street, where memories are short and the "new" usually masks its antiquity, that by 1615 Greene was almost forgotten. In that year his *Disputation between a He Cony-Catcher and a She Cony-Catcher* appeared under the title *Thieves Falling Out . . . Or, The Bellman Wanted a Clapper.* The tract contains a spurious preface signed with the initials "R. G.," but written by a printer or a hack. The reprint was obviously intended to capitalize upon the popularity of Dekker's underworld pamphlets: "Albeit (about some two or three yeares past) the ugly faces of divers dambde abuses, were set naked upon every Post, their Vizards being flead off, both by *Lanthorne and Candlelight,* and by the *Belman of London.*" Thus, Greene bowed to Dekker, as Dekker was to bow to his successors.[31]

Though many a hack barely altered a phrase when he borrowed, a few were actually ingenious. Rid, who had the effrontery to upbraid Dekker publicly for his borrowings from Harman in *The Bellman of London,* and then patched together his own "compositions," has an unusual passage in *Martin Markall, Beadle of Bridewell* (1610):

. . . Brokers *I meane and Usurers, that like vultures prey upon* the simple, those that are *moaths in a Commonwealth,* living upon *the spoile of young gentlemen, as thirstie as a horse-leech, that will never leave drinking untill he burst: A Knave that hath the interest in the leases of fortie bawdie houses, and a receiver of lifts, and a dishonourable supporter of Cut-purses,*

sleeping with his neighbours pledges all night in his bosome, and feeding upon forfeits and penalties, as Ravens doe upon carrion,

one that is *a bowzie, bawdie miser, good for none but himself, and his trugge, the scumme of your seaven deadly sinnes, and an enemy to all good mindes* (p. 14).

With a few minor alterations, Rid wove together material from Greene's *Defense of Cony-Catching* and *A Quip for an Upstart Courtier.*

. . . those miserable *Usurers* (*I meane*) *that like Vultures pray uppon* the spoyle of the poore (*Defense,* p. 14).

This base churle [the broker] is one of the *moaths of the common wealth,* hee is *the spoile of young Gentlemen,* a bloud sucker of the poore, *as thirsty as a horse leach that will never leave drinking while hee burst, a knave that hath intrest in the leases of forty baudy houses, a receiver for lifts, and a dishonorable supporter of cut purses* (*Quip,* p. 243).

sleeping with his neighbors pledges all night in his bosome, and feeding upon forfaits and penalties, as the ravens doe upon carren? (*Defense,* p. 14).

. . . hee [the broker] is (sir) . . . *a bowsie bawdy miser, good for none but himselfe and his trug,* . . . *the scum of the seven deadly sins, an enemy to all good mindes* (*Quip,* pp. 244–245).

This passage illustrates to what lengths hacks were willing to go in order to conceal the poverty of their wit.[32]

It is superfluous, however, to illustrate further or to poke fun at the infantile trickery of hacks. For in analyzing the literary underworld we are no longer discussing literature, only subterfuge. Greene borrowed from his predecessors, it is true, but most of the material in his conycatching tracts is his own; furthermore, he brought to his task the expert skills of a journalist. Dekker borrowed more heavily than Greene, but such was his cleverness in creating an unusual framework for his cant and his rogues that his literary skill at least partly redeemed his thefts. But Rowlands, Nixon, and Rid had little literary skill. They were manufacturers of vendible literary products. They have been disinterred because they throw light on the seamy aspects of Grub Street when it was new. Or perhaps Grub Street was never new; from the beginning it consisted of shreds and patches gathered from dusty, and sometimes not so dusty, books of others.

CHAPTER EIGHT.

CONCLUSION

IT took but little more than a century to produce Grub Street, the inevitable offshoot of the mechanical reproduction of books as well as the inevitable slum that hordes of untalented writers were destined to create. Stationers greedy for gain and commerce were not solely to blame. Young Elizabethans came to London to achieve fame and riches. Those without talents (or interest) in business or in military service saw publication as an avenue to the success that Deloney's characters invariably achieved in the bourgeois fairyland he imposed upon a reality that offered more promises than tangible rewards. But these aspiring authors could not escape into fantasy. The lives of hacks (and often of geniuses) followed an inexorable pattern: idealism fused with social and literary ambitions, the journey to London and St. Paul's Churchyard, haggling with stationers and publication, expectations of patronage — soon disillusionment, then poverty, finally death. In September 1592, Greene, then about thirty-five, died in a squalid tenement of Shoreditch, attended only by his disheveled mistress. In the following year Marlowe was killed in a tavern brawl. Nashe disappeared about 1600 — still a young man. Lodge took refuge in a more lucrative profession. Churchyard undoubtedly died in poverty, still pleading for "charitie." After 1603 nothing more is known of that pathetic translator, Richard Robinson, who recorded almost with tears in his *Eupolemia* the tale of his prolonged bout with poverty and humiliation. Robinson and his fellows had moved from one slum to another until they were buried in unmarked graves somewhere in London. Yet, despite their ordeals these sons of the middle class had achieved some distinction; unlike their forebears they were not to be completely forgotten.

With them had come a diversfied middle-class audience which aristocrats and bourgeois writers flayed intemperately — and repetitively. This rapidly expanding public evidenced the defects characteristic of a mass audience: it craved verse rather than poetry, entertainment rather than profundity, practical treatises rather than philosophical or theological theory. It was an audience which sought the fare supplied in our century by newspapers and magazines. But, as we have seen, it was not so tasteless as its critics alleged. For Spenser and Shakespeare were revered, even if for reasons which made aesthetes cringe, and its desire to be amused (and even to indulge in essentially harmless wish-fullfilment) was not absurd, only human. Regardless of our opinions and reservations, this was to be the audience of the emerging capitalistic era.

The new patron was also from the middle class, the publisher, that businessman much maligned by artists for his exclusive interest in what was marketable and at the same time profitable. (Long before 1600, he had become more important than the handful of nobles who dispensed favors to writers.) Authors invariably refused to recognize that printing was a complex and expensive undertaking requiring organizational and financial acumen. Nor would they often admit that what they deemed the sordid trade of mercenary men had created a new occupation, or profession, for ambitious middle-class men. At the same time these businessmen, without any pretense of altruism, made a tangible contribution to the ideals verbalized by early sixteenth-century humanists. Publishers were never so naive as to overestimate the potentialities of Erasmus' plowboy, but they, inadvertently perhaps, accelerated, by producing in large quantities relatively inexpensive grammars and manuals, the cultural evolution from ignorance to enlightenment. That this "enlightenment" was frequently an euphemism for self-interest is unimportant.

And so it was that middle-class businessmen dominated the Elizabethan literary profession, that middle-class authors accepted (howbeit reluctantly and contemptuously) the hire of these businessmen, and that readers from the same class purchased their wares and imposed to a large extent their tastes upon the new trade. Aristocrats continued to warble for a time in the luxurious confines of estates like that at Wilton, but the professional writer, though he looked enviously at the ivy-clad walls beyond his reach, frequented St. Paul's Churchyard, where he was unceremoniously treated by stationers and readers, but where, despite his paltry pecuniary returns and his trials, he achieved a token of the acclaim he craved.

NOTES

INDEX

NOTES

CHAPTER ONE

AUTHORS IN THEIR MILIEU

1. *The Compound of Alchemy* (1591), sig. M4v.
2. Barnaby Rich, *A New Description of Ireland* (1610), sig. A4.
3. Aubrey, *Brief Lives,* ed. Oliver Lawson Dick (London, 1949), p. 279; Parker, *Correspondence,* ed. John Bruce and T. T. Perowne (Cambridge, 1853), p. 290; Arthington, sig. A3; Tyler, sig. A3v. And see William Webbe, in *Elizabethan Critical Essays,* ed. G. Gregory Smith (Oxford, 1904), I, 226–227.
4. Florio, quoted by Frances A. Yates, *John Florio* (Cambridge, 1934), p. 337; King James, quoted by F. S. Siebert, *Freedom of the Press in England, 1476–1776* (Urbana, 1952), p. 142; Ascham, *The Schoolmaster,* ed. W. A. Wright (Cambridge, 1904), p. 290. And see Hake, *News out of Paul's Churchyard* (1579), sigs. A3v–A4; Cross, *Virtue's Commonwealth* (1603), sig. N2v; Hall, *Virgidemiarum* (1598), sig. G6v; Daniel, *The Complete Works in Verse and Prose,* ed. A. B. Grosart (Spenser Society, 1885–1896), I, 285–286.
5. Lyly, *The Complete Works,* ed. R. W. Bond (Oxford, 1902), I, 4. See Franklin B. Williams, Jr., "Robert Tofte," *RES,* XIII (1937), 292.
6. For Mabbe, see A. L. Rowse, *The England of Elizabeth* (London, 1950), p. 213.
7. For discussions of the Inns of Court, see Rowse, *The England of Elizabeth,* pp. 523–526; C. H. Conley, *The First English Translators of the Classics* (New Haven, 1927), pp. 23–33; Eleanor Rosenberg, *Leicester — Patron of Letters* (New York, 1955), pp. 177–180. Also see "A Young Gentleman of the University," in Earle's *Micro-cosmography* (1628).
8. Burghley, quoted by G. B. Harrison, in his edition of Henry Percy's *Advice to His Son* (London, 1930), p. 39; Alfred Harbage, *Shakespeare and the Rival Tradition* (New York, 1952), p. 98. For the status of university graduates, see William Segar, *Honor Military and Civil* (1602), sig. T6v; and "A Younger Brother" in Earle's *Micro-cosmography.* Interesting discussions of Tudor class fluidity

appear in Lewis Einstein, *Tudor Ideals* (New York, 1921), pp. 131–139; Mildred Campbell, *The English Yeoman* (New Haven, 1942); James A. Williamson, *The Tudor Age* (London, 1953).

9. *The Three Parnassus Plays,* ed. J. B. Leishman (London, 1949), p. 144.

10. Harvey, in Smith, I, 113.

11. See George Burke Johnston, " 'An Epistle Mendicant' by Ben Jonson," *N & Q,* n.s., I (1954), 471; Lane, quoted by Ray Heffner, "Did Spenser Die in Poverty?" *MLN,* XLVIII (1933), 223. Heffner's acceptance of Spenser's destitution is, correctly I believe, disputed by Josephine Waters Bennett, "Did Spenser Starve?" *MLN,* LII (1937), 400–401.

12. Drayton, *Works,* ed. J. William Hebel (Oxford, 1931–1941), IV, 391; Peacham, quoted by Bernard H. Newdigate, *Michael Drayton and His Circle* (Oxford, 1941), p. 221. In contrasting Munday and Drayton, Celeste Turner naively observes that "Henslowe's shillings meant little" to the latter; see *Anthony Mundy — An Elizabethan Man of Letters* (Berkeley, 1928), p. 115.

13. Lodge, *The Complete Works* (Hunterian Club, [1879–1888]), I, 37; Wood, *Athenae Oxonienses,* II, 383; Lodge, *The Works of Seneca* (1614), sig. [ ] 5v. Like other scholars I am heavily indebted to Charles J. Sisson's exemplary study of Lodge, *Thomas Lodge and Other Elizabethans* (Cambridge, Mass., 1933). However, Sisson's assertion (pp. 109–110) that *A Treatise of the Plague* "was an attempt to make up from Lodge's real profession of literature what he was failing to achieve in his new profession," appears to be as whimsical as Wood's statement.

14. Nashe, *The Works,* ed. R. B. McKerrow (London, 1910), I, 303; I, 157; III, 30–31.

15. Harvey, *Four Letters,* ed. G. B. Harrison (London, 1923), p. 19; Jonson, ed. C. H. Herford and Percy Simpson (Oxford, 1925–1952), I, 142. Also compare a similar observation of Horace Walpole, quoted by A. S. Collins, *Authorship in the Days of Johnson* (London, 1927), pp. 189–190.

16. Quoted by C. T. Prouty, *George Gascoigne* (New York, 1942), p. 61; Fletcher, in *Elizabethan Sonnets,* ed. Sidney Lee (New York, n.d.), II, 27; Harvey, *The Works,* ed. A. B. Grosart (The Huth Library, 1884–1885), I, 289.

17. Nashe, in Smith, I, 317; Turbervile, quoted by J. E. Hankins, *The Life and Works of George Turbervile* (Lawrence, Kansas, 1940), p. 28; *The Three Parnassus Plays,* ed. Leishman, p. 240; Webbe, in Smith, I, 246, and note I, 255. Similar accusations of drunkenness

appear in Nashe, *Works*, III, 333; R. W.'s *Martin Mar-Sixtus* (1591), sig. A3v; Marston, quoted by Turner, *Anthony Mundy*, p. 130; and Earle, *Micro-cosmography* (1628), sigs. F1v–F3.

18. Meres, ed. Don Cameron Allen, in *University of Illinois Studies in Language and Literature*, XVI (1933), 84, 75; Harvey, *Four Letters*, ed. Harrison, p. 20.

19. See Harvey, *Four Letters*, ed. Harrison, pp. 19–20; Greene, *Groatsworth of Wit*, ed. G. B. Harrison (London, 1923), p. 41.

20. Elyot, *The Governor*, ed. H. H. S. Craft (London, 1880), pp. 58, 63–64, 70. Probably the classic expression of the utility of history appears in William Baldwin's preface to *The Mirror for Magistrates*, ed. Lily B. Campbell (Cambridge, 1938), pp. 65–66.

21. Smith, I, 65, 237, 173, 264. Note the puritanical tirade against Aeneas' behavior in Rich, *Room for a Gentleman* (1609), sigs. D3–D3v.

22. *Marginalia*, ed. G. C. Moore Smith (Stratford-upon-Avon, 1913), p. 148.

23. Smith, I, 76, 332. J. E. Spingarn, in *A History of Literary Criticism in the Renaissance* (New York, 1899), pp. 267–268, notes the similarity between the views of artists and their opponents.

24. Agrippa, *Of the Vanity and Uncertainty of Arts and Sciences* (1569), sig. D3; Nashe and Harvey, in Smith, I, 337, 94. Harington replied at length to Agrippa in his preface to *Orlando Furioso*.

25. *The Letters of John Chamberlain*, ed. N. E. McClure (Philadelphia, 1939), p. 24; Harvey, *Marginalia*, pp. 144–145; Greville, quoted by Geoffrey Bullough, "Fulk Greville, First Lord Brooke," *MLR*, XXVIII (1933), 12.

26. See Castiglione, ed. Walter Raleigh (London, 1900), p. 85. Note Ascham's comment on the neglect of the *Courtier* in noble circles, in *The Schoolmaster*, p. 218. See also J. W. Saunders, "The Stigma of Print. A Note on the Social Basis of Tudor Poetry," *Essays in Criticism*, I (1951), 139–164.

27. Spenser, in Smith, I, 88. And note Lyly's feigned amateurism, in *Works*, I, 182.

28. Wood, *Athenae Oxonienses*, I, 683. I have included Barnfield among amateurs because he appears to be a writer who dabbled in verse for an aristocratic coterie.

29. Quoted by Hankins, *The Life and Works of George Turbervile*, p. 20.

30. Pettie, *The Civil Conversation of M. Stefano Guazzo* (1586), ed. Edward Sullivan (London, 1925), p. 8; Puttenham, in Smith, II, 22, 23–24.

CHAPTER TWO

THE AUDIENCE

1. Churchyard, *The Mirror of Man and Manners of Men* (1594), sig. A2v.

2. Webster, *The Complete Works*, ed. F. L. Lucas (London, 1927), I, 107; Rowlands, *'Tis Merry When Gossips Meet* (1602), in *The Complete Works* (Hunterian Club, 1872–1880), pp. 6–8. Note also Rich, *Faults, Faults* (1606), sig. B3v; R. C., *The Time's Whistle*, ed. J. M. Cowper (London, 1871), pp. 28–29.

3. Dekker, *The Wonderful Year* (1603), in *The Plague Pamphlets*, ed. F. P. Wilson (Oxford, 1925), p. 4.

4. Dekker, *The Seven Deadly Sins of London* (Cambridge, 1905), p. 3; Florio, *A World of Words* (1598), sig. a5v; Marston, *The Scourge of Villainy*, ed. G. B. Harrison (London, 1925), pp. 48, 3–4. See also Vaughan, *The Spirit of Detraction* (1611), sig. *4.

5. Drayton, *Works*, I, 211; Middleton, *The Works*, ed. A. H. Bullen (London, 1886), VIII, 8–9; Marston, *The Scourge of Villainy*, pp. 3–4. Cf. Niccols, *The Furies* (1614), sig. A5.

6. Dekker, *The Non-Dramatic Works*, ed. A. B. Grosart (The Huth Library, 1884–1886), II, 89; Gascoigne, *The Complete Works*, ed. J. W. Cunliffe (Cambridge, 1907–1910), I, 11. Cf. Rich, *Faults, Faults*, sig. L4.

7. *The Letters and Epigrams of Sir John Harington*, ed. N. E. McClure (Philadelphia, 1930), pp. 276–277, and note Breton's variation in *The Works in Verse and Prose*, ed. A. B. Grosart (Edinburgh, 1879), I, lxii; Marston, *The Scourge of Villainy*, ed. Harrison, p. 48.

8. Hollyband, quoted by M. St. Clare Byrne, *The Elizabethan Home* (London, 1925), p. 4; Statute of 1406, quoted by Clara P. McMahon, *Education in Fifteenth-Century England* (Baltimore, 1947), p. 99.

9. Goldsmiths, quoted by Sylvia L. Thrupp, *The Merchant Class of Medieval London* (Chicago, 1948), p. 158, and see her interesting study of a fifteenth-century literacy test, pp. 156–158; Campbell, *The English Yeoman*, pp. 263, 268. For much of the material in this paragraph I am indebted to Plant, *The English Book Trade* (London, 1939), p. 36. See also G. E. and K. R. Fussell, *The English Countryman . . . 1500–1900* (London, 1955), p. 22. J. W. Adamson has an excellent discussion of commerce and literacy in *A Short History of Education* (Cambridge, 1919), pp. 77–80.

10. *A Moral Method of Civil Policy* (1576), sigs. C4–C4v.

11. Lever, *Sermons* (1550), ed. Edward Arber (London, 1870), p. 81; and see J. W. Adamson, "The Extent of Literacy in the Fifteenth

and Sixteenth Centuries," *The Library*, 4th series, X (1929–30), 171–173). In *A Short History of Education*, p. 135, Adamson has some cautionary remarks on this subject. In *Tudor Puritanism* (Chicago, 1939), pp. 466–469, M. M. Knappen, I believe, is much too pessimistic about sixteenth-century literacy and much too generous in his praise of Puritans.

12. See H. S. Bennett, *English Books & Readers, 1457–1557* (Cambridge, 1952), p. 188; Fritz Caspari, *Humanism and the Social Order in Tudor England* (Chicago, 1954), p. 62. There is an interesting discussion of humanism in Adamson, pp. 107–132; for a sharply different interpretation of More's *Utopia*, see J. W. Allen, *A History of Political Thought in the Sixteenth Century* (London, 1941), pp. 153–156.

13. Plant, pp. 37–38; J. Howard Brown, *Elizabethan Schooldays* (Oxford, 1933), pp. 7–8.

14. Harrison, *A Description of England*, ed. F. J. Furnivall (London, 1877–1881), II, 83; Lever, *Sermons*, ed. Arber, p. 123; Magnus, quoted by Cornelius Brown, *A History of Newark-on-Trent* (Newark, 1904–1907), II, 186; *The English Courtier and the Country Gentleman*, sig. C4; Tawney, *The Agrarian Problem in the Sixteenth Century* (London, 1912), p. 135. Adamson (pp. 73–88) discusses the growth of popular education in the fifteenth century.

15. Neale, *Queen Elizabeth* (London, 1947), p. 22. For accounts of female education up to the sixteenth century, see Dorothy Gardiner, *English Girlhood at School* (London, 1929), and Mary Agnes Cannon, *The Education of Women During the Renaissance* (Washington, 1916). Note also Robert Vaughan, *A Dialogue Defensive for Women against Malicious Detractors*, quoted by Louis B. Wright, *Middle-Class Culture in Elizabethan England* (Chapel Hill, N. C., 1935), p. 468.

16. Thrupp, p. 171, and see pp. 169–174; Becon, *A New Catechism*, quoted by Foster Watson, *Report of the Commissioner of Education for the Year 1902* (Washington, 1903), I, 503; Mulcaster, ed. R. H. Quick (London, 1888), p. 167; Adamson, p. 61, and Rowse, *The England of Elizabeth*, p. 502, but note Godfrey Davies, *The Early Stuarts, 1603–1660* (Oxford, 1937), p. 355; Hyrde, quoted by Watson, *Vives and the Renascence Education of Women* (London, 1912), p. 166. For an account of educated women in the sixteenth century, see Myra Reynolds, *The Learned Lady in England, 1650–1760* (Boston, 1920), pp. 1–37.

17. Adamson, pp. 171–172. Stephen Gardiner, Bishop of Winchester, averred, absurdly, that "not the hundreth part of the realme" was able to read; see Bennett, p. 28. Miss Thrupp (p. 158) conjectures after her examination of a literacy test administered in the

fifteenth century that 50 per cent of lay male Londoners could read English. Wright, in *Middle-Class Culture,* pp. 43–80, is especially good in his discussion of the contributions of livery companies to sixteenth-century education. Also see Davies, *The Early Stuarts, 1603–1660,* p. 356; and William Nelson, "The Teaching of English in Tudor Grammar Schools," *SP,* XLIX (1952), 119–143.

18. Fletcher, in *Elizabethan Sonnets,* ed. Lee, II, 27; Bacon, quoted by Wright, *Middle-Class Culture,* p. 67.

19. Thrupp, p. 161; Breton, *The Court and Country,* in *Works,* ed. Grosart, II, 10.

20. Pace, quoted by Caspari, pp. 136–137; Fenton, *A Form of Christian Policy* (1574), sig. 2D4v. But see J. H. Hexter, "The Education of the Aristocracy in the Renaissance," *The Journal of Modern History,* XXII (1950), 1–20.

21. Quoted by Plant, p. 45.

22. Harrison, *A Description of England,* II, 105–106, 128; Wilson, *The State of England, 1600,* ed. F. J. Fisher (London, 1936), pp. 23–24; Tawney, quoted by Alfred Harbage, *Shakespeare's Audience* (New York, 1941), p. 54. Tawney's division of Tudor society is as follows:

Gentry, professional men, officials	6.3 per cent
Dealers and retailers	19.3
Craftsmen	52.0
Laborers, carriers, etc.	c. 15.0
Servants and miscellaneous	c. 7.4

23. Manningham, *Diary,* ed. John Bruce (Westminster, 1868), p. 63; Bodley, *Letters . . . to Thomas James,* ed. G. W. Wheeler (Oxford, 1926), p. xliii.

24. *A Description of England,* II, 133.

25. Nashe, quoted by Violet A. Wilson, *Society Women of Shakespeare's Time* (New York, 1925), pp. 137–138; Meres, ed. Allen, p. 81.

26. *Brief Lives,* ed. Dick, pp. 138, 146.

27. Aubrey, quoted by Frances Berkeley Young, *Mary Sidney, Countess of Pembroke* (London, 1912), pp. 39–40; Earl of Bedford, see Gladys Scott Thomson, *Life in a Noble Household, 1641–1700* (New York, 1937), pp. 263–265.

28. Warwick, Hist. Mss. Comm., Appendix, II, 102; Howard, see David Mathew, "The Library at Naworth," in *For Hilaire Belloc* (London, 1942), pp. 117–130; Coke, see David Rogers, "The Holkham Collection," *Bodleian Library Record,* IV (1952–53), 258; Percy, see Hist. Mss. Comm., VI, Appendix, 226–231, and Edward de Fonblanque, *Annals of The House of Percy* (London, 1887). Also see

Phoebe Sheavyn, *The Literary Profession in the Elizabethan Age* (Manchester, 1909), pp. 150–152.

29. Quoted by Conyers Read, *Mr. Secretary Cecil and Queen Elizabeth* (London, 1955), p. 30.

30. *The Three Parnassus Plays*, ed. Leishman, pp. 306–307, 192, and see Marston, *The Scourge of Villainy,* ed. Harrison, pp. 3–4; Leslie Hotson, *Shakespeare's Sonnets Dated and Other Essays* (London, 1950), pp. 34–35; Moffett, *Nobilis,* ed. Virgil B. Heltzel and Hoyt H. Hudson (San Marino, 1940), p. 83.

31. *The Furies,* sig. A3.

32. *The Letters of John Chamberlain,* ed. McClure, I, 276, 24, 45, 57, 67, 70, 191. For additional comments see McClure's introduction and E. P. Statham, *A Jacobean Letter-Writer: The Life and Times of John Chamberlain* (London, n.d.).

33. Rich, *Faults, Faults,* sig. F2; Jonson, III, 305; Osborne, quoted by A. W. Reed, "Chivalry and the Idea of a Gentleman," in *Chivalry,* ed. Edgar Prestage (London, 1928), p. 225; *The English Courtier and the Country Gentleman,* sig. H4. See also Brathwaite, *The English Gentleman* (1630), sigs. 2F2–2F3.

34. F. E. Halliday, *Richard Carew of Antony* (London, 1953), pp. 23, 308. See also Leslie Hotson's account of Richard Stonley's library, in *SB,* II (1949–50), 49–61.

35 Whetstone, *An Heptameron of Civil Discourses* (1582), sigs. R4v–S1v; Rowse (London, 1941), pp. 428–429; Ramsey's library is described in Louis B. Wright's "William Perkins: Elizabethan Apostle of 'Practical Divinity,' " *HLQ,* III (1940), 195. Note the praise of learning by John Oglander, a country squire living on the Isle of Wight, in Cecil Aspinall-Oglander, *Nunwell Symphony* (London, 1945), pp. 48–49.

36. Yonge, quoted by Bruce Pattison, *Music and Poetry of the English Renaissance* (London, 1948), p. 7; Whiteways, see Thomas D. Murphy, ed., "The Diary of William Whiteway of Dorchester, County Dorset, from the Year 1618 to the Year 1635," unpubl. diss. (Yale), pp. xxx–xxxi. See also Thrupp, pp. 247–249. For favorable portraits of merchants in literature (mostly drawn from the seventeenth century), see Wright, *Middle-Class Culture,* pp. 21–34.

37. S. I., *Bromleion,* sig. *4v.

38. Davies, *A Scourge for Paper-Persecutors,* sig. B4.

39. Coote, sig. A3. One of the commendatory verses in Hilles' treatise was written by Robert Hanley, "merchant."

40. Nashe, *Works,* III, 84, and also see I, 280; *The Defense of Cony-Catching* (1592), ed. G. B. Harrison (London, 1924), p. 10. I have attributed this passage in the *Defense* to Nashe in "The Relationship of Robert Greene and Thomas Nashe (1588–1592)," *PQ,*

NOTES TO CHAPTER TWO

XXXIII (1954), 360–361. In "Best Sellers in Seventeenth-Century Fiction," *PBSA*, XLVII (1953), 362–363, Charles C. Mish conjectures that in the seventeenth century *Jack of Newbury* went through fourteen editions and *The Gentle Craft* sixteen editions. Harvey refers favorably to the latter in his *Marginalia*, pp. 227–228.

41. *Captain Cox, His Ballads and Books,* ed. F. J. Furnivall (London, 1871), pp. 28–31.

42. Donne, quoted by Wilson, *Society Women of Shakespeare's Time*, p. 144; Jonson, *Volpone*, V, 73–74. Note also Harrison, *A Description of England*, II, 271–272.

43. Nashe, *Works*, I, 173; Northampton and King James, quoted by Wilson, *Society Women of Shakespeare's Time*, pp. 172, 176–177; Powell, quoted by John Buxton, *Sir Philip Sidney and the English Renaissance* (London, 1954), p. 182.

44. *Vives and the Renascence Education of Women,* ed. Watson, p. 33; Platt (1640 ed.), sig. A3v, and note Tusser, *Five Hundred Points of Good Husbandry*, ed. W. Payne and S. J. Herrtage (London, 1878), pp. 159, 161. Markham was indebted to Thomas Dawson's *The Good Housewife's Jewel* (1587), from which he occasionally lifted material verbatim; see Dawson, sigs. E8v–F1, and Markham's *The English Housewife*, in *A Way to Get Wealth* (1630), sigs. E5v–E6. See D'Arcy Power's excellent discussion of the international popularity of Rosslin, "*The Birth of Mankind* or *The Woman's Book* — A Bibliographical Study," *The Library*, 4th series, VIII (1927–28), 1–37. Wright deals with feminine taste in *Middle-Class Culture*, pp. 103–118, 201–227.

45. *Vives and the Renascence Education of Women*, p. 203; Lyly, *Works*, II, 8–10. See Wright's description of feminine interest in romances, *Middle-Class Culture*, pp. 110–112, 116–117.

CHAPTER THREE

THE TASTE OF THE AUDIENCE

1. See Conley, *The First English Translators of the Classics*, pp. 78–80; Beard, *The Theater of God's Judgments* (1612 ed.), sigs. A5v–A6; Dering, *A Brief and Necessary Catechism* (1590 ed.), sig. A1v. Also see Fenton, *Golden Epistles* (1575), sig. 2¶1; and Vaughan, *The Spirit of Detraction* (1611), sigs. P3–P3v. There is an interesting discussion in Wright, *Middle-Class Culture*, pp. 231 ff.

2. Udall, *The First Tome of the Paraphrase of Erasmus* (1548), sig. B3v; Robinson, *A Record of Ancient Histories* (1595 ed.), sigs. A2v–A3.

3. Nashe, *Works*, III, 324; Daniel, *Poems and A Defence of Ryme,*

ed. A. C. Sprague (Cambridge, Mass., 1930), p. 82; Drayton, *Works*, III, 175–177; Davies, *A Scourge for Paper-Persecutors* (1625), sigs. A3v–B1. See also Hall, *Virgidemiarum* (1598), sigs. B1–B1v; *Certain Elegies, Done by Sundry Excellent Wits* (1620), sigs. A7v–A8v; and Reynolds, *Mythomystes* (1623), sigs. B1v–B2.

4. *Letters and Epigrams*, ed. McClure, pp. 276–277.

5. H. B. Lathrop, "The First English Printers and Their Patrons," *The Library*, 4th series, III (1922–23), 76–78; E. Gordon Duff, *A Century of the English Book Trade* (London, 1905), p. xiv.

6. *Wynkyn de Worde & His Contemporaries* (London, 1925), p. 61.

7. Quoted by H. R. Plomer, "Robert Copland," *Trans. of the Bibliog. Soc.*, III (1895–96), 219.

8. Klotz, "A Subject Analysis of English Imprints for Every Tenth Year from 1480 to 1640," *HLQ*, I (1937–38), 418. For discussions of Elizabethan fondness for religious works, see F. P. Wilson, *Elizabethan and Jacobean* (Oxford, 1945), pp. 20, 88, and "Guides to Godliness" in Wright, *Middle-Class Culture*, pp. 228–296. See also the excellent discussion of books printed before 1557 in Bennett, *English Books & Readers, 1475 to 1557*, pp. 65–151. For studies of the popularity of fiction, see Charles C. Mish, "Best Sellers in Seventeenth-Century Fiction," *PBSA*, XLVII (1953), 356–373, and *"Reynard the Fox* in the Seventeenth Century," *HLQ*, XVII (1953–54), 327–344.

9. *The Three Parnassus Plays*, ed. Leishman, p. 247; Cross, sigs. O4v–P1; Rogers, quoted by Wright, *Middle-Class Culture*, p. 231; Stubbes, quoted in *Shakespeare's England* (Oxford, 1916), II, 222. Wright (p. 101) does not accept Stubbes's statement that religious books were not in demand. See also Breton, *The Mother's Blessing*, in *Works*, ed. Grosart, I, 4.

10. Robinson, quoted by Wright, p. 236; anonymous writer, quoted by A. F. Pollard, *The History of England from the Accession of Edward VI. to the Death of Elizabeth (1547–1603)* (London, 1910), pp. 442–443; Sisson, *The Judicious Marriage of Mr Hooker* (Cambridge, 1940), pp. 50, 51, and see pp. 70–73. Sisson (pp. 51, 117) notes that in 1601 booksellers remaindered 1000 copies of Dr. Henry Smith's *Sermons* (1592).

11. Stephens, quoted by Wright, p. 235; Rich, *Opinion Defied* (1613), sig. A4v, and *My Lady's Looking Glass* (1616), sig. I2.

12. Nashe, *Works*, III, 329–330; *The Three Parnassus Plays*, ed. Leishman, p. 207; Spenser, *The Tears of the Muses*, lines 319–326; Stanyhurst, quoted by Vernon Hall, Jr., *Renaissance Literary Criticism* (New York, 1945), p. 198; Chettle, *Kind-Heart's Dream*, ed. G. B. Harrison (London, 1923), p. 16; Marston, quoted by Turner, *Anthony Mundy*, p. 130.

13. Holcroft, quoted by A. S. Collins, *The Profession of Letters* (London, 1928), pp. 31–32; Breton, *Pasquill's Madcap*, in *Works*, ed. Grosart, I, 12; and cf. William Turner, in *A Pepysian Garland*, ed. Hyder E. Rollins (Cambridge, Mass., 1922), p. 34. Wright discusses ballads in *Middle-Class Culture*, pp. 418–433.

14. In *Spanish and Portuguese Romances of Chivalry* (Cambridge, 1920), pp. 262, 293, Henry Thomas is much too dogmatic in his insistence that romances attracted only vulgar readers. Although he grants the popularity of romances among all readers until roughly 1560, Ronald S. Crane has set his terminal date too early; see "The Vogue of *Guy of Warwick* from the Close of the Middle Ages to the Romantic Revival," *PMLA*, XXX (1915), 165–167. Wright discusses romances under "Popular Literary Taste," in *Middle-Class Culture*, pp. 84–90, 110–117, 375–396, and asserts (p. 376) that during the sixteenth century the appeal was primarily to "the less favored classes." See also Sheavyn, pp. 186–188.

15. Quoted in *The Thought & Culture of the English Renaissance*, ed. Elizabeth M. Nugent (Cambridge, 1956), pp. 566–567.

16. *Vives and the Renascence Education of Women*, ed. Watson, p. 196; Tyndale, quoted by Elizabeth J. Sweeting, *Early Tudor Criticism* (Oxford, 1940), p. 162; Perkins, quoted by Wright, *Middle-Class Culture*, p. 248; Fenton, quoted by Wright, p. 346; Ascham, *Toxophilus*, pp. xiv–xv, and repeated in *The Schoolmaster*, pp. 230–231; Dering, *A Brief and Necessary Catechism* (1590 ed.), sig. A1v; Nashe, in Smith, I, 323; Rich, *A New Description of Ireland*, sigs. A3–A3v; *Summary Declaration*, quoted by Frank A. Mumby, *The Romance of Bookselling* (London, 1910), p. 64.

17. Harvey, *A Discursive Problem Concerning Prophecies* (1588), sigs. K2v–K3; Fenton, quoted by Wright, *Middle-Class Culture*, p. 346. See also Martin Parker, *Harry White's Humor*, ed. J. O. Halliwell [Oxford, 1846], p. 11; Cross, *Virtue's Commonwealth* (1603), sigs. O1v–O2; and Davies, *A Scourge for Paper–Persecutors* (1625), sigs. B1–B1v. Hall, in *Renaissance Literary Criticism*, p. 207, notes the snobbery in many of the criticisms of romances.

18. Wilson, quoted by Hall, p. 206; Burghley, in Read, *Mr. Secretary Cecil and Queen Elizabeth*, p. 114; Drayton, *Works*, III, 240; but see Newdigate, *Michael Drayton and His Circle*, p. 22; Tofte, quoted by Williams, "Robert Tofte," *RES*, XIII (1937), 424; Sidney, in Smith, I, 173; Robert Sidney, in Dick Taylor, Jr., "The Third Earl of Pembroke as a Patron of Poetry," *Tulane Studies in English*, V (1955), 42.

19. Cumberland and Essex, in G. C. Williamson, *George, Third Earl of Cumberland (1558–1605)* (Cambridge, 1920), p. 18, and G. B. Harrison, *The Life and Death of Robert Devereux, Earl of Essex*

(London, 1937), p. 74, where the date is given as February 26, 1592; Peele, quoted by Charlotte C. Stopes, *The Life of Henry, Third Earl of Southampton* (Cambridge, 1922), p. 95; *The Letters of John Chamberlain*, ed. McClure, pp. 230–231; De Vere, quoted by Turner, *Anthony Mundy*, p. 43.

20. Aubrey, *Brief Lives*, ed. Dick, p. 149; Segar, *Honor Military and Civil* (1602), sig. E5v; Cockaine, paraphrased by G. B. Harrison, *An Elizabethan Journal, 1591–1594* (London, 1928), p. 17; Ashley, *Of Honour*, ed. Virgil B. Heltzel (San Marino, 1947), pp. 8–9, from the editor's summary of Ashley's autobiography; Puttenham, in Smith, II, 43–44, and note 87; Laneham, *Captain Cox, His Ballads and Books*, ed. Furnivall, pp. 28–30, xii–xiii; Parrot, *The Mastive* (1615), sig. I1; Overbury, quoted by Thomas, *Spanish and Portuguese Romances of Chivalry*, p. 293. See also the autobiography of a London merchant's son, in Wright, *Middle-Class Culture*, pp. 86–87.

21. For Sidney, see Zandvoort, *Sidney's Arcadia*, p. 194; for Jonson, see I, 47, where his editors observe that "the vein of chivalrous romance which undoubtedly ran in Jonson's nature disengaged itself so freely from the obsessions of realism and satire."

22. Ascham, *The Schoolmaster*, p. 230; Dering, *A Brief and Necessary Catechism* (1590 ed.), sigs. A1v–A2; Robinson, *The Reward of Wickedness* (1574), sig. A4; Bastard, *Chrestoleros*, sig. C4; Rich, *My Lady's Looking Glass* (1616), sig. I2, and cf. *Faults, Faults* (1606), sig. L3v. Note also Davies, *Sir Martin Mar-People* (1590), sigs. A3v–A4; and Evans, *Oedipus* (1615), sigs. A5–A5v.

23. See A. C. Judson, *The Life of Edmund Spenser* (Baltimore, 1945), pp. 52–53; Ashley, *Of Honour*, ed. Heltzel, pp. 8–9; Laneham, *Captain Cox, His Ballads and Books*, ed. Furnivall, pp. xii–xiii; Gascoigne's printer, quoted by Clara Gebert, *An Anthology of Elizabethan Dedications and Prefaces* (Philadelphia, 1933), p. 37. See also the account of a rustic's reading in Nash, *Quaternio*, sigs, E1v–E2.

24. *Churchyard's Charge* (1580), sigs. *3–*3v; Saunders, "The Façade of Morality," in *That Soueraine Light* (Baltimore, 1952), p. 14.

25. Cutwode, *Caltha Poetarum* (1599), sigs. A5–A5v; Greene, *The Complete Works*, ed. A. B. Grosart (Huth Library, 1881–1885), XII, 195–196, 215, 270, 201, 273. For the date of the *Vision*, consult McNeir, *N & Q*, CXCV (1950), 137.

26. Dekker, *Non-Dramatic Works*, ed. Grosart, III, 309, and note Nash's similar observation in *Quaternio*, sigs. A2v–A3; Rich, *The Fruits of Experience*, sig. A2; Bastard, *Chrestoleros*, sig. E8.

27. Sig. A3v.

28. *Wit's Trenchmor* (1597), in *Works*, ed. Grosart, II, 6; *No*

NOTES TO CHAPTER THREE

Whipping Nor Tripping, I, xxxv; *The Pilgrimage to Paradise,* I, 4; *The Strange Fortunes,* II, 4; *The Miseries of Mamillia,* II, 35.

29. Harvey, *Four Letters,* ed. Harrison, p. 41; Greene, *Works,* II, 10; III, 5; V, 145; V, 9, 6; VI, 6; IV, 229.

30. Greene, *Works,* V, 241; VII, 219; XII, 281, 195; VIII, 8; IX, 119; VIII, 109; XI, 113.

31. *A Notable Discovery of Cosenage,* ed. Harrison, pp. 7–8; *The Repentance of Robert Greene,* ed. Harrison, pp. 25–26; *Groatsworth of Wit,* ed. Harrison, p. 6.

32. See, for example, Quentin Reynolds, *The Fiction Factory, or From Pulp Row to Quality Street* (New York, 1955), pp. 74–75.

CHAPTER FOUR

PATRONAGE: "MECOENAS IS YCLAD IN CLAYE"

1. See Samuel Moore, "General Aspects of Literary Patronage in the Middle Ages," *The Library,* 3rd series, IV (1913), 369–392, and Bennett, *English Books & Readers, 1475 to 1557,* pp. 1–18.

2. Cockaine, ed. W. R. Halliday (Oxford, 1932), sigs. A2–A2v; Robinson, *Part of the Harmony of King David's Harp* (1582), sig. A4v.

3. Quoted by Stopes, *The Life of Henry, Third Earl of Southampton,* p. 55. In "The Literature of Patronage, 1580–1630," *Essays in Criticism,* II (1952), 273, Patricia Thomson attributes the tone of dedications to Petrarch.

4. *The Knaves of Spades and Diamonds,* in *Works,* pp. 3–4.

5. Robinson, *Eupolemia,* in *SP,* XXI (1924), 638, 644; Evans, *Oedipus,* sig. A3; Donne, *Poems,* ed. H. J. C. Grierson (Oxford, 1912), I, 150.

6. *The Art of Flattery* (1579), sig. E2v.

7. Anton, *The Philosopher's Satires* (1616), sig. A2; Meres, ed. Allen, p. 70; Barnfield, *The Complaint of Poetry* (1598), sig. A3v; *Eupolemia,* p. 638.

8. Sig. G3v.

9. See H. W. Garrod's excellent discussion, "Erasmus and His English Patrons," *The Library,* 5th series, IV (1949–50), 13, 7; see also the extravagant praise of English patronage by Udall, quoted by Bennett, *English Books & Readers, 1475 to 1557,* p. 40.

10. See Conley, *The First English Translators of the Classics,* pp. 38–41. Conley perhaps accepts too literally the statements of these translators that they sought fame and an "immortall crown" rather than money (pp. 43–44). The dedications of Turbervile and Studley were often unauthorized (pp. 42–43), and Golding candidly admitted

the advertising value of his dedication to the Earl of Bedford (pp. 44–45).

11. Gamzue, "Elizabeth and Literary Patronage," *PMLA*, XLIX (1934), 1049; Puttenham, in Smith, II, 16–18, 21, and note 66; Peele, *The Works*, ed. Alexander Dyce (London, 1828), II, 141; Platt, *The Jewel House of Art and Nature* (1594), sigs. B2–B2v. The poem is quoted by Gamzue, p. 1045 and n.; see also *CSP, Domestic, 1595–1597*, p. 466; Thomas Birch, *Memoirs of the Reign of Queen Elizabeth* (London, 1754), I, 131; Chester, "Thomas Churchyard's Pension," *PMLA*, L (1935), 902; Manningham, *Diary*, ed. Bruce, p. 43.

12. See Neale, *Queen Elizabeth*, pp. 284–287; Daniel, *Works* (1601), sig. A2. See also Conyers Read, *The Tudors* (New York, 1936) p. 51: "Without them [Elizabeth and her predecessors] the finest fruits of the English genius in the sixteenth century might have been trampled under foot in the battle of contending creeds."

13. See Buxton, *Sir Philip Sidney and the English Renaissance*, p. 172. For this discussion of the Sidneys and Herberts, in addition to Buxton, I have drawn upon Sheavyn, pp. 13–15; D. Nichol Smith, "Authors and Patrons," in *Shakespeare's England*, II, 192–195, 197–199, 202–203; Young, *Mary Sidney, Countess of Pembroke*; Thomson, *Essays in Criticism*, II (1952), 267–284; Taylor, *Tulane Studies in English*, V (1955), 41–67.

14. Nashe, *Works*, III, 331, a quotation from Nashe's preface to an unauthorized printing of *Astrophel and Stella* (see footnote 19 below); Daniel, *A Defense of Rime*, in *Poems*, ed. Sprague, p. 129; Thomson, *Essays in Criticism*, II (1952), 277.

15. Spenser, *The Ruins of Time*, lines 261–262; Jonson, quoted by Buxton, p. 230. Drayton's criticism of the countess appears in his *Pastorals* (1606), quoted by Newdigate, *Michael Drayton and His Circle*, p. 59. Sheavyn (p. 17) briefly discusses the Countess of Bedford and Lady Clifford.

16. Smith, *Shakespeare's England*, II, 188–191; Rosenberg, *Leicester — Patron of Letters*, pp. 352–362; *Prothalaminon*, lines 137–138; Florio, *Second Fruits* (1591), ed. R. C. Simioni, Jr. (Gainesville, Fla., 1953), sigs. A3–A3v. See also Sheavyn, pp. 15–16; Judson, *The Life of Edmund Spenser*, p. 67.

By far the most important work on Leicester is Miss Rosenberg's recent study. She has presented cogently many interesting theories, though without adequate corroborative data in many instances. Her view that many "chiefs of state" subsidized propaganda is most attractive and plausible, but she fails to offer sufficient documentation. Miss Rosenberg too often assumes, I believe erroneously, that Leicester approved in advance books dedicated to him. On this question, see Franklin B. Williams, Jr., "An Index of Dedications and Commendatory Verses," *The Library*, 5th series, XII (1957), 14.

17. Florio, *A World of Words* (1598), sig. a3v. Southampton and Essex are discussed by Sheavyn, pp. 16–17, and by Smith, in *Shakespeare's England*, II, 199–202, 195–196. A partial list of books dedicated to Hatton appears in Eric St. John Brooks, *Sir Christopher Hatton* (London, 1946), pp. 124–144. Smith discusses Walsingham and Burghley, II, 196–197, 191–192, and see Conyers Read, *Mr Secretary Walsingham and the Policy of Queen Elizabeth* (Cambridge, Mass., 1925), III, 433–437. About Burghley there is a sharp difference of opinion; see Rowse, *The England of Elizabeth*, pp. 52–53, and Read, *Mr. Secretary Cecil and Queen Elizabeth*, p. 11. Miss Rosenberg, in effect, supports Rowse; see p. 101, n. Professor Virgil Heltzel, who is preparing what will undoubtedly be a definitive study of Elizabethan patronage, discusses "Sir Thomas Egerton as Patron" in *HLQ*, XI (1947–48), 105–127.

18. Sig. A2v.

19. Spenser, in Smith, I, 89; Turbervile, in Chambers, *The Works of the English Poets* (London, 1810), II, 581; Ascham, *The Schoolmaster* (1570), pp. 229–230; Brathwaite, *Nature's Embassy* (1621), ed. J. W. Ebsworth (Boston, Lincolnshire, 1877), p. 287. Another notorious instance of an unauthorized dedication is Nashe's to the Countess of Pembroke (quoted earlier in this chapter) in the first printing of *Astrophel and Stella* (1591); his preface did not appear in the corrected edition of the sonnets issued later in the year. See also Coke's protest against a dedication "published without my privity," quoted in *N & Q*, 1st series, VII (1853), 434.

20. Greene, *Works*, II, 252, and Grosart's note, II, 335–336; II, 141; VIII, 6; VIII, 115–117. Although *Mamillia* was formally dedicated to Lord Darcy, probably Portington or his sister (or both) rewarded Greene. Nicholas Storojenko discusses Greene's patrons in *Works*, I, 20–25.

21. *Works*, III, 176; VI, 152–153; V, 239; VII, 5.

22. *Works*, IV, 6; VII, 224; III, 49. Storojenko (I, 20), however, believes that the Derby family (Lady Margaret and Ferdinando Stanley, the fifth Earl) was actively interested in Greene.

23. *Works*, VI, 5–6, XI, 109; XIV, 299.

24. *Works*, IX, 227. Greene appended no dedications to the five cony-catching tracts of 1591–1592 and to *The Debate between Folly and Love* (1587), a translation which may have been commissioned by printer William Ponsonby.

25. For Churchyard's relations with Hatton, see Brooks, pp. 125–129, and Harris Nicolas, *Memoirs of the Life and Times of Sir Christopher Hatton* (London, 1847), pp. 172, 175–176, 180, 253–254,

304–305; for the poet's relations with Howard, see Conley, pp. 41–42.

26. In my compilations I have included the dedicatees of the twenty sections in his miscellany *Churchyard's Challenge* (1593), which includes books written over a period of thirty years. If the epitaphs in collections such as *The Reviving of the Dead* and *A Feast Full of Sad Cheer* were presented separately to kinsmen and friends of the deceased, the number of Churchyard's patrons would considerably exceed twenty-nine.

27. *The Honor of the Law,* sig. A1v. Epitaphs are discussed in Chapter 7.

28. *A Praise and Report of Master Martin Forbisher's Voyage,* sig. A3; *A Spark of Friendship,* sigs. A2v–A3; and see also *Churchyard's Charge,* sig. **2.

29. Sheavyn, pp. 33–34; *A Warning for the Wise,* sig. A2; *Churchyard's Charge,* sigs. **1v, C3.

30. D'Israeli, "Dedications," in *Curiosities of Literature* (London, 1834), II, 126. See also H. B. Wheatley, *The Dedication of Books to Patron and Friend* (London, 1887), pp. 16–18.

31. *Non-Dramatic Works,* III, 224–246, and see *The Honest Whore, Part II,* ed. Fredson Bowers (Cambridge, 1955), II, 142. This subject is discussed by Wheatley, pp. 28–32, Sheavyn, pp. 36–37; Smith, in *Shakespeare's England,* II, 209.

32. Garrod, p. 2. Garrod notes that the first draft of Erasmus' *De Conscribendis Epistolis* was dedicated to Robert Fisher; another copy to a wealthier patron, Adolphus Veere; a third, in Erasmus' autograph, to William Blount, Lord Mountjoy; and the printed book to Nicholas Bérauld. On multiple dedications, see Williams, *The Library,* 5th series, XII (1957), 20–21.

33. Bailey, see F. P. Wilson, in *Joseph Quincy Adams: Memorial Studies* (Washington, 1948), pp. 559–560; Rich, *The Honesty of This Age,* ed. Peter Cunningham (London, 1844), p. xvi; F. P. Wilson, "Ralph Crane, Scrivener to the King's Players," *The Library,* 4th series, VII (1926–27), 197; Herman R. Mead, "Three Issues of *A Buckler against the Fear of Death,*" *The Library,* 4th series, XXI (1940–41), 199–206. See also Franklin B. Williams, Jr., "Special Presentation Epistles: A Preliminary Check-list," *The Library,* 5th series, VII (1952), 16.

34. See Fred Ives Carpenter, *A Reference Guide to Edmund Spenser* (Chicago, 1923), p. 70; Sheavyn, pp. 17–19; Smith, in *Shakespeare's England,* II, 205, 210–211; Buxton, p. 248; Leila Parsons, "Prince Henry (1594–1612) as Patron of Literature," *MLR,* XLVII (1952), 503–504; and Cecil C. Seronsy, "Daniel's *Panegyrike* and the

Earl of Hertford," *PQ*, XXXII (1953), 342–344; Newdigate, *Michael Drayton and His Circle*, p. 160.

35. Aubrey, *Brief Lives*, ed. Dick, p. 180; Jonson, quoted by Mumby, *The Romance of Bookselling*, p. 131. See also *Ben Jonson*, I, 86, 96, 245–247.

36. Camden, *CSP, Domestic, 1591–1594*, p. 479, and Sheavyn, pp. 31–32; Hakluyt, *APC, 1599–1600*, p. 331; Sadler, sigs. iii–iv; Parker, *Correspondence*, p. xiii.

37. *The Spending of the Money of Robert Nowell*, ed. A. B. Grosart (Manchester, 1877), p. 276; *Roll of Accounts of Duke of Northumberland*, Hist. Mss. Comm., VI, Appendix, pp. 227, 229. See also Sheavyn, p. 26, n.; Smith, in *Shakespeare's England*, II, 211; and Parsons, *MLR*, XLVII (1952), 503; Wilson, in *Joseph Quincy Adams: Memorial Studies*, p. 556.

38. From the Goldsmiths' Company James Mabbe received £10 for *The Diet of Health*; see Rowse, *The England of Elizabeth*, p. 213.

39. Thynne, *Emblems and Epigrams*, ed. F. J. Furnivall (London, 1876), p. 3; Peacham, *The Truth of Our Times* (1638), ed. R. R. Cawley (New York, 1942), pp. 39, 33–34.

40. Howell, quoted by Buxton, p. 137. The use of the dedication as advertisement is discussed by Bennett, *English Books & Readers, 1475 to 1557*, pp. 47–53, and *The Library*, 5th series, IV (1949–50), 155–165. Conley (pp. 84–94) has an excellent discussion of references to Zoilus and Momus.

41. Hall, sigs. E5–E5v, B2; *The Institution of a Gentleman*, sigs. *4–*4v; Rich, sig. A2; Lodge, *Works*, III, 26.

42. Ed. Edward F. Rimbault (London, 1842), p. 76.

43. *Works*, I, 195, 241.

44. *Works*, II, 9, 202.

45. Davies, *A Scourge for Paper-Persecutors*, sig. C3v; Dekker, in *The Plague Pamphlets*, ed. Wilson, p. 65. See also the attacks on the language of dedications in the following: Carew, *The Survey of Cornwall* (1602), in Halliday, *Richard Carew of Antony*, p. 79; Woodhouse, *The Contention between the Elephant and the Flea* (1605), ed. A. B. Grosart (Manchester, 1877), sig. A2; J. S., *Cynthia's Revenge* (1613), sig. A2; Thomas Heywood, *The Fair Maid of the West, Part I* (1631), in *Works*, II, 257.

46. Middleton, *Works*, VIII, 51–52; Dekker, *A Knight's Conjuring*, ed. Rimbault, p. iii, and compare *Non-Dramatic Works*, II, 87–88. See also Brathwaite, *A Strappado for the Devil*, ed. J. W. Ebsworth (Boston, Lincolnshire, 1877), p. 63; Peacham, *Thalia's Banquet* (1620), sig. B3v; *The Three Parnassus Plays*, ed. Leishman, pp. 103, 125–126, 142, 146–147, 150, 180–187.

47. Rowlands, *A Fool's Bolt Is Soon Shot* (1614), in *Works*, p. 5;

Davies, *A Scourge for Paper-Persecutors,* sig. B3; Bacon, quoted in *Shakespeare's England,* II, 208.

CHAPTER FIVE

WRITERS AND STATIONERS

1. The literature relating to stationers is too voluminous to be cited in detail here. Convenient condensations are H. G. Aldis' "The Book Trade, 1557–1625," *CHEL,* IV, 378–414; McKerrow's "Booksellers, Printers, and the Stationers' Trade," in *Shakespeare's England,* II, 212–239; Ernest A. Savage, *Old English Libraries* (Chicago, 1912), pp. 199–208. I have found useful Alfred W. Pollard's *Shakespeare's Fight with the Pirates* (London, 1917); Siebert's *Freedom of the Press in England, 1476–1776;* Leo Kirschbaum's "Author's Copyright in England before 1640," *PBSA,* XL (1946), 43–80, and *Shakespeare and the Stationers* (Columbus, Ohio, 1955); and, above all, Greg's *The Shakespeare First Folio* (Oxford, 1955) and *Some Aspects and Problems of London Publishing between 1550 and 1650* (Oxford, 1956).

2. Wither, *The Scholar's Purgatory,* quoted by Arber, *S. R.,* IV, 18.

3. Nashe, *Works,* I, 341; Pollard, *Shakespeare's Fight with the Pirates,* pp. 33–34. See also Kirschbaum, *Shakespeare and the Stationers,* pp. 339–340.

4. Cooper, quoted by Beatrice White, "Printers and Authors in the Sixteenth Century: Some Sidelights," *N & Q,* CLXII (1932), 114–115.

5. Googe, ed. Edward Arber (London, 1871), 24–25; Percy, in *Elizabethan Sonnets,* ed. Lee, II, 139; R. F., *School of Slovenry,* quoted by Kirschbaum, *Shakespeare and the Stationers,* p. 125. Kirschbaum, however, cites R. F.'s words as evidence that authors could not halt publication of their works.

6. Blenerhasset, ed. Lily B. Campbell (Cambridge, 1946), pp. 379, 383, 382–383, and see Professor Campbell's comment, p. 363; Grove, sig. A3v.

7. Robson, sig. A2; *The Schoolmaster,* attributed to Michael Scott, sig. A3; *The English Courtier and the Country Gentleman,* sig. A2v.

8. Tofte, in *Elizabethan Sonnets,* ed. Lee, II, 355, 424, and see Percy Simpson, "Literary Piracy in the Elizabethan Age," *Oxford Bibliog. Soc. Publ.,* n.s., I (1947–48), 4–5; *Greene's Funerals,* ed. R. B. McKerrow (Stratford-upon-Avon, 1922), p. 69. See also Henry Bynneman's preface to George Best's *A True Discourse of the Late Voyages . . . to Cathay* (1578), in M. A. Shaaber, *Some Forerunners of the Newspaper in England, 1476–1622* (Philadelphia, 1929), p. 281.

9. Ed. G. B. Harrison (London, 1926), pp. 5, 15, 238–239.

10. *Gorboduc*, quoted by Gebert, *An Anthology of Elizabethan Dedications and Prefaces*, pp. 34–35; Daniel, *Poems*, ed. Sprague, p. 9; Webbe, in Smith, I, 266; Breton, quoted by Kirschbaum, *Shakespeare and the Stationers*, p. 115; Heywood, see Mumby, *The Romance of Bookselling*, p. 106; Hall, see *The Discovery of a New World*, ed. Huntington Brown (Cambridge, Mass., 1937), pp. xxix, 143; Bacon, in Gebert, p. 120. Thomas Playfere refers to the unauthorized publication of a sermon, quoted by Wright, *Middle-Class Culture*, p. 278, n.

11. Blount, quoted by Kirschbaum, pp. 105–106. The most complete discussion of surreptitious publication appears in Kirschbaum, *Shakespeare and the Stationers*, pp. 87–153. I do not, however, share his conclusions (pp. 147–148) that unauthorized publication was commonplace and not deemed reprehensible either by stationers or by authors. Stationers were businessmen with a marketplace morality, certainly, but they were too acute to antagonize and to cut themselves off from writers by pilfering on such a scale as prefaces (that is, until one reads between the lines) indicate.

12. Bastard, *Chrestoleros*, sig. B7v; Plant, *The English Book Trade*, p. 100; Nashe, *Works*, III, 128.

13. Marriot, sig. A3; petition in 1643, quoted in *S. R.*, I, 587.

14. See my "The Editions of Robert Greene's *A Quip for an Upstart Courtier* (1592)," *SB*, VI (1953–54), 107–116. I am assuming that the price was 6d., and that 6000 copies were run off. The gross from this number of copies would have been £250; Wolfe's expenses probably averaged 3d. per copy. However, since all the type was not distributed after each impression, Wolfe's expenses were probably somewhat less than £125. If he printed the permissible 1250 copies each time, his profit would have been correspondingly greater. Wolfe, who was only as honest as he had to be, may even have printed more than 1250 copies.

15. Elyot, sig. a2v; Peacham, *The Truth of Our Times* (1638), p. 32; Gascoigne, *Works*, I, 4.

16. *The Return from Parnassus* and Wither, quoted in *Shakespeare's England*, II, 182; Aubrey, *Brief Lives*, ed. Dick, p. 23; J. S., *Cynthia's Revenge*, sig. A2v.

17. For publication costs, see Edwin Eliott Willoughby, *The Printing of the First Folio of Shakespeare*, in *Trans. of the Bibliog. Soc.*, Supplements, VIII (1932), 25–26; and Sisson, *The Judicious Marriage of Mr Hooker*, pp. 53–55.

There has been a great deal of scholarly controversy as to the size of editions in the sixteenth century. As R. B. McKerrow acknowledges, in *An Introduction to Bibliography* (Oxford, 1928), pp. 131–132, evidence is virtually nonexistent. In *A Printer of Shakespeare: The Books and Times of William Jaggard* (London, 1934), p. 27, Willoughby assumes that "the maximum [permissible] size of an edition was . . . the normal one." For the opposite view, see Plant, *The English Book Trade*, p. 93. Bennett, in *English Books & Readers, 1475–1557*, p. 228, argues that in the first seventy-five years of printing, editions of ordinary books rarely exceeded "600–700 copies."

18. Bastard, sigs. L2v, B7v, E8. See Rowlands, *'Tis Merry When Gossips Meet* (1602), p. 8; and Turner, *Nosce Te* (1607), sig. A3.

19. See W. W. Greg and E. Boswell, *Records of the Court of the Stationers' Company* (London, 1930), p. 90, and Introduction, pp. lxx–lxxi and notes.

20. Nashe, *Works*, I, 287; Pollard, *Shakespeare's Fight with the Pirates*, p. 25; Greene, *The Defense of Cony-Catching*, ed. Harrison, p. 7, quoted by Sheavyn, p. 73.

21. Greene, *Works*, VIII, 129; *Groatsworth of Wit*, ed. Harrison, pp. 34, 36. Chambers, in *The Elizabethan Stage*, I, 373, estimates that "a play by Greene would fetch £6 13s. 4d. about 1592."

22. See Margaret Dowling's excellent article, "The Printing of John Dowland's *Second Booke of Songs or Ayers*," *The Library*, 4th series, XII (1931–32), 365–380.

23. Earle, *Micro-cosmography*, sigs. Flv–F2.

24. *S. R.*, I, 587. For discussion of payments in kind, see Sheavyn, p. 73; G. H. Putnam, *Books and Their Makers during the Middle Ages* (New York, 1897), II, 276, 432–434; Plant, *The English Book Trade*, pp. 217–218; Kirschbaum, in *PBSA*, XL (1946), 61, n.

25. *Eupolemia*, pp. 636, 644.

26. *Eupolemia*, pp. 635, 636.

27. *The Three Parnassus Plays*, ed. Leishman, p. 155; Churchyard, *A Spark of Friendship*, sig. A3; *Fennor's Descriptions*, sig. A2v. In a letter to Aubrey (*Brief Lives*, ed. Dick, p. c.), Tanner notes that seventeenth-century booksellers refused to give Sir Henry Spelman "five pounds in books for his incomparable Glossary." Either the booksellers did not want to print the glossary, or, more probably, they feared that Spelman, with so many copies of his book at his disposal, would spoil the market for dealers.

28. Parrot and Cotton, quoted by Kirschbaum, *PBSA*, XL (1946), 60–61; Nashe, *Works*, I, 258, 261, and see III, 71, 96, 128; *The Three Parnassus Plays*, ed. Leishman, p. 248.

29. Stell, sig. ¶3v; Barwick, sig. L2; Edmund Gosse, *The Life and Letters of John Donne* (New York, 1899), II, 68; Harington, in Smith, II, 219; Daniel, quoted by Kirschbaum, *Shakespeare and the Stationers*, p. 85. For other instances of subsidy, see Mumby, *The*

NOTES TO CHAPTER FIVE

Romance of Bookselling, p. 131, *CSP, Domestic, 1591–1594,* p. 342; John Taylor, *The Carriers' Cosmography* (1637), sig. A2; M. A. Shaaber, "The Meaning of the Imprint in Early Printed Books," *The Library,* 4th series, XXIV (1943–44), 137–138; Willoughby, *A Printer of Shakespeare,* p. 19. While he languished in prison, John Clavell subsidized the printing of his lurid confession, *A Recantation of an Ill-Led Life* (1628).

30. Caxton, quoted by H. L. R. Edwards, *Skelton: The Life and Times of an Early Tudor Poet* (London, 1949), p. 34; Golding, sig. **3. For this discussion of the employment of authors by printers I have drawn upon Shaaber, *Some Forerunners of the Newspaper in England, 1476–1622,* pp. 225–226; Percy Simpson, *Proof-Reading in the Sixteenth, Seventeenth, and Eighteenth Centuries* (London, 1935), pp. 31–32; *CHEL,* IV, 388–389; Yates, *John Florio,* pp. 175–176; Pollard, *Shakespeare's Fight with the Pirates,* pp. 25–26; Harry R. Hoppe, "John Wolfe, Printer and Publisher, 1579–1601," *The Library,* 4th series, XIV (1933–34), 241–288.

Stow prepared his *Summary of Chronicles* (1567) "at the requeste of the Printer and other of my loving frends"; see *Survey of London,* ed. C. L. Kingsford (Oxford, 1908), I, lxxvi. Hall's *Mundus Alter et Idem* (*c.* 1605) was printed at the expense of Ascanio Renialme, a publisher or a son of a publisher; see Edward A. Petherick, *The Gentleman's Magazine,* CCLXXXI (1896), 76–77.

31. Harvey, *Works,* II, 243, and Nashe's reply, *Works,* III, 127; Middleton, *Works,* VIII, 82.

32. *The Three Parnassus Plays,* ed. Leishman, pp. 143, 228.

33. Chettle, *Kind-Heart's Dream,* ed. Harrison, p. 16; Nashe, *Works,* V, 194–195; Rich, *Faults, Faults* (1606), sig. L4.

CHAPTER SIX

CENSORSHIP

1. This notorious incident is discussed by many commentators; see Harington, *Nugae Antiquae,* ed. Thomas Park (London, 1904), I, 143–165.

2. Sheavyn, p. 39. Also see J. S. Burn, *The Star Chamber* (London, 1870), p. 73. In addition to the authorities cited in succeeding footnotes, I have found the following discussions of censorship useful: McKerrow, in *Shakespeare's England,* II, 212–239; Frank Fowell and Frank Palmer, *Censorship in England* (London, 1913); Siebert, *Freedom of the Press in England, 1476–1776;* Percy Simpson, *Studies in Elizabethan Drama* (Oxford, 1955).

3. "The Façade of Morality," in *That Soueraine Light,* pp. 10, 7.

4. *S. R.*, III, 11; *Sidney Papers*, ed. Arthur Collins (London, 1746), I, 358. Norman Wood takes the opposite position in *The Reformation and English Education* (London, 1931), p. 263. But see Neale's more judicious appraisal in *Elizabeth I and Her Parliaments, 1584–1601* (London, 1957), p. 241.

5. North and Becon, quoted by Russell A. Fraser, in *The Court of Venus* (Durham, N. C., 1955), pp. 63–64; Ascham, *The Schoolmaster* (1570), p. 230; Vaughan, *The Golden Grove*, sigs. Y6v–Y7, and *The Spirit of Detraction*, sig. P1, and see sigs. P2–P2v. See also Dering, *A Brief and Necessary Catechism* (1590 ed.), sigs. A1v–A2; Perkins, *Works* (1605 ed.), quoted by Wright, *Middle-Class Culture*, p. 180, n.

6. Lodge and Webbe, in Smith, I, 76, 254; F. S., *The Picture of a Wanton* (1615), quoted by Wright, *Middle-Class Culture*, pp. 233–234; Heywood, quoted by A. M. Clark, *Thomas Heywood — Playwright and Miscellanist* (Oxford, 1931), p. 60; Nashe, in Smith, I, 328; *Certain Elegies, Done by Sundry Excellent Wits*, sig. A8v. See also Reynolds, *Mythomystes* (1632), sigs. B1v–B2v, and Stubbes, *A Motive to Good Works* (1593), quoted by Kirschbaum, *Shakespeare and the Stationers*, p. 391.

7. Bk. V, Canto ix, sts. 25–26. And note the vulgar ditty on the grave of John Penry, who was hanged for treason in 1593, recorded by John Weever, *Ancient Funeral Monuments* (1631), sig. F4v.

8. Puckering, quoted by Neale, *Elizabeth I and Her Parliaments, 1584–1601*, p. 249; Allen, *A History of Political Thought*, p. 209. See also in this connection Wilson, *Elizabethan and Jacobean*, pp. 7, 14; Knappen, *Tudor Puritanism*, p. 467; and, particularly, R. G. Usher, *The Rise and Fall of the High Commission* (Oxford, 1913), p. 20.

9. Wolfe, quoted by H. R. Plomer, "An Examination of Some Existing Copies of Hayward's 'Life and Raigne of King Henrie IV,'" *The Library*, n.s., III (1902), 15.

10. "The Regulation of the Book Trade before the Proclamation of 1538," *Trans. of the Bibliog. Soc.*, XV (1917–19), 172–173. In this paragraph I am indebted to the excellent discussion of censorship in Wood, *The Reformation and English Education*, pp. 228–241. See also Franklin Le Van Baumer, *The Early Tudor Theory of Kingship* (New Haven, 1940), pp. 211–224.

11. *APC, 1547–1550*, p. 312.

12. Act of 1555, in Arber, *S. R.*, I, 52, and Cyril Bathurst Judge, *Elizabethan Book-Pirates* (Cambridge, Mass., 1934), pp. 15–16; Act of 1558, in Wood, *The Reformation and English Education*, p. 236.

13. Arber, *S. R.*, I, xxxviii, and G. W. Prothero, *Select Statutes and Other Constitutional Documents* (2nd ed., Oxford, 1898), pp.

NOTES TO CHAPTER SEVEN

4. Greene, *Works*, V, 6; Turner, *The Garland of a Green Wit* (1595), sig. A2; Danter, preface to R. B.'s *Greene's Funerals* (1594), ed. McKerrow, p. 69.

5. Sig. H1. Note also the ambiguous references to money on sigs. N4v, U2v. In *Zelauto* appear woodcuts from Stephen Batman's *The Traveled Pilgrim* (1569), altered and adapted to suit Munday's text.

6. Sigs. a3v–a4. For comments on advertisements in books, all of which repeat the same misinformation, see *Shakespeare's England*, II, 230–232; Sheavyn, p. 73; Mumby, *The Romance of Bookselling*, p. 125, which quotes Aldis in *CHEL*, IV, 408; Plant, *The English Book Trade*, p. 248.

7. Sigs. 2H7v–2I4. The earlier list in *The Profitable Art of Gardening* includes three books omitted in the later volume.

8. *A Compendium of the Rational Secrets of . . . Fioravanti* (1582), sig. *5. See also Paul H. Kocher, "John Hester, Paracelsan (fl. 1576–93)," in *Joseph Quincy Adams: Memorial Studies*, pp. 621–638; and Francis R. Johnson, "Thomas Hill: An Elizabethan Huxley," *HLQ*, VII (1943–44), 329–351.

To *A Discovery of Certain English Wants* (1595), in *The Harleian Miscellany*, ed. Thomas Park (London, 1812), IX, 110, Hugh Platt appends the following notice: "All those that are desirous to have any conference with the publisher hereof, may bee advertised of his abode by William Ponsonby, stationer, in Paules churchyard."

9. Quoted by Thomas C. Izard, *George Whetstone* (New York, 1942), p. 133.

10. *A Watchword to England,* sig. N2v; *The Third and Last Part of Palmerin of England*, sig. 4C3v.

11. *A Disputation between a He Cony-Catcher and a She Cony-Catcher,* ed. G. B. Harrison (London, 1923), p. 31; *The Black Book's Messenger*, ed. Harrison (London, 1924), p. 1; *The Defense of Cony-Catching*, ed. Harrison, p. 64. See Jordan, *Robert Greene*, pp. 102–103, notes.

12. Greene, ed. Harrison, p. 7; Styward, sig. A3; Roberts, *A Defiance to Fortune* (1590), sig. A4; Markham, sig. I2. Cf. Deloney, *The Gentle Craft*, in *Works*, ed F. O. Mann (Oxford, 1912), p. 140.

13. Greene, *The Second Part of Cony-Catching*, ed. Harrison, p. 7; Elyot, sig. a2v; Gosson, *The Ephemerides of Phialo* (1579), sig. [ ]4.

14. *A . . . Dialogue between Mercury and an English Soldier,* sig. A2; *Alarm to England*, sigs. *2–*2v, *3v; *A Short Survey of Ireland*, sig. A3v; *The Honesty of This Age*, ed. Cunningham, p. 5.

15. Johnson, quoted by Wright, *Middle-Class Culture*, p. 329; Pricket, *A Soldier's Wish unto His Sovereign Lord, King James* (1603), sig. C2; Shute, *The First Part of the Christian Instruction*

(1565), quoted by Rosenberg, *Leicester — Patron of Letters,* p. 209; Barret, *The Theoric and Practice of Modern Wars* (1598), sig. ¶4.

16. Stanyhurst, *The First Four Books of Vergil's Aeneid* (1583), sig. A4v; Nashe, *Works,* I, 9–10.

17. *A Spark of Friendship,* sig. A3.

18. Sig. A2, quoted by Bennett, *English Books & Readers, 1475–1557,* p. 49. Brief discussions of New Year's books appear in Bennett, pp. 48–50, and in Garrod, "Erasmus and His English Patrons," *The Library,* 5th series, IV (1949–50), 1–13. Most of the books cited were printed before 1558.

19. Gascoigne, *Works,* II, 515, and see Prouty, *George Gascoigne,* p. 97, and Rosenberg, *Leicester — Patron of Letters,* p. 172.

20. *Churchyard's Charge,* sigs. C2, C3; *A Pleasant Discourse of Court and Wars,* sig. C2; *A Pleasant Conceit,* quoted by Gebert, *An Anthology of Elizabethan Dedications and Prefaces,* p. 103. Collier suggest that *The Misery of Flanders* (1579) may have been a New Year's gift to the queen; see G. G. Langsam, *Martial Books and Tudor Verse* (New York, 1951), p. 148.

21. See Hyder E. Rollins, *An Analytical Index to the Ballad-Entries (1557–1709) in the Registers of the Company of Stationers of London* (Chapel Hill, N. C., 1924), nos. 1917, 1919, 1920; *The Three Parnassus Plays,* ed. Leishman, p. 185.

22. Nashe and Puttenham, in Smith, I, 316, II, 59; A. H., additions to Davies' *A Scourge for Paper-Persecutors* (1625), sig. A3.

23. Guilpin, *Skialetheia,* ed. G. B. Harrison (Oxford, 1931), sig. B8; Hall, *The Discovery of a New World* (1609), ed. Brown, p. 56; *Wither's Motto* (1621), sigs. B1v–B2. Note also *The Three Parnassus Plays,* ed. Leishman, p. 178.

24. Whetstone, quoted by Izard, *George Whetstone,* p. 243; for Lodge, see Sisson, *Thomas Lodge and Other Elizabethans,* p. 149, and Paradise, *Thomas Lodge,* pp. 74–75; for Taylor, see Plant, *The English Book Trade,* p. 238; D'Israeli, in *Curiosities of Literature,* II, 130; Williams, "Richard Johnson's Borrowed Tears," *SP,* XXXIV (1937), 186–190.

25. There is a lengthy discussion of Whetstone's elegies in Izard, pp. 227–261.

26. Greene, *Works,* IX, 232; Drayton, *Works,* I, 84; Donne, *Poems,* ed. Grierson, I, 150.

27. I have arranged in tabular form the borrowings pointed out by Frank Aydelotte, *Elizabethan Rogues and Vagabonds* (Oxford, 1913), pp. 135–136, 175–177. The references are to the 1614 edition of *The Art of Juggling,* the original editions of Scot and of *Mihil Mumchance,* and J. O. Halliwell's reprint of *A Manifest Detection . . . of Dice Play* (London, 1850).

28. Walker, "The Reading of an Elizabethan: Some Sources of the Prose Pamphlets of Thomas Lodge," *RES*, VIII (1932), 266. For Rowlands, see F. W. Chandler, *The Literature of Roguery* (Boston, 1907), I, 103–104; Edward D. McDonald, *Indiana University Studies*, IX (1911), 143–170; A. Davenport, "Samuel Rowlands and Thomas Lodge," *N & Q*, CLXXXIV (1943), 13–16; John Leon Lievsay, "Newgate Penitents: Further Aspects of Elizabethan Pamphlet Sensationalism," *HLQ*, VII (1943–44), 47–69; *The Three Parnassus Plays*, ed. Leishman, pp. 48–49. For Deloney, see Mann's introduction to *Works*, and Rollins, "Thomas Deloney's Euphuistic Learning and *The Forest*," *PMLA*, L (1935), 679–686, and "Deloney's Sources for Euphuistic Learning," *PMLA*, LI (1936), 399–406.

29. The page references are to the following: Dekker, *Non-Dramatic Works*, ed. Grosart, III; Harman and Awdeley, in *The Rogues and Vagabonds of Shakespeare's Youth*, ed. Edward Viles and F. J. Furnivall (London, 1907); *The Works of Samuel Rowlands*; Greene, The Bodley Head Quartos, ed. Harrison. The titles of Greene's tracts are shortened. I have in this table utilized the findings of Chandler, *The Literature of Roguery*, I, 103–108; McDonald, *Indiana University Studies*, IX (1911), 143–170; Aydelotte, *Elizabethan Rogues and Vagabonds*, pp. 130–134; Lievsay, *HLQ*, VII (1943–44), 47–69. For a detailed discussion of Dekker's pamphlets see my article, "Thomas Dekker, Hack Writer," *N & Q*, n.s., II (1955), 145–150.

Anthony Nixon composed, one might say not unfairly, with a pair of scissors and a pot of paste; see F. P. Wilson, "Some English Mock-Prognostications," *The Library*, 4th series, XIX (1938–39), 30; Ennis, "Anthony Nixon: Jacobean Plagiarist and Hack," *HLQ*, III (1939–40), 377–401; and my "Another Source for Anthony Nixon's *The Scourge of Corruption* (1615)," *HLQ*, XVII (1953–54), 173–176. For Rich's manufactured tracts, see Lievsay, "A Word about Barnaby Rich," *JEGP*, LV (1956), 389–391.

30. I have drawn upon the critics cited in the preceding footnote. In addition I have used John J. O'Connor's "On the Authorship of the Ratsey Pamphlets," *PQ*, XXX (1951), 381–386. Page references are to the texts cited above. *Jests to Make You Merry* appears in Dekker, *Non-Dramatic Works; The Life and Death of Gabriel Ratsey* and *Ratsey's Ghost*, ed. S. H. Atkins (London, 1935).

31. Sigs. A2–A2v.

32. The italics are mine. The two passages in the *Defense of Cony-Catching* are continuous. See my "Samuel Rid's Borrowings from Robert Greene," *N & Q*, n.s., I (1954), 236–238.

INDEX

INDEX

INDEX

INDEX

Lloyd, Lodowick, 11–12

Lodge, Thomas, 7, 8, 9, 11, 13–14, 17, 19, 20, 21, 115, 131, 167, 177, 193, 201, 204, 205, 210, 227, 233

Lok (or Lock), Henry, 8

Luther, Martin, 183

Lyly, John, 7, 8, 11, 17, 61–62, 105, 205

McClure, Norman Egbert, 250 (n. 7), 255 (n. 4)

McDonald, Edward D., 272 (n. 28, 29)

McKerrow, R. B., viii, 138, 159, 197, 248 (n. 14), 264–265 (n. 17), 268 (n. 18)

McMahon, Clara P., 250 (n. 8)

McNeir, Waldo F., 257 (n. 25)

Mabbe, James, 8, 262 (n. 38)

Magnus, Thomas, 37

A Manifest Detection of Dice Play, 232, 233, 236

Mann, F. O., 270 (n. 12), 272 (n. 28)

Manners, Edward, Earl of Rutland, 127

Manningham, John, 43, 259 (n. 11)

Margaret of Navarre, 196

Markham, Gervase, 60–61, 120, 206, 210, 216–217

Marlowe, Christopher, 7, 8, 10, 11, 18, 84, 196, 197, 200, 201, 243

Marquino, Francesco, 167

Marriot, John, bookseller, 151

Marston, John, 8, 9, 11, 30–31, 77, 196, 200, 201, 253 (n. 30)

Martin, Gregory, 189

Marprelate Controversy, 11, 172, 190–191

Mary, Queen, 104, 185–186, 189, 191, 195

Mathew, David, 252 (n. 28)

Mead, Herman R., 122, 261 (n. 33)

Meadows, Denis, 268 (n. 15)

Meres, Francis, 8, 11, 16–17, 45–46, 68, 85, 100

Middleton, Thomas, 30, 132, 135, 168

Mihil Mumchance, 210, 232, 234–235, 236–239

Miller, Edwin H., 253–254 (n. 40), 264 (n. 14), 272 (n. 29, 32)

Miller, John, warden of the Leather-sellers' Company, 127

The Mirror for Magistrates, 249 (n. 20)

Mish, Charles C., 254 (n. 40), 255 (n. 8)

Moffett, Thomas, 49, 51

Monson, William, judge of the Common Pleas, 191, 268 (n. 20)

Moore, Samuel, 258 (n. 1)

More, Margaret, 38

More, Sir Thomas, 35, 39, 191

Mulcaster, Richard, 35, 39, 218

Mumby, Frank A., 256 (n. 16), 262 (n. 35), 264 (n. 10), 265–266 (n. 29), 270 (n. 6)

Munday, Anthony, 7, 9, 11, 17, 76, 167, 205, 209, 211–212, 214–215, 248 (n. 12)

Murphy, Thomas D., 253 (n. 36)

Nash, Thomas, *Quaternio*, 257 (n. 23, 26)

Nashe, Thomas, 8, 11, 14, 15, 18, 21, 26, 32, 45, 56, 57, 60, 66, 67, 68, 72, 76, 79, 84, 107, 114, 119, 124, 132–134, 135, 141, 142, 150, 154, 157, 164, 167–168, 178, 180, 182, 193–194, 196, 197, 199–200, 201, 204, 205, 207, 221, 225–226, 233, 243

Neale, J. E., 38, 105, 267 (n. 4, 8), 268 (n. 17)

Nelson, William, 252 (n. 17)

Newdigate, Bernard H., 248 (n. 12), 256 (n. 18), 259 (n. 15), 262 (n. 34)

Newman, Thomas, printer, 142, 148

New Year's Day gift books, 222–225

Niccols, Richard, 49, 250 (n. 5)

Niclas, Henrik, 188

Nicolas, Harris, 260 (n. 25)

Nixon, Anthony, 205, 210, 236, 241

Norrys, Sir Thomas, 12

North, Sir Thomas, 9, 176

Norton, Thomas, 148, 149, 189, 192

Nowell, Alexander, Dean of St. Paul's, 127

Nowell, Robert, 125

Nugent, Elizabeth M., 255 (n. 15)

Ockland, Christopher, 105

[278]

INDEX

INDEX